ESTATE PUBLICATIONS

STAFFORDSHIRE

C000093489

Street maps with index
Administrative Districts
Population Gazetteer
Road Map with index
Postcodes

COUNTY RED BOOKS

This atlas is intended for those requiring street maps of the historical and commercial centres of towns within the county. Each locality is normally presented on one or two pages and although, with many small towns, this space is sufficient to portray the whole urban area, the maps of large towns and cities are for centres only and are not intended to be comprehensive. Such coverage in Super and Local Red Books (see page 2).

Street plans prepared and published by ESTATE PUBLICATIONS, Bridewell House, TENTERDEN, KENT, and based upon the ORDNANCE SURVEY mapping with the permission of the Controller of H. M. Stationery Office.

The Publishers acknowledge the co-operation of the local authorities of towns represented in this atlas.

Estate Publications 231 C   ISBN 0 86084 835 3   Crown Copyright 398713

COUNTY RED BOOK

STAFFORDSHIRE

contains street maps for each town centre

SUPER & LOCAL RED BOOKS

are street atlases with comprehensive local coverage

BURTON UPON TRENT

including: Ashby-de-la-Zouch, Barton-under-Needwood, Linton, Repton, Swadlincote, Tutbury etc.

STAFFORD

including: Hopton, Penkridge, Stone, Walton-on-the-Hill etc.

STOKE-ON-TRENT

including: Alsager, Audley, Biddulph, Blythe Bridge, Kidsgrove, Madeley, Newcastle-under-Lyme etc.

CONTENTS

LEGEND TO STREET MAPS

One-Way Street	→	**Post Office**	●
Pedestrianized	▨	**Public Convenience**	Ⓒ
Car Park	Ⓟ	**Place of Worship**	✛

Scale of street plans: 4 Inches to 1 mile (unless otherwise stated on the map).

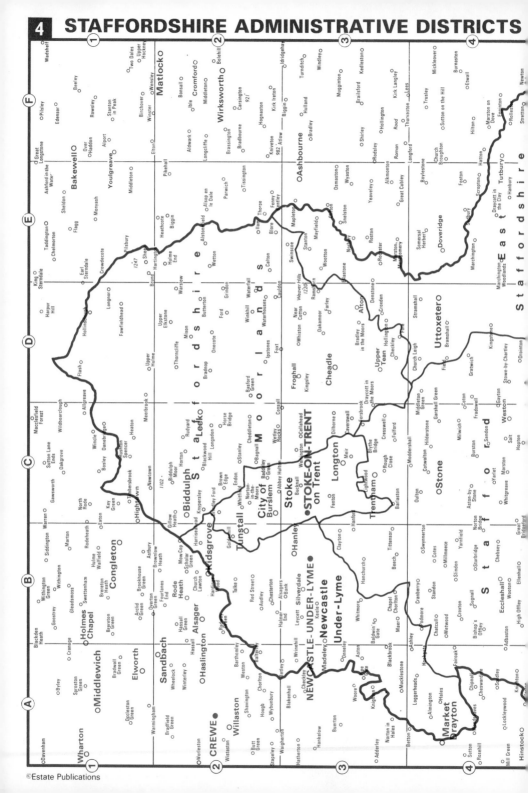

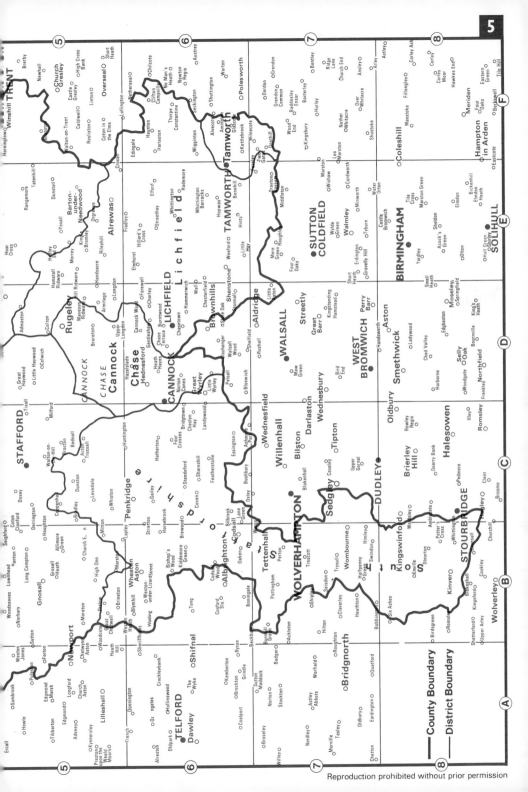

GAZETTEER INDEX TO ROAD MAPS
with Populations

County of Staffordshire population **1,031,135**

Districts:

Cannock Chase **88,833**

East Staffordshire **97,105**

Lichfield **92,679**

Newcastle-under Lyme **119,091**

South Staffordshire **105,487**

Stafford **117,788**

Staffordshire Moorlands **95,450**

Stoke-on-Trent **244,637**

Tamworth **70,065**

Place	Ref
Abbey Hulton	8 D3
Abbots Bromley **1,700**	9 F6
Acton Trussell & Bednall **1,156**	10 D2
Adbaston **551**	8 B6
Admaston	11 E1
Allimore Green	10 C1
Almington	8 A5
Alrewas **4,037**	11 G2
Alsagers Bank	8 B3
Alstonefield **273**	9 F2
Alton **1,321**	9 E4
Amington	11 H3
Anslow **578**	9 G6
Anslow Gate	9 G6
Armitage with Handsacre **4,426**	11 F2
Ashley	8 B5
Aston	8 B4
Aston-by-Stone	8 D6
Audley **8,358**	8 B3
Baddeley Green	8 D3
Bagnall **833**	8 D3
Baldwin's Gate	8 B4
Balterley **210**	8 B3
Barlaston **2,946**	8 C5
Barton-under-Needwood **4.664**	11 G2
Basford Green	9 E3
Bednall & Acton Trussel **1,156**	10 D2
Beech	8 C5
Berkswich **1,938**	*
Betley **1,000**	8 B3
Biddulph **19,237**	8 C2
Biddulph Moor	8 D2
Bilbrook **4,991**	10 C3
Bishop's Offley	8 B6
Bishop's Wood	10 C3
Blackbrook	8 B5
Blackwood Hill	8 D2
Blithfield **235**	*
Blore with Swinscoe **122**	9 F3
Blymhill & Weston-under-Lizard **581**	10 B2
Blythe Bridge	8 D4
Bobbington **535**	10 B5
Bonehill	11 G3
Bradley **396**	10 C2
Bradley in the Moors	9 E4
Bradnop **319**	9 E3
Bramshall	9 E5
Branston **3,384**	11 G1
Brereton & Ravenhill **6,461**	11 E2
Brewood **7,151**	10 C3
Bridgtown **628**	10 D4
Brindley Ford	10 C3
Brindley Heath **936**	*
Brineton	10 B2
Brocton **1,044**	10 D1
Brown Edge **2,539**	8 D3
Brund	9 F2
Bucknull	8 D4
Burntwood **25,617**	11 E3
Burslem	8 C3
Burston & Sandon **382**	8 D6
Burton-upon-Trent **47,240**	11 H1
Butterton **226**	9 F2
Calton	9 F3
Cannock **46,754**	10 D4
Cannock Wood **1,052**	11 E2
Castle Church **3,200**	*
Cauldon	9 F3
Caverswall **1,058**	8 D4
Cellahead	8 D4
Chapel & Hill Chorlton **341**	8 B5
Chase Terrace	11 E3
Chasetown **4,273**	11 E3
Chatcull	8 B5
Cheadle **11,265**	9 E4
Chebsey **510**	8 C6
Checkley **4,328**	9 E5
Cheddleton **5,896**	8 D3
Cheslyn Hay **7,015**	10 D3
Chesterfield	11 H3
Chesterton	8 B3
Chorley & Farewell **313**	11 F2
Church Eaton **623**	10 C2
Church Leigh	9 E5
Clayton	8 C4
Clifton Campville **695**	11 H3
Codsall **7,854**	10 C3
Codsall Wood	10 C3
Colton **713**	11 E1
Colwich **4,749**	11 E1
Consall **150**	8 D3
Coppenhall **218**	10 D1
Cotes	8 C5
Coton & Hopton **1,854**	8 D6
Coton Clanford	10 C1
Cotton **354**	*
Cotwalton	8 D5
Coven	10 C3
Cranberry	8 B5
Cresswell **1,239**	8 D5
Croxall	11 G2
Croxden **220**	9 E5
Croxton	8 B6
Curborough & Elmhurst **172**	11 F2
Denstone **899**	9 F4
Derrington	10 C1
Dilhorne **519**	8 D4
Dosthill	11 G4
Doxey	10 D1
Draycott in the Clay **829**	9 G6
Draycott in the Moors **1,151**	8 D4
Drayton Bassett **820**	11 G4
Drointon	9 E6
Dunstall **234**	11 G1
Dunston **229**	10 D2
Eccleshall **4,606**	8 B6
Edingale **547**	11 G2
Elford **549**	11 G3
Ellastone **287**	9 F4
Ellenhall **109**	8 C6
Elmhurst & Curborough **172**	11 F2
Endon & Stanley **3,397**	8 D3
Enville **397**	10 C6
Essington **4,750**	10 D3
Etchinghill	11 E1
Fairoak	8 B5
Farewell & Chorley **313**	11 F2
Farley **190**	9 E4
Fawfieldhead **300**	9 E1
Fazeley **4,548**	11 G4
Featherstone **3,922**	10 D3
Fenton **13,394**	8 C4
Field	9 E5
Fisherwick **174**	*
Flash	9 E1
Fole	9 E5
Ford	9 E3
Forsbrook **5,497**	8 D4
Forton **241**	10 B1
Four Crosses	10 D4
Foxt	9 E3
Fradley	11 F2
Fradswell **182**	9 E6
Froghall	9 E4
Fulford **5,670**	8 D5
Gailey	10 D2
Garshall Green	8 D5
Gayton **154**	8 D6
Gentleshaw	11 E2
Gillow Heath	8 C2
Glascote	11 G3
Gnosall **5,026**	10 B1
Gnosall Heath	10 C1
Goldenhill	8 C3
Gratwich	9 E6
Great Bridgeford	8 C6
Great Haywood	11 E1
Great Wyrley **11,002**	11 E3
Grindon **242**	9 F3
Hadley End	11 F1
Hademore	11 G3
Hales	8 A5
Halfpenny Green	10 C5
Halmer End	8 B3
Hammerwich **4,201**	11 E3
Hamstall Ridware **289**	11 F1
Hanbury **556**	9 G6
Hanchurch	8 C4
Hansacre with Armitage **4,426**	11 F2
Hanford	8 C4
Hanley	8 C4
Harlaston **318**	11 G3
Harriseahead	8 C2
Hatherton **584**	10 D3
Haughton **1,010**	*
Haunton	11 G2
Hazelslade	11 E2
Heath Hayes & Wimblebury **9,410**	11 E3
Heathylee **259**	*
Heaton **286**	8 D2
Hednesford	11 E2
High Offley **872**	8 B6
High Onn	10 C2

Hilderstone **409**	8 D5	
Hillard's Cross	11 F2	
Hill Ridware	11 F2	
Hilton **279**	*	
Himley **946**	10 C5	
Hints **319**	11 F4	
Hixon	9 E6	
Hoar Cross **196**	11 F1	
Hollington	9 E5	
Hollingsclough **165**	9 E1	
Hookgate	8 B5	
Hopton & Coton **1,854**	8 D6	
Hopwas	11 G3	
Horninglow **5,990**	11 G1	
Horse Bridge	8 D3	
Horsebrook	10 C3	
Horton **733**	8 D2	
Hulme End	9 F2	
Huntington **2,892**	10 D2	
Ilam **127**	9 F3	
Ingestre **127**	8 D6	
Ipstone **1,422**	9 E3	
Keele **1,203**	8 B4	
Kettlebrook	11 G4	
Kiddemore Green	10 C3	
Kidsgrove **24,132**	8 C3	
King's Bromley **1,076**	11 F2	
Kingsley **2,336**	9 E4	
Kingstone **614**	9 E6	
Kinver **6,748**	10 C6	
Knighton	8 A4	
Knighton	8 A6	
Knypersley	8 C2	
Landywood	10 D3	
Lane Green	10 C4	
Lapley & Stretton **2,781**	10 C2	
Lawnhead	10 C1	
Leek **19,850**	8 D2	
Leekfrith **362**	*	
Leigh **806**	*	
Levedale	10 C2	
Leycett	8 B4	
Lichfield **28,666**	11 F3	
Lightwood	8 D4	
Little Aston **2,566**	11 F4	
Little Hay	11 F4	
Little Haywood	11 E1	
Little Wyrley	11 E3	
Loggerheads **4,355**	8 A5	
Longdon **1,542**	11 F2	
Longnor **392**	9 F1	
Longsdon **563**	8 D3	
Longton **12,860**	8 D4	
Lower Penn **1,639**	*	
Madeley **3,796**	8 B4	
Maer **550**	8 B5	
Marchington **1,253**	9 F6	
Marchington Woodlands	9 F6	
Marston **152**	10 C2	
Marston	8 D6	
Mavesyn Ridware **991**	11 F2	
Mayfield **1,260**	9 F4	
Meerbrook	9 E2	
Meir **14,413**	8 D4	
Middleton	11 G4	
Middleton Green	9 E5	
Milford	10 D1	
Millmeece	8 C5	
Milwich **433**	8 D5	
Mitton	10 C2	
Mixon	9 E2	
Moddershall	8 D5	
Moreton	10 B2	
Morrey	11 F1	
Mucklestone	8 A5	
Near Cotton	9 E4	
Newborough **382**	9 F6	
Newcastle-under-Lyme **73,872**	8 C4	
Newton	9 E6	
Newtown	8 D2	
Norbury **310**	10 B1	
Norton Bridge	8 C6	
Norton Canes **6,549**	11 E3	
Norton in the Moors	8 C3	
Oakamoor **663**	9 E4	
Oaken	10 C4	
Okeover **76**	*	
Onecote **241**	9 E3	
Onneley	8 B4	
Orgreave	11 F2	
Orslow	10 B2	
Oulton	8 C5	
Outwood **1,889**	*	
Pattingham & Patshull **2,283**	10 B4	
Penkridge **8,565**	10 D2	
Perton **11,336**	10 C4	
Pipe Gate	8 B4	
Podmore	8 B5	
Potter's Cross	10 C6	
Quarnford **230**	*	
Ramshorn **17**	9 F4	
Rangemore	11 G1	
Ranton **415**	10 C1	
Red Street	8 C3	
Riley Hill	11 F2	
Rocester **1,432**	9 F5	
Rolleston **3,203**	9 G6	
Rough Close	8 D5	
Rudyard	8 D2	
Rugeley **17,043**	11 E1	
Rushton Spencer **444**	8 D2	
Salt & Enson **438**	8 D6	
Sandon & Burston **382**	8 D6	
Saredon **693**	*	
Seighford **2,483**	10 C1	
Seisdon & Trysull **1,095**	10 C5	
Shareshill **698**	10 D3	
Shebdon	8 B6	
Sheen **234**	9 F2	
Shenstone **6,890**	11 F3	
Silverdale **7,124**	8 B4	
Six Ashes	10 B5	
Slindon	8 C5	
Stafford **53,079**	10 D1	
Standeford	10 D3	
Standon **776**	8 B5	
Stanley & Endon **3,397**	8 D3	
Stanton **202**	9 F4	
Stoke on Trent **177,099**	8 C4	
Stone **12,645**	8 D5	
Stone Rural **2,295**	*	
Stonnall **1,636**	11 E3	
Stourton	10 C6	
Stowe-by-Chartley **1,688**	10 C6	
Stramshall	9 F5	
Streethay **372**	11 F3	
Stretton **7,432**	9 H6	
Stretton & Lapley **2,781**	10 C2	
Sugnall	8 B6	
Sturbridge	8 C6	
Sutton	10 B1	
Swindon **1,360**	10 B5	
Swinfen & Packington **479**	*	
Swinscoe with Blore **122**	9 F3	
Swynnerton **4,208**	8 C5	
Talke **4,447**	8 B3	
Tamworth **70,065**	11 G3	
Tatenhill **550**	11 G1	
Teddesley Hay **76**	*	
Tettenhall	10 C4	
Thorncliffe	9 E2	
Thorpe Constantine **101**	11 H3	
Tittensor	8 C5	
Tittesworth **301**	*	
Tixall **196**	10 D1	
Trentham **15,588**	8 C4	
Trescott	10 C4	
Trysull & Seisdon **1,095**	10 C5	
Tunstall **11,283**	8 C3	
Tutbury **3,249**	9 G6	
Two Gates	11 G4	
Upper Elkstone	9 E2	
Upper Hulme	9 E2	
Upper Longdon	11 E2	
Upper Tean	9 E5	
Uttoxeter **10,329**	9 F5	
Uttoxeter Rural **1,378**	*	
Wall **448**	11 F3	
Walton-on-the-Hill	10 D1	
Warslow & Elkstones **310**	9 F2	
Waterfall	9 F3	
Waterhouses **1,060**	9 F3	
Weeford **192**	11 F3	
Wergs	10 C4	
Werrington **6,100**	8 D4	
Weston **677**	8 D6	
Weston Jones	10 B1	
Weston-under-Lizard & Blymhill **581**	10 B2	
Wetley Rocks	8 D3	
Wetton **155**	9 F3	
Wetwood	8 B5	
Wheaton Aston	10 C2	
Whiston	9 E4	
Whiston	10 C2	
Whitfield	8 C3	
Whitgreave **155**	8 C6	
Whitmore **1,274**	8 B4	
Whittington	10 C6	
Whittington **3,188**	11 G3	
Whittington Barracks	11 G3	
Wiggington **996**	11 G3	
Wilnecote	11 G4	
Winkhill	9 E3	
Winshill **6,746**	11 H1	
Wombourne **13,711**	10 C5	
Woodseaves	10 B1	
Wooton	8 B6	
Wootton **134**	9 F4	
Wrinehill	8 B4	
Wychnor **75**	*	
Yarlet	8 D6	
Yarnfield	8 C5	
Yoxall **1,802**	11 F1	

Population figures are based upon the 1991 census and relate to the local authority area or parish as constituted at that date. Boundaries of the districts are shown on pages 4-5. Places with no population figure form part of a larger local authority area or parish.

Population figures in bold type.

*Place not included on map due to limitation of space

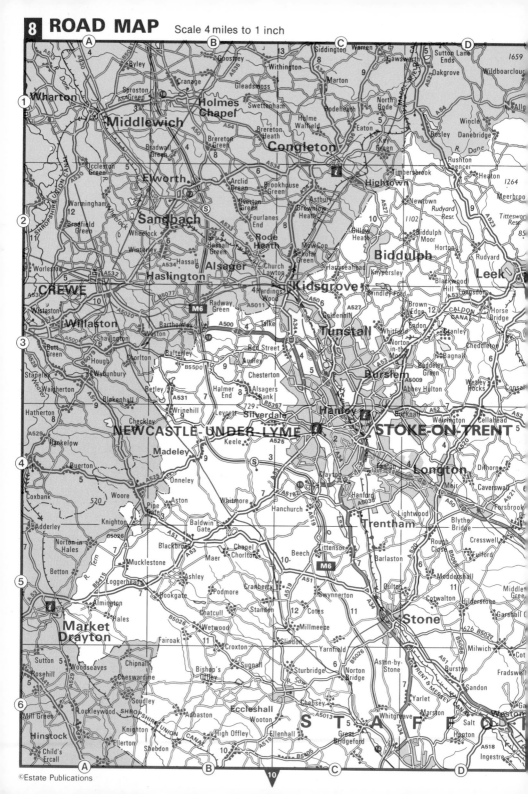

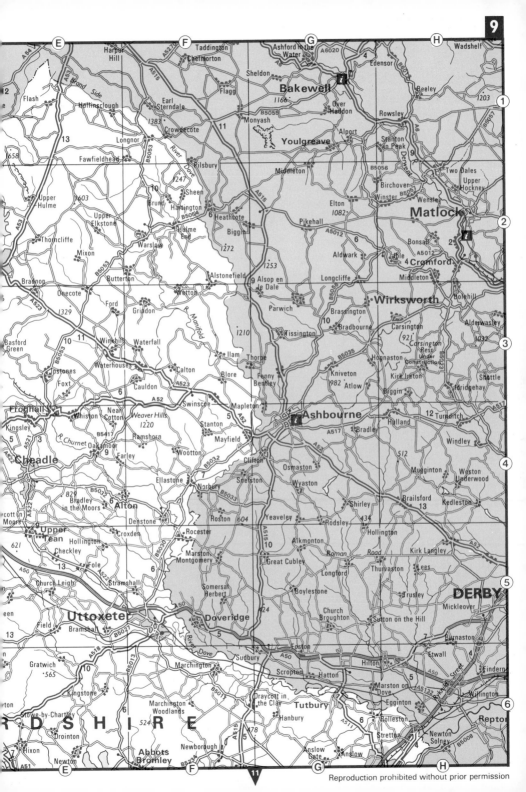

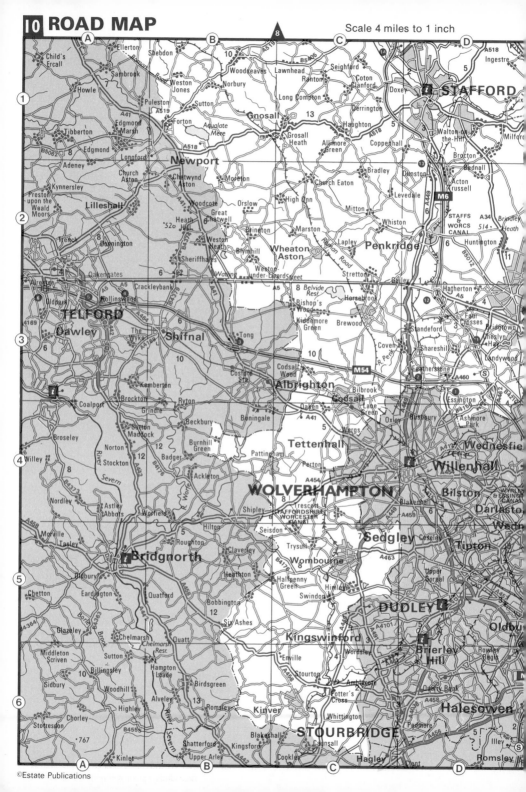

Scale 4 miles to 1 inch

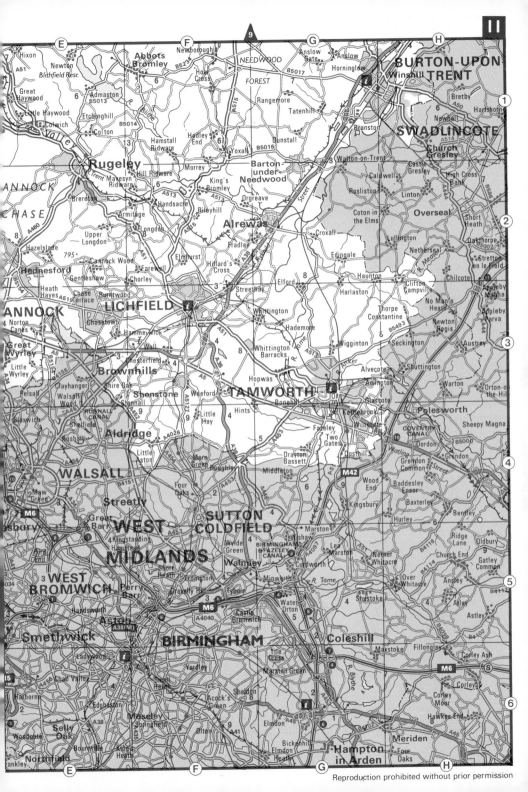

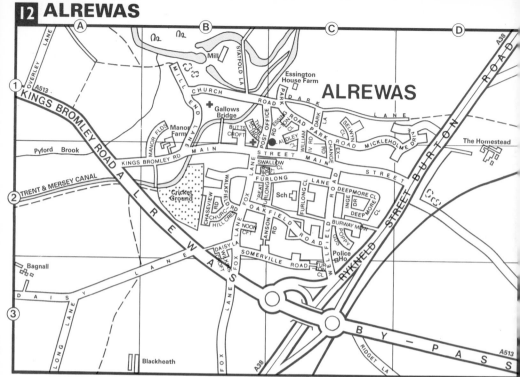

ALTON

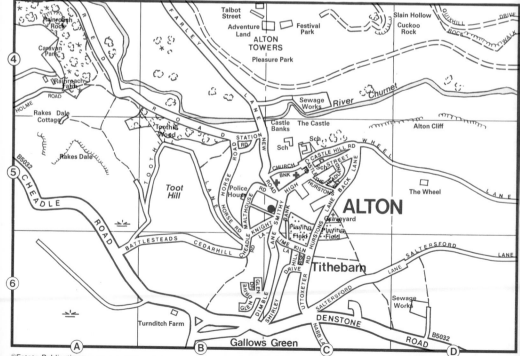

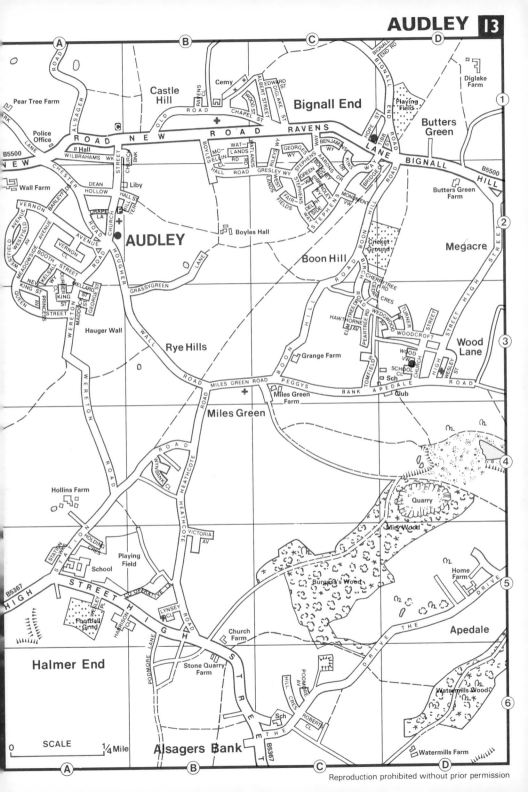

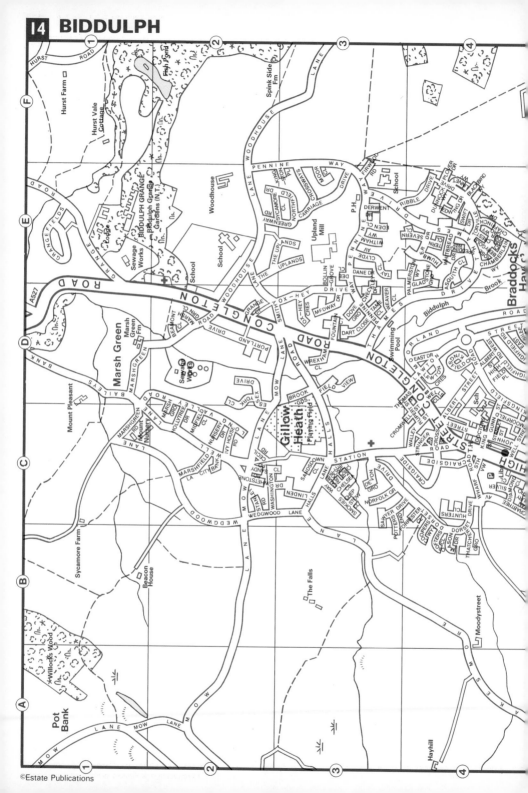

14 BIDDULPH

©Estate Publications

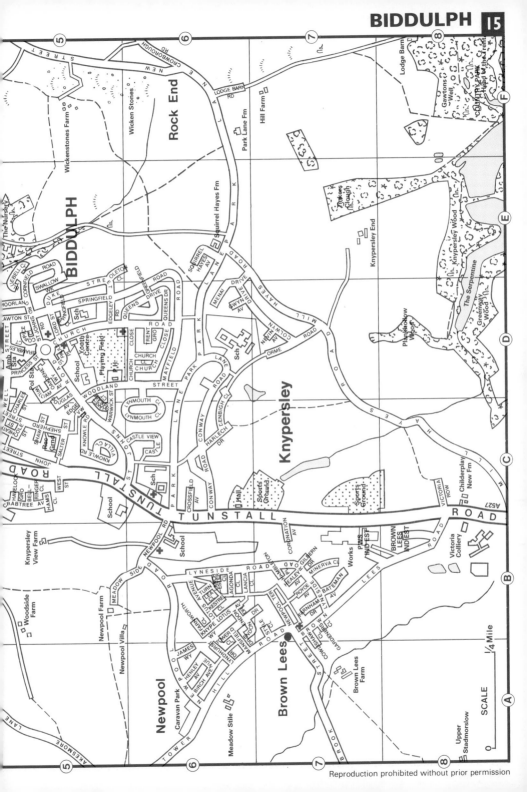

BLYTHE BRIDGE

Forsbrook

Moor Green

Moor Green Farm

Heath House

River Blythe

Foxfield Light Railway

Creda

Stallington Grange

Playing Field

Mullox Ltd

Works

SCALE

0   1/4 Mile

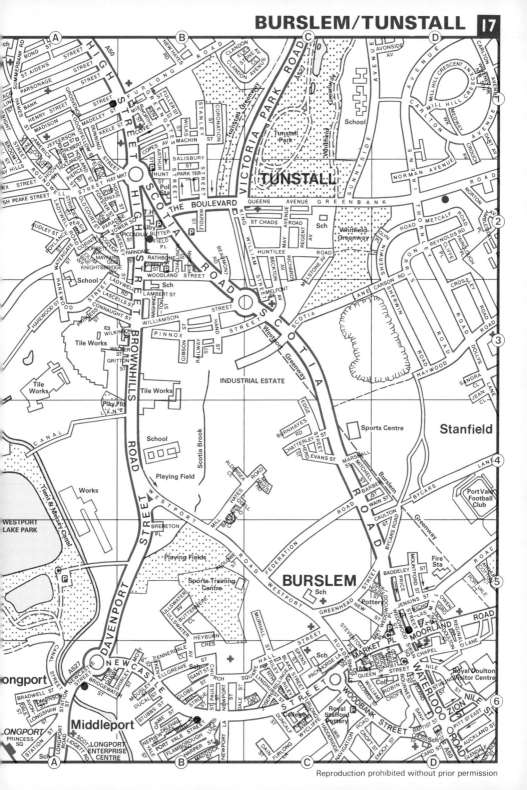

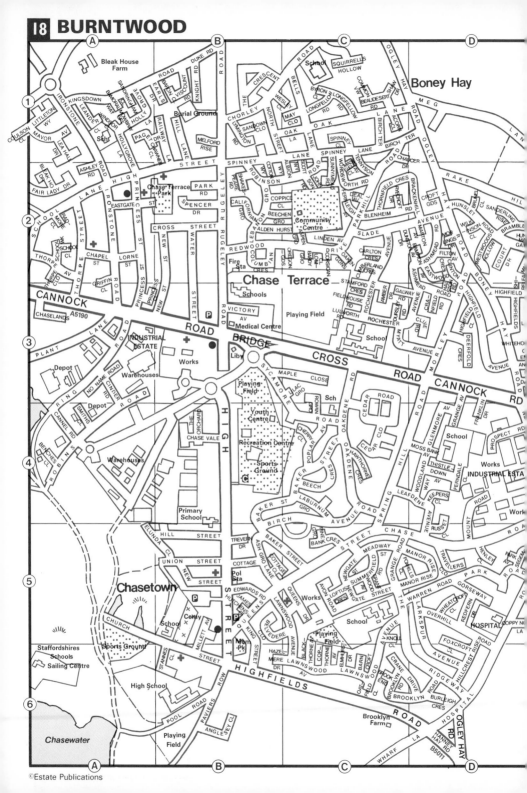

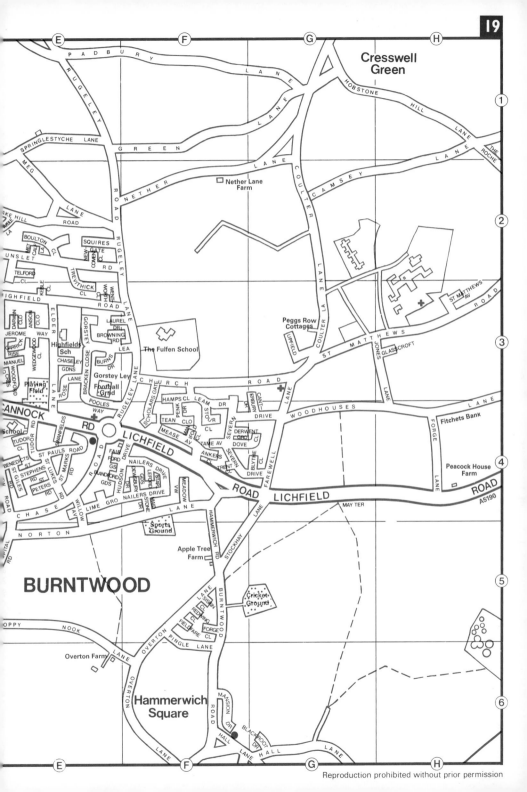

Cresswell
Green

BURNTWOOD

Hammerwich
Square

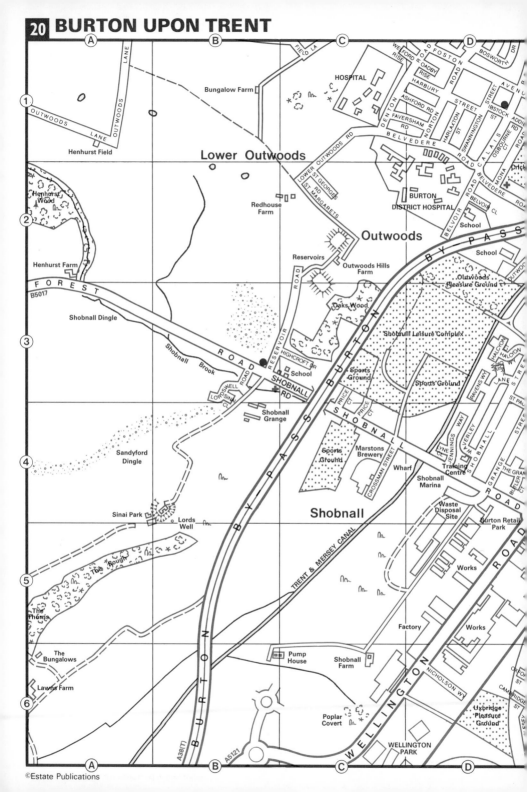

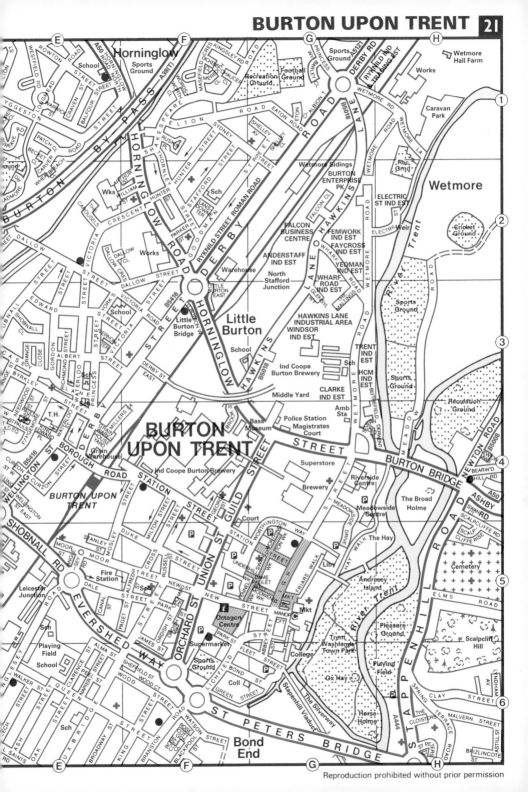

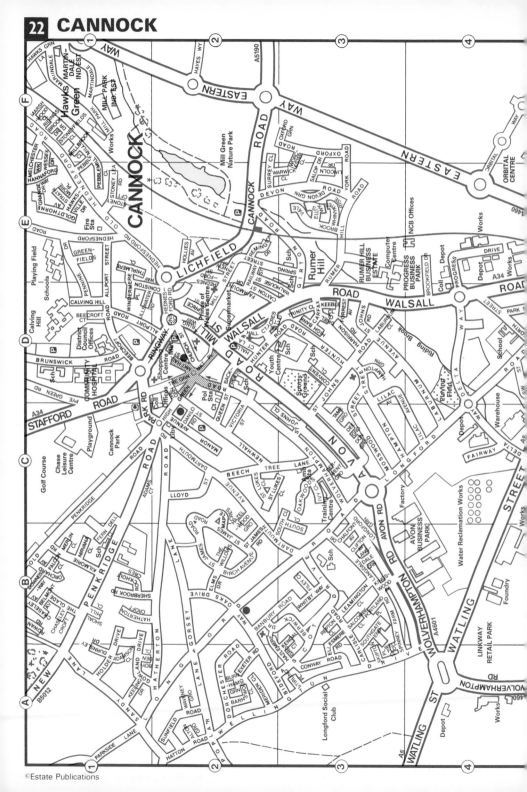

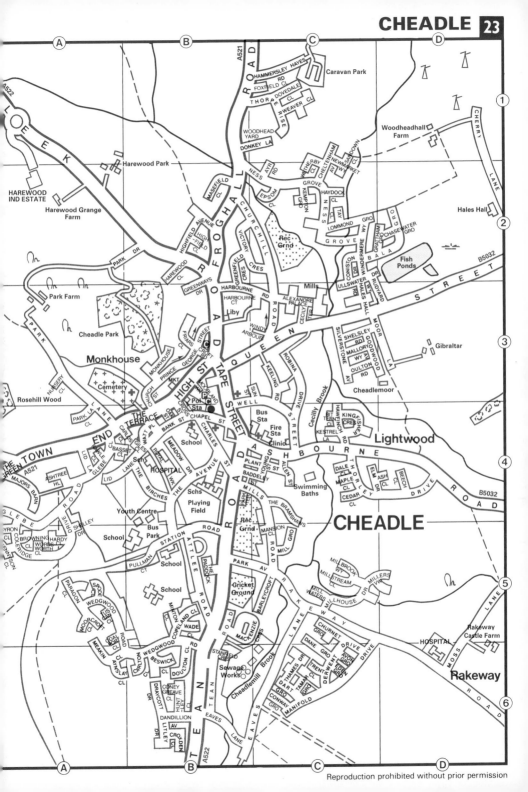

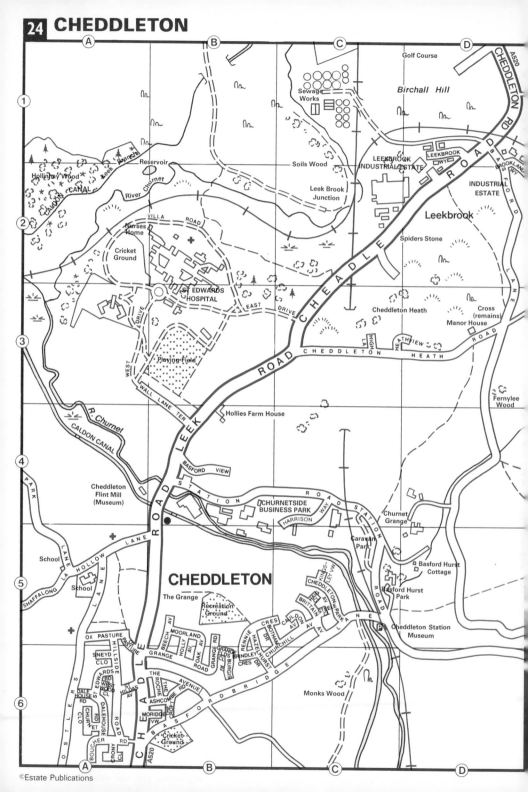

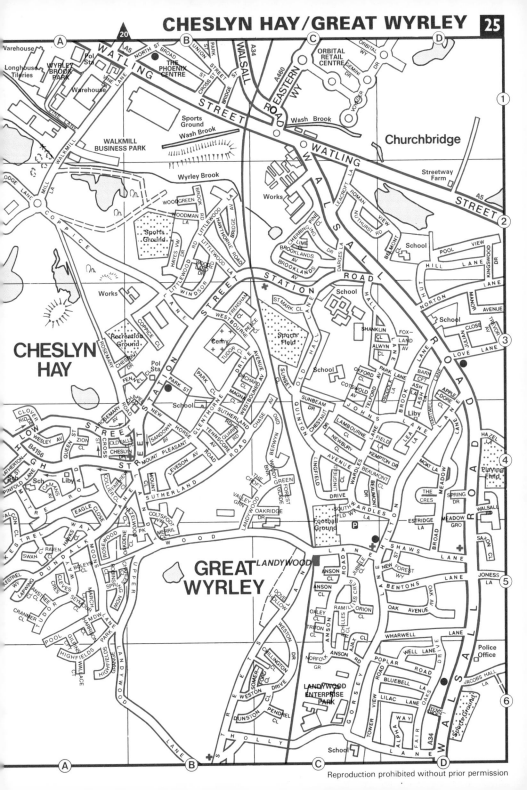

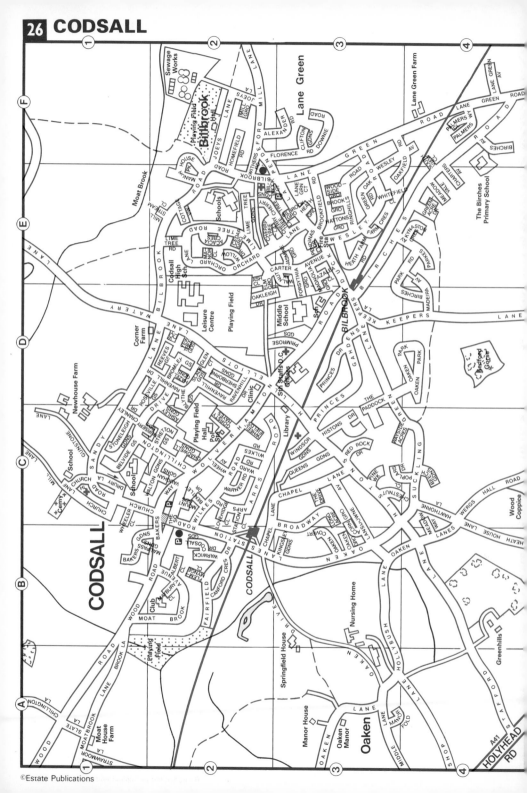

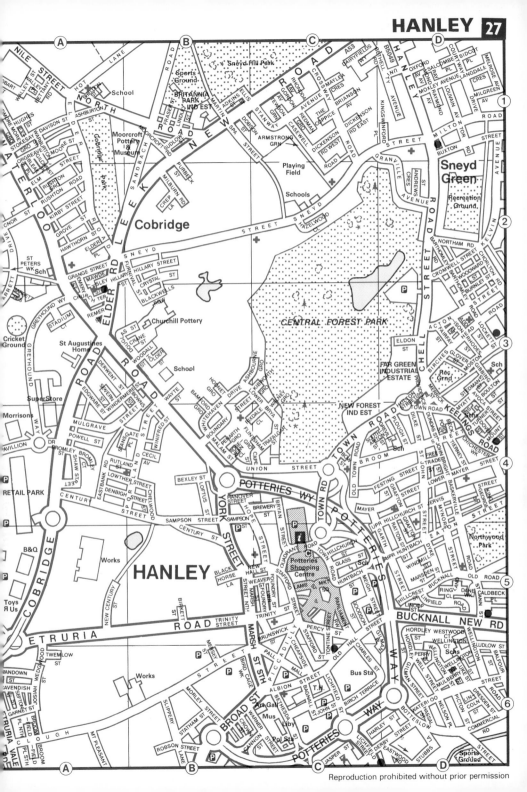

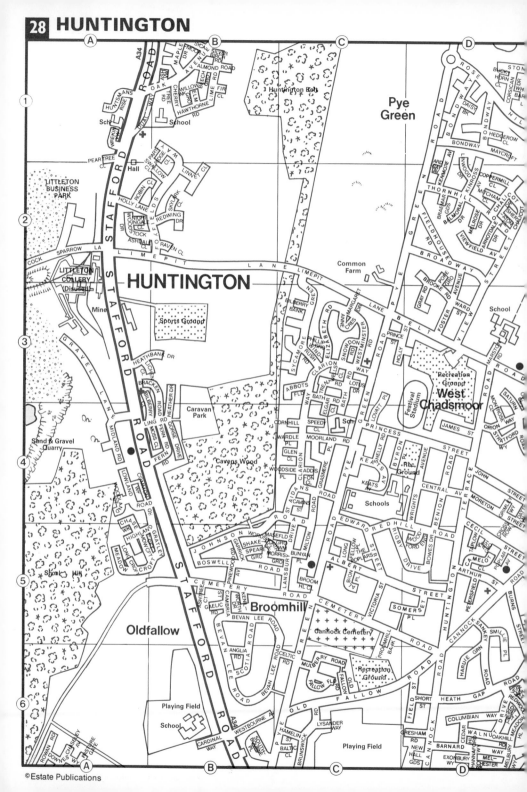

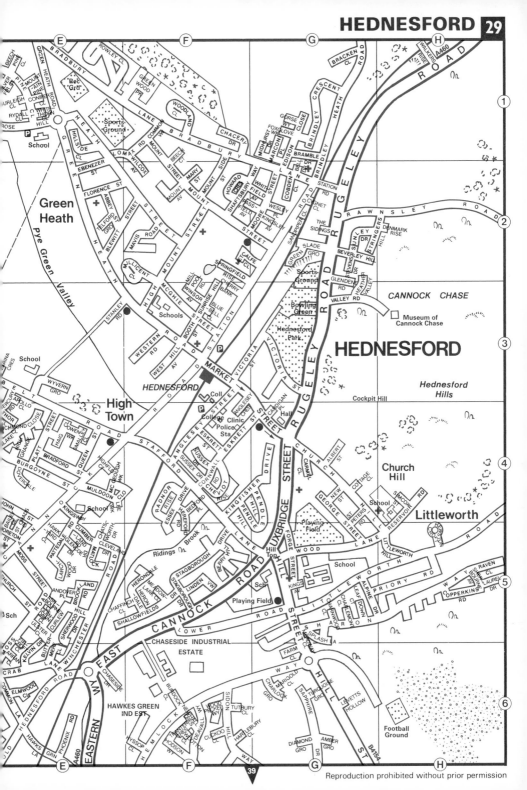

Green Heath

Pye Green Valley

HEDNESFORD

CANNOCK CHASE

Museum of Cannock Chase

High Town

HEDNESFORD

Hednesford Hills

Cockpit Hill

Church Hill

Littleworth

Chaseside Industrial Estate

Hawkes Green Ind Est

Football Ground

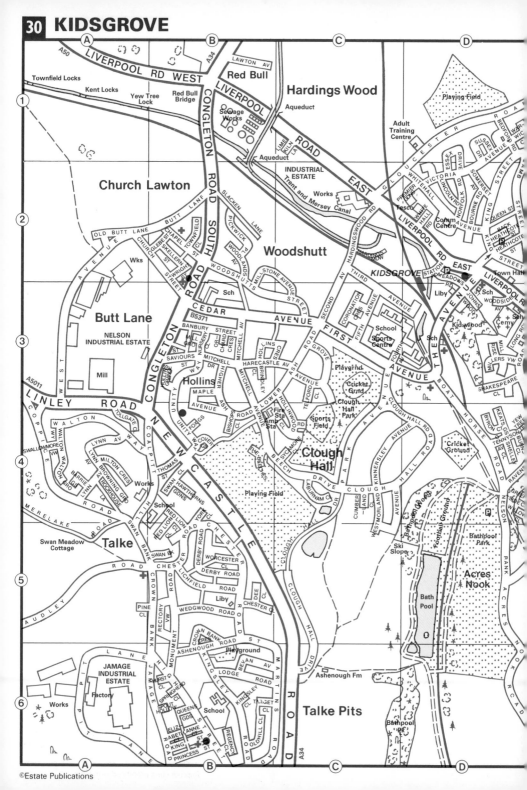

Reproduction prohibited without prior permission

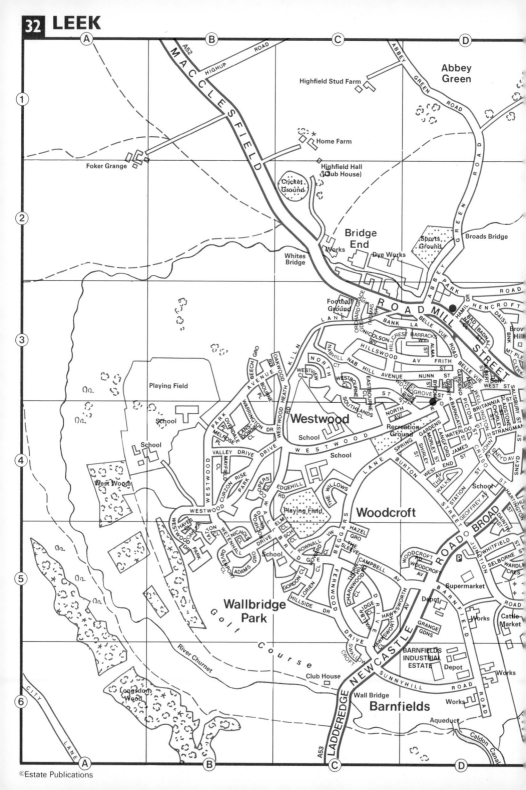

©Estate Publications

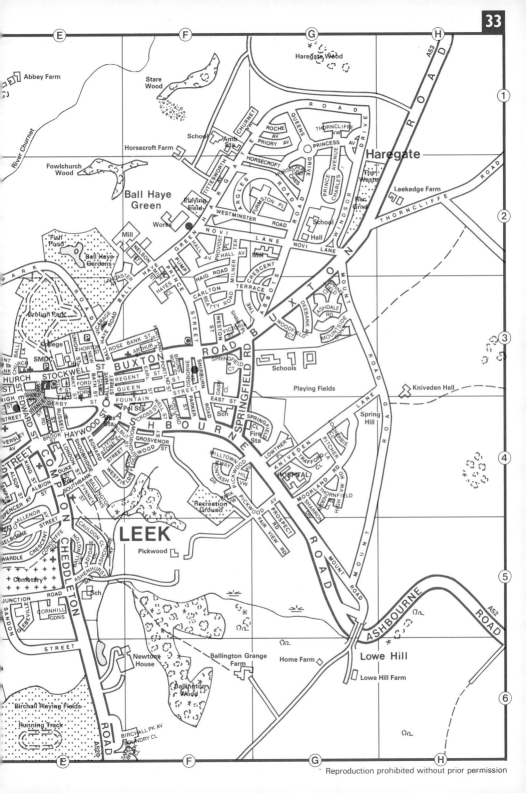

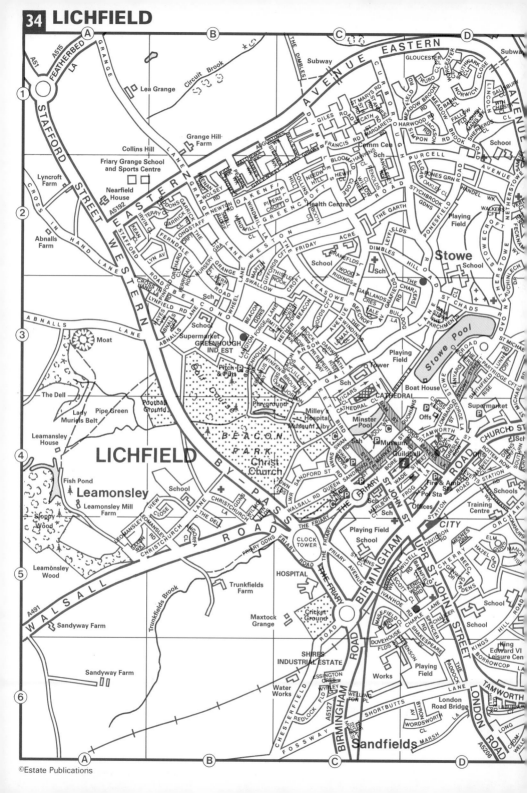

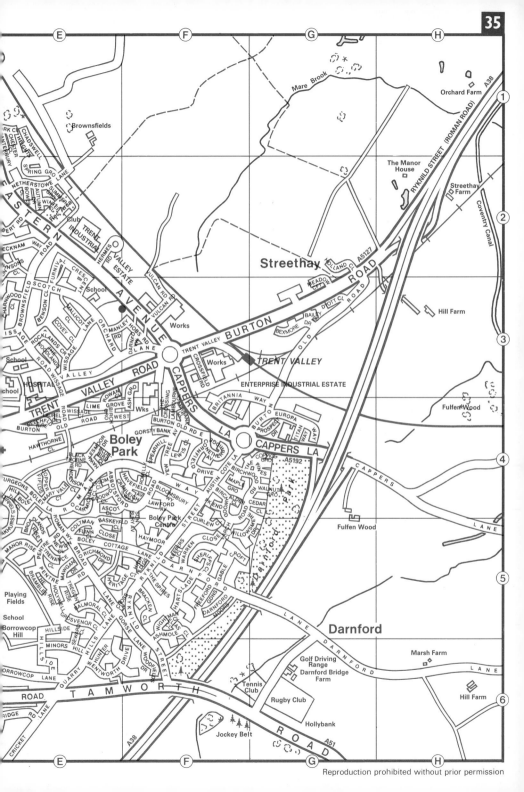

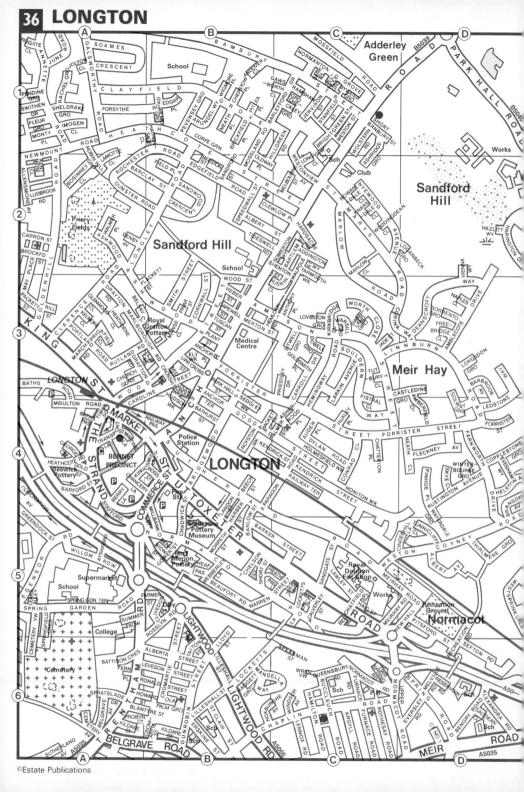

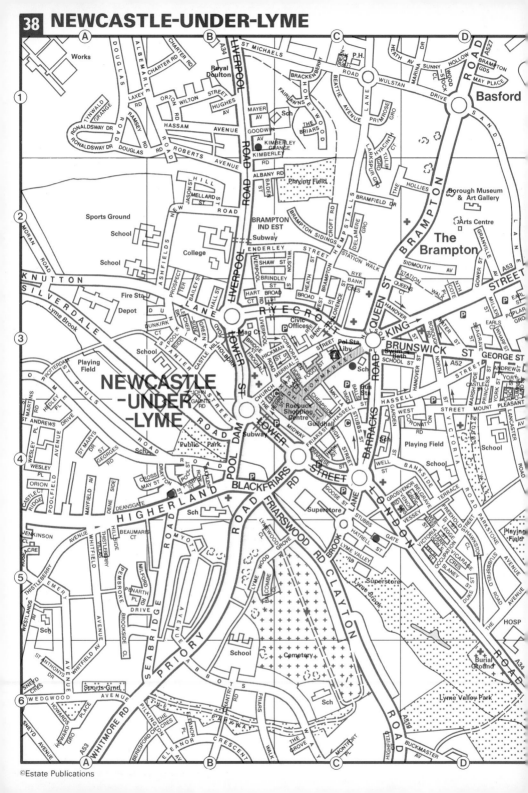

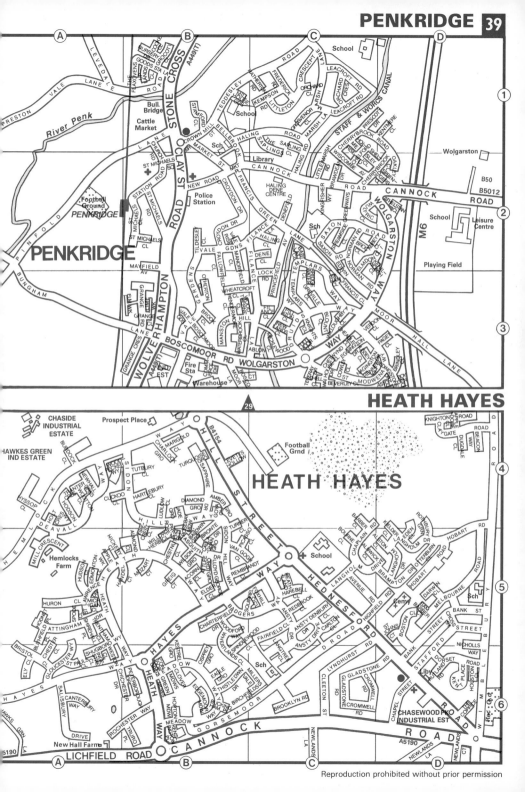

PENKRIDGE

HEATH HAYES

40 RUGELEY

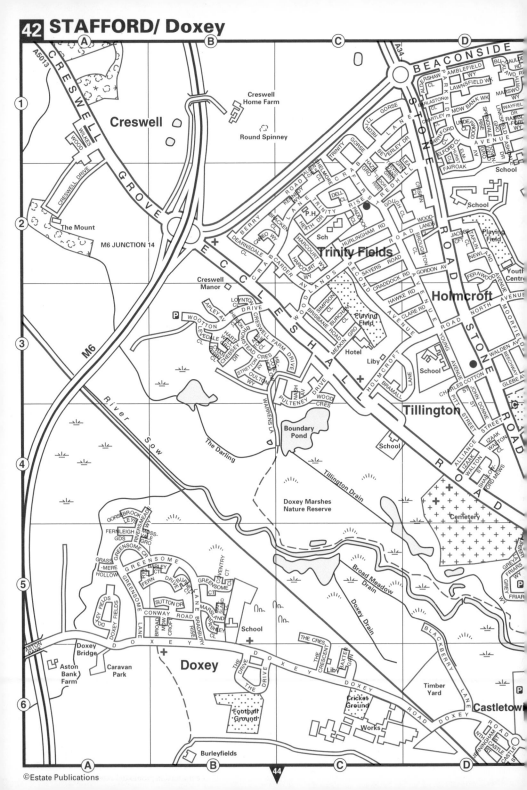

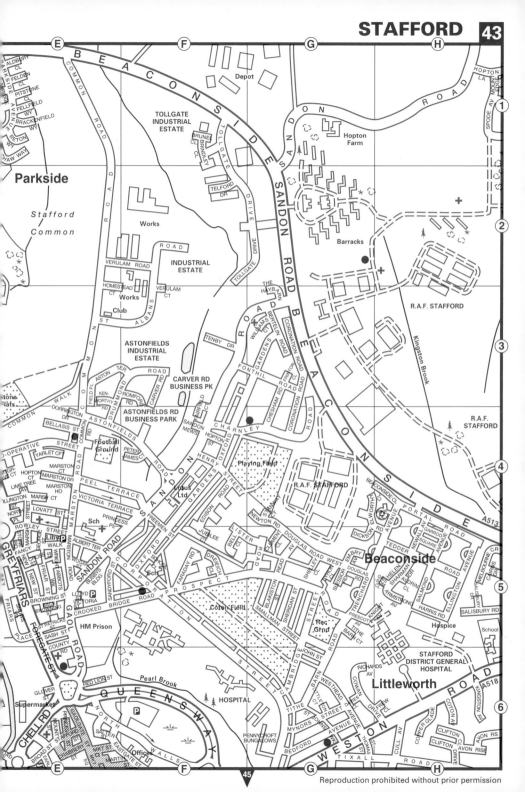

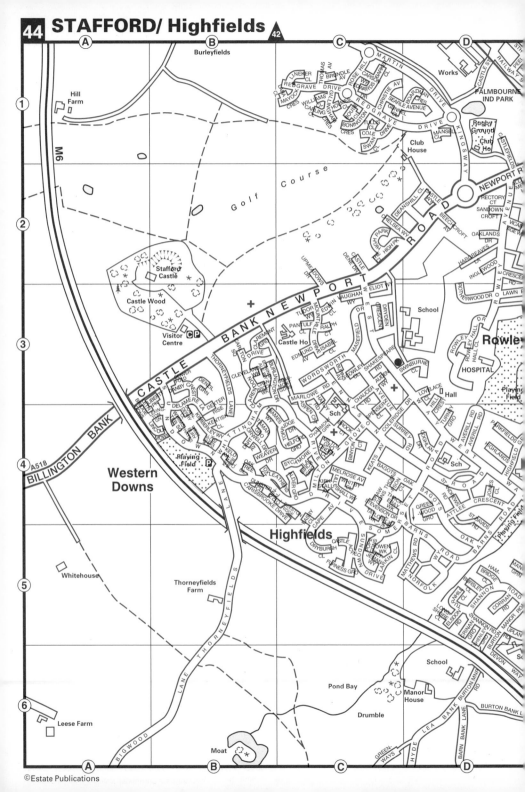

A B C D

Burleyfields

1

Hill Farm

M6

Works

PALMBOURNE IND PARK

Golf Course

Rugby Ground

Club Ho

2

Club House

NEWPORT

Stafford Castle

Castle Wood

Visitor Centre CP

CASTLE BANK

NEWPORT ROAD

School

3

Rowle

HOSPITAL

Hall

Playing Field

Castle Ho

4

A518

Western Downs

Playing Field P

Sch

Sch

BILLINGTON BANK

5

Whitehouse

Thorneyfields Farm

THORNEYFIELDS LANE

Highfields

School

6

Leese Farm

BIGWOOD

Pond Bay

Manor House

Drumble

BURTON BANK

Moat

A B C D

©Estate Publications

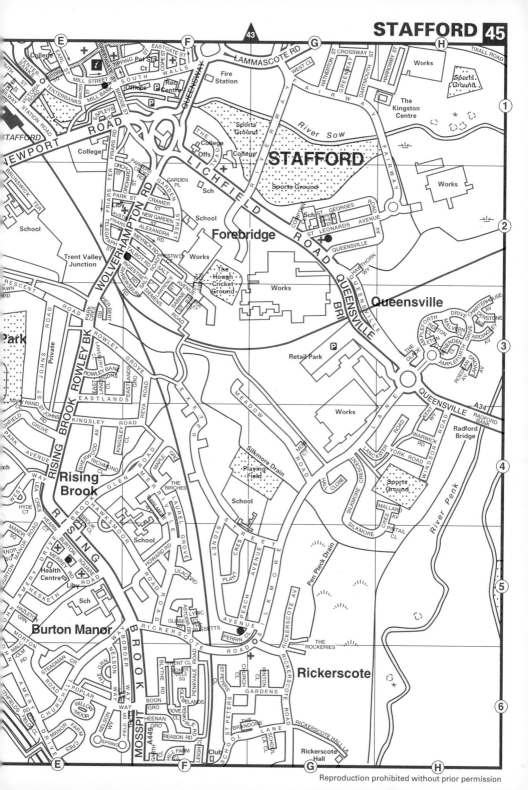

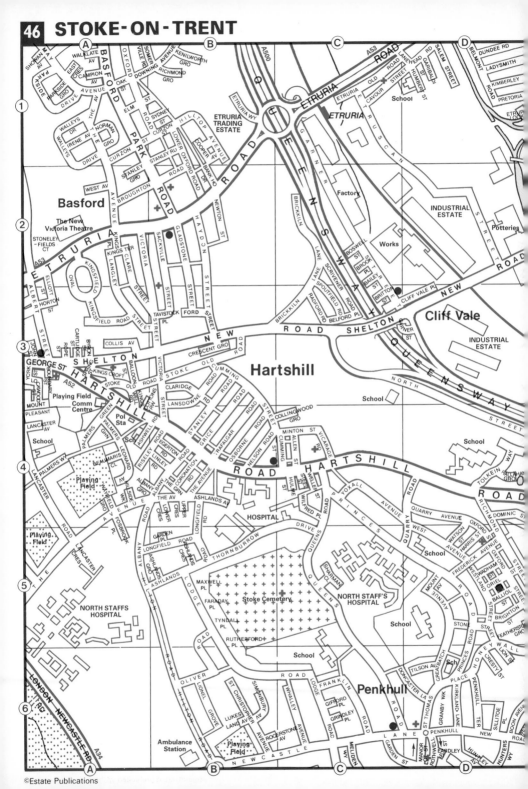

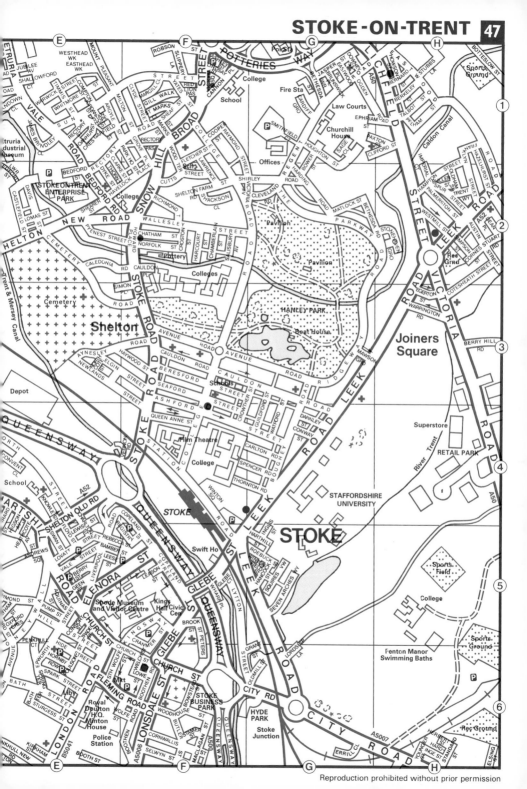

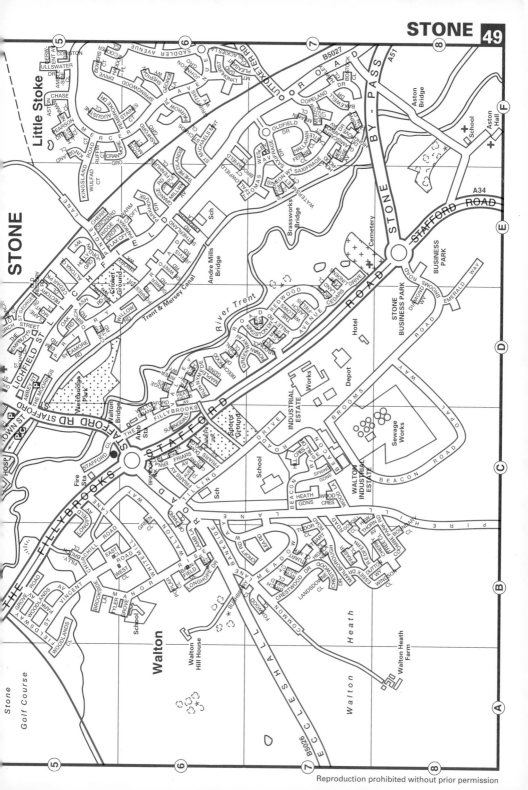

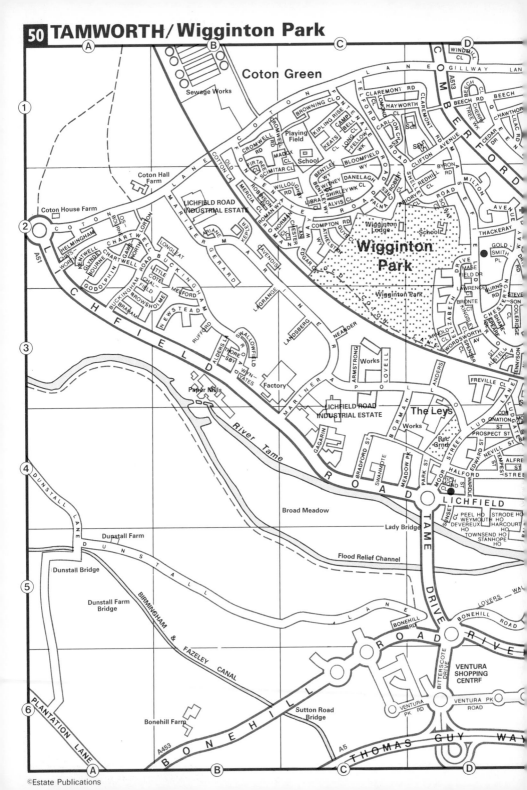

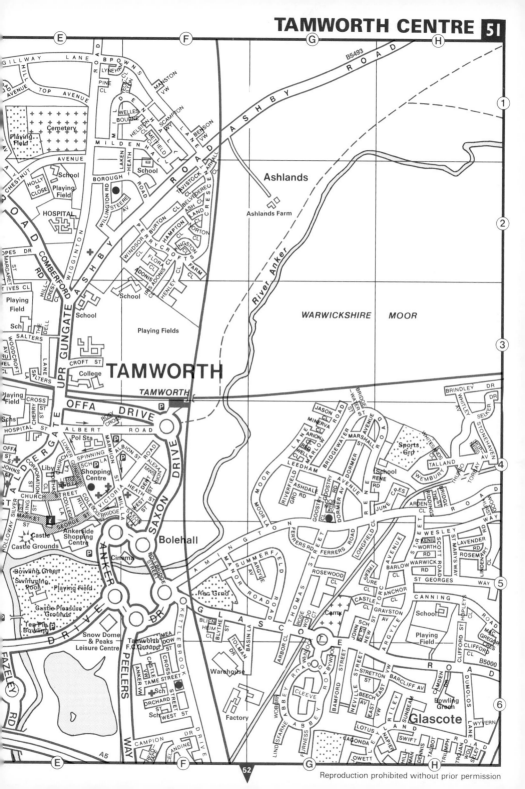

Ashlands

Ashlands Farm

River Anker

WARWICKSHIRE MOOR

TAMWORTH

TAMWORTH

Cemetery

Playing Field

School

School

HOSPITAL

Playing Fields

College

OFFA DRIVE

ALBERT ROAD

Pol Sta

Shopping Centre

Ankerside Shopping Centre

Castle

Castle Grounds

Bolehall

Bowling Green

Swimming Pool

Playing Field

Castle Pleasure Grounds

Ten Pin Bowling

Snow Dome & Peaks Leisure Centre

Tamworth F.C.Ground

Cinema

Rec Grd

Warehouse

Factory

Sports Grd

School

School

Playing Field

Bowling Green

Glascote

Cemy

ASHBY ROAD

B5493

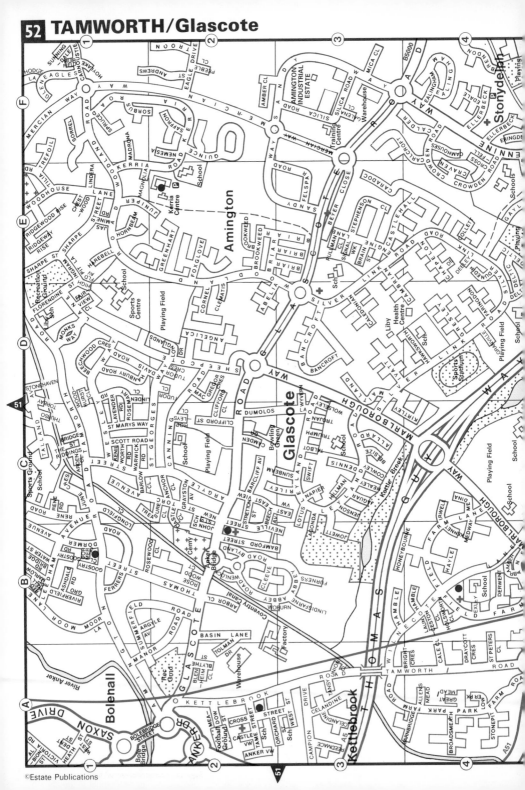

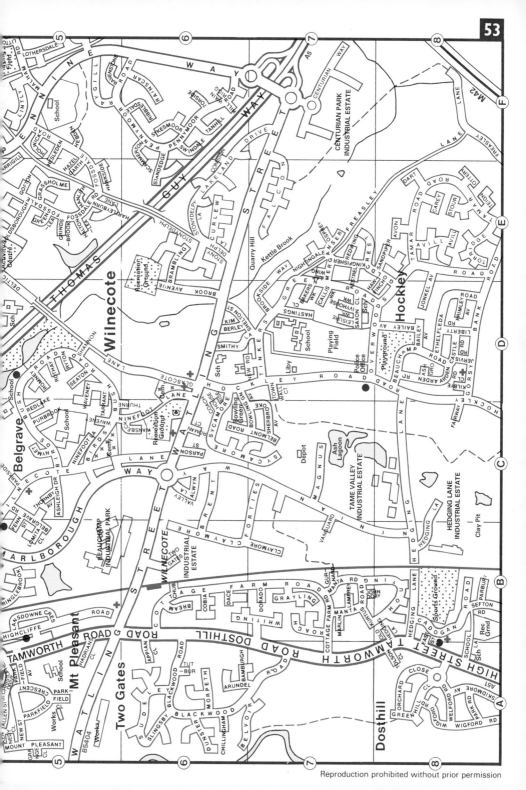

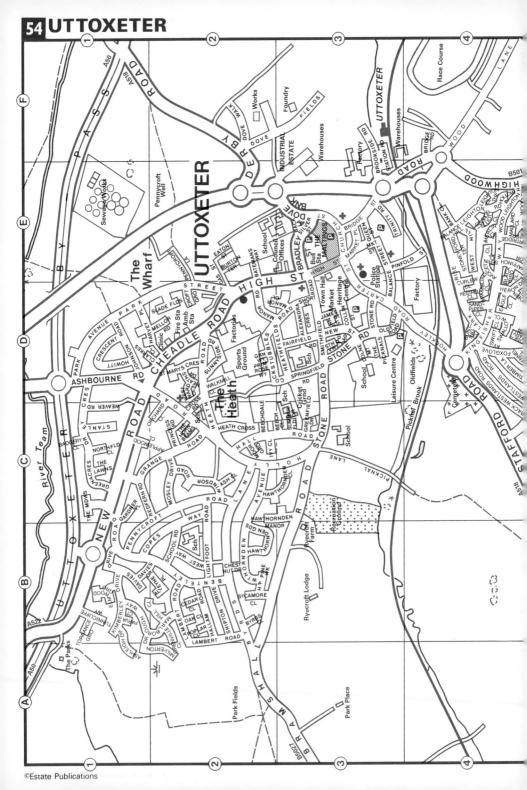

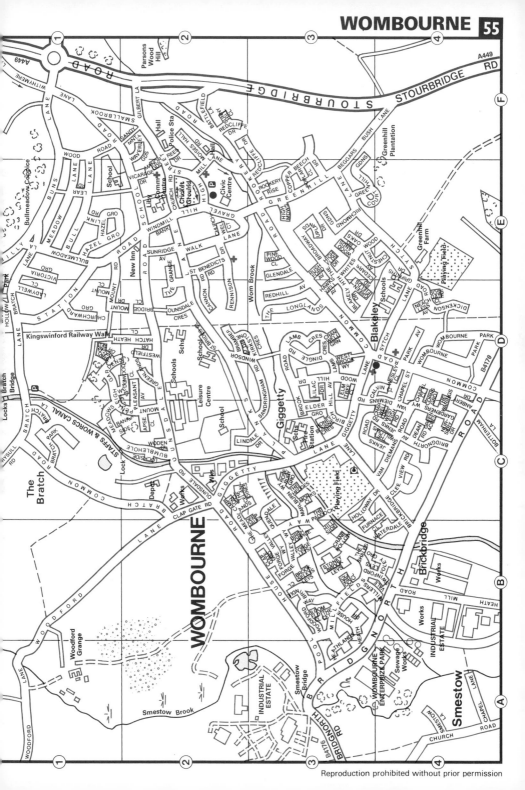

A - Z INDEX TO STREETS
with Postcodes

The Index includes some names for which there is insufficient space on the maps. These names are preceded by an * and are followed by the nearest adjoining thoroughfare.

ALREWAS

Alrewas By-Pass. DE13 12 A2
Anson Rd. DE13 12 B2
Audley Clo. DE13 12 C1
Burton Rd. DE13 12 D2
Burway Meadow. DE13 12 C2
Butts Croft. DE13 12 B1
Chaseview Rd. DE13 12 B2
Church Rd. DE13 12 B1
Churchill Cres. DE13 12 B2
Daisy La. DE13 12 A3
Dark La. DE13 12 C1
Deepmore Clo. DE13 12 C2
Essington Clo. DE13 12 C1
Exchange Rd. DE13 12 C2
Fox La. DE13 12 B2
Furlong Clo. DE13 12 C2
Furlong La. DE13 12 B2
Great Furlong. DE13 12 B2
Heron Ct. DE13 12 B2
Inge Dri. DE13 12 C2
Kings Bromley Rd. DE13 12 A1
Long La. DE13 12 A3
Main St. DE13 12 B2
Manor Fields. DE13 12 B2
Mickleholme Dri. DE13 12 C1
Mill End La. DE13 12 B1
Noon Croft. DE13 12 B2
Oakfield Rd. DE13 12 B2
Overley La. DE13 12 A1
Park Rd. DE13 12 C1
Poppy Gdns. DE13 12 C2
Post Office Rd. DE13 12 B2
Ridget La. DE13 12 C3
Rykneld St. DE13 12 C3
Selwyn Clo. DE13 12 C1
Somerville Rd. DE13 12 B2
Statfold La. DE13 12 B1
Swallow Clo. DE13 12 B2
The Moorings. DE13 12 B1
Turton Clo. DE13 12 C3
Walkfield Rd. DE13 12 B2
Wellfield Rd. DE13 12 C3
Wilkins Croft. DE13 12 B2
William IV Rd. DE13 12 C2

ALTON

Back La. ST10 12 C5
Battlesteads. ST10 12 A6
Castle Hill Rd. ST10 12 C5
Castle Rd. ST10 12 C5
Cedarhill. ST10 12 B6
Cheadle Rd. ST10 12 A5
Cheadle Rd. ST10 12 B6
Church Bnk. ST10 12 C5
Denstone Rd. ST10 12 C6
Dimble La. ST10 12 B6
Farley La. ST10 12 B4
Glen Dri. ST10 12 B6
Headland Way. ST10 12 C5
High St. ST10 12 C5
Hill Rise Rd. ST10 12 C6
Holme Rd. ST10 12 A4
Horse Rd. ST10 12 B5
Hurstons La. ST10 12 C6
Knight La. ST10 12 B5
Lime Kiln La. ST10 12 C6
Malthouse Rd. ST10 12 B5
Nabb La. ST10 12 C6
New Rd. ST10 12 B5
Quixhill Dri. ST10 12 D4
Red Rd. ST10 12 A4
Rock Walk. ST10 12 D4
Saltersford La. ST10 12 C6
Shirley Dri. ST10 12 C6
Smithy Bank. ST10 12 C5
Station Rd. ST10 12 B5
The Hurstons. ST10 12 C5
Toothill La. ST10 12 B5
Uttoxeter Rd. ST10 12 C6
Wheel La. ST10 12 C5

AUDLEY

Aarons Dri. ST7 13 C2
Albert St. ST7 13 C1
Alsager Rd. ST7 13 A1
Apedale Rd. ST7 13 D3
Barleyfields. ST7 13 A2
Benjamins Way. ST7 13 C1
Bignall End Rd. ST7 13 D1
Bignall Hill. ST7 13 D2
Birch Rd. ST7 13 C2
Boon Hill Rd. ST7 13 C3
Booth St. ST7 13 A2
Boughey Rd. ST7 13 C2
Boyles Hall Rd. ST7 13 B1
Bridge Clo. ST7 13 C2
Brindley Way. ST7 13 C2
Cedar Cres. ST7 13 C3
Chapel La. ST7 13 A2
Chapel St. ST7 13 B1
Cherrytree Rd. ST7 13 C2
Chester Rd. ST7 13 A2
Church Bank. ST7 13 B1
Church St, Audley. ST7 13 A2
Church St, Wood Lane. ST7 13 D3
Co-operative La. ST7 13 B5
Dean Hollow. ST7 13 A2
Delph Side. ST7 13 C2
Diglake St. ST7 13 C1
Durber Clo. ST7 13 A3
Edward St. ST7 13 C1
Elm Tree Dri. ST7 13 C3
Fairfields. ST7 13 C2
George St. ST7 13 A3
Georges Way. ST7 13 C1
Grassygreen La. ST7 13 B3
Greenways. ST7 13 C2
Gresley Way. ST7 13 C2
Hall St. ST7 13 B2
Harrison Clo. ST7 13 A5
Hawthorne Av. ST7 13 C3
Heathcote Rd. ST7 13 B4
High St, Alsagers Bank. ST7 13 A5
High St, Wood La. ST7 13 D3
Hill Cres. ST7 13 C6
Hill Ter. ST7 13 B2
Holding Cres. ST7 13 A5
Hope St. ST7 13 C1
Hougher Wall Rd. ST7 13 A2
Ikins Dri. ST7 13 C2
Kelsall Way. ST7 13 A2
King St. ST7 13 A3
Lynsey Clo. ST7 13 B5
McEllin Clo. ST7 13 B1
Maddock St. ST7 13 A3
Meadowside Av. ST7 13 A2
Mellard St. ST7 13 A3
Miles Green Rd. ST7 13 B3
Monument Vw. ST7 13 C2
New King St. ST7 13 A3
New Rd. ST7 13 A2
Old Rd. ST7 13 B1
Park La. ST7 13 A1
Peartree Rd. ST7 13 C3
Peggys Bank. ST7 13 C3
Podmore Av. ST7 13 C6
Podmore La. ST7 13 B6
Princess Av. ST7 13 A3
Queen St. ST7 13 A3
Ravens Clo. ST7 13 B1
Ravens La. ST7 13 C1
Rileys Way. ST7 13 C1
Roberts Clo. ST7 13 C6
School Clo. ST7 13 D3
Station Rd. ST7 13 A5
Station Walks. ST7 13 A5
Stephens Way. ST7 13 C2
The Drive. ST7 13 C6
Tibb St. ST7 13 D1
Tomfields. ST7 13 C3
Turner Av. ST7 13 D3
Vernon Av. ST7 13 A2
Vernon Clo. ST7 13 A2
Victoria Av. ST7 13 B5
Watlands Rd. ST7 13 B1
Wedgwood Av. ST7 13 D3
Wereton Rd. ST7 13 A3
Wesley Pl. ST7 13 A5
Wesley St. ST7 13 D3
Westfield Av. ST7 13 A2
Westlands. ST7 13 C2
Wilbrahams Walk. ST7 13 A1
Wood St. ST7 13 C1
Wood Vw. ST7 13 D3
Woodcroft. ST7 13 D3
Wynbank Clo. ST7 13 B4

BIDDULPH

Akesmore La. ST8 15 A5
Albert St. ST8 14 C4
Asquith Clo. ST8 14 E4
Baileys Bank. ST8 14 D1
Balfour Gro. ST8 14 E4
Banbury Gro. ST8 14 C4
Bateman Av. ST8 15 B7
Beaumont Clo. ST8 14 D2
Bellringer Clo. ST8 15 C5
Birch Av. ST8 15 A6
Blackbird Way. ST8 14 E4
Bluebell Clo. ST8 15 E5
Bollin Gro. ST8 14 E3
Bowmere Clo. ST8 14 C3
Brambles Ct. ST8 15 D5
Brook Gdns. ST8 14 D3
Brook St. ST8 15 A7
Brown Lees Rd. ST8 15 B7
Cambridge Clo. ST8 14 C3
Carriage Dri. ST8 14 E3
Castle View. ST8 15 C6
Cecil Rd. ST8 14 C2
Chaffinch Dri. ST8 14 E4
Chamberlain Way. ST8 14 E4
Charles St. ST8 15 C5
Checkley Dri. ST8 14 D3
Chelsea Clo. ST8 14 C3
Chepstow Clo. ST8 14 C3
Church Clo. ST8 15 D6
Church Rd. ST8 15 D5
City Bank. ST8 14 C2
Clyde Av. ST8 14 E3
Cole St. ST8 15 C5
Colwyn Dri. ST8 15 D7
Congleton Rd. ST8 14 D4
Conway Rd. ST8 15 C6
Coopers Way. ST8 14 C4
Coppice Clo. ST8 15 D5
Cornfield Rd. ST8 15 D5
Coronation Av. ST8 15 B7
Cowlishaw Clo. ST8 15 B7
Crabtree Av. ST8 15 C5
Craigside. ST8 14 C4
Crofters Clo. ST8 14 B4
Cromwell St. ST8 14 C4
Cross St. ST8 14 C4
Crossfield Av. ST8 15 C6
Crossways. ST8 14 E3
Crowborough Rd. ST8 15 F6
Dane Dri. ST8 14 E3
Dart Clo. ST8 14 D3
Dee Clo. ST8 14 E3
Denbigh Clo. ST8 15 C6
Derwent Dri. ST8 14 E3
Devon Gro. ST8 14 C3
Diamond Clo. ST8 14 C4
Doctors Clo. ST8 14 C4
Dorset Dri. ST8 14 C4
Douglas Av. ST8 15 D5
Dove Gro. ST8 14 D3
Duke St. ST8 15 D5
Dunnock Way. ST8 14 E4
East Dri. ST8 14 D4
Eden Clo. ST8 14 E3
Edgeley Rd. ST8 15 D5
Edgeview Ct. ST8 15 C5
Endon Dri. ST8 15 B6
Essex Dri. ST8 14 D2
Farnham Dri. ST8 15 B7
Farnworth Clo. ST8 15 B6
Field View. ST8 14 D3
Firwood Rd. ST8 14 E3
Forrester Clo. ST8 14 C4
Fountain Ct. ST8 14 D3
Gardeners Clo. ST8 15 B7
Gilbern Dri. ST8 15 B7
Gladstone Gro. ST8 14 E4
Goldcrest Way. ST8 14 E4
Grange Ct. ST8 14 D2
Grange Rd. ST8 14 E1
Grangefields. ST8 14 E1
Greenfield. ST8 15 D6
Greenway Rd. ST8 14 E3
Gunn St. ST8 14 C4
Gwyn Av. ST8 15 D6
Halls La. ST8 14 C3
Halls Rd. ST8 14 C3
Hambleton Pl. ST8 15 B7
Hams Clo. ST8 15 C5
Harlech Dri. ST8 15 C6
Havelock Gro. ST8 15 C5
Healey Av. ST8 15 B7
Heath St. ST8 15 C5
Henley Av. ST8 15 A6
High St. ST8 14 C4
Highfield Pl. ST8 14 D4
Highfield Rd East. ST8 14 D4
Highfield Rd West. ST8 14 D4
Hollytree Dri. ST8 14 C2
Humber Dri. ST8 14 E4
Hunters Clo. ST8 14 C4
Hurst Rd. ST8 14 F1
INDUSTRIAL ESTATES:
Brown Lees Ind Est. ST8 15 B8
PWS Ind Est. ST8 15 B7
Ivy House Rd. ST8 14 C2
James Way. ST8 15 A6
John St. ST8 14 C4
John St. ST8 15 C5
Jubilee Clo. ST8 14 D4
Kestrel Clo. ST8 15 B6
King St. ST8 14 C4
Kingsfield Cres. ST8 14 D4
Kingsfield Rd. ST8 14 C4
Kingston Pl. ST8 14 E3
Knowle Rd. ST8 15 C5
Knype Way. ST8 15 B6
Lagonda Clo. ST8 15 B6
Lanchester Clo. ST8 15 B6
Lancia Clo. ST8 15 B6
Lawton Cres. ST8 14 D4
Lawton St. ST8 14 D4
Linden Dri. ST8 14 C3
Linnet Way. ST8 14 E4
Lodge Barn Rd. ST8 15 F6
Long Valley Rd. ST8 14 C2
Lord St. ST8 15 D5
Lotus Av. ST8 15 B6
Lyndhurst Dri. ST8 15 A6
Lyneside Rd. ST8 15 B6
Lynmouth Clo. ST8 15 C6
Mansfield Dri. ST8 15 A6
Marsh Green Clo. ST8 14 D2
Marsh Gro. ST8 14 C2
Marshfield La. ST8 14 C2
Marshgreen Rd. ST8 14 C1
Mason Dri. ST8 14 B4
Mayfield Rd. ST8 15 D6
Meadowside. ST8 15 B6
Medway Dri. ST8 14 D3
Menai Dri. ST8 15 D6
Midfield Clo. ST8 14 C2
Mill Hayes Rd. ST8 15 C8
Minerva Clo. ST8 15 B7
Moor Clo. ST8 14 E3
Moorfield. ST8 14 C4
Moorland Rd. ST8 14 D4
Mow La. ST8 14 A1
Nevin Av. ST8 15 D7
New St. ST8 15 F6
Newpool Rd. ST8 15 A6
Newpool Ter. ST8 15 B7
Norfolk Gro. ST8 14 C3
Northfield Dri. ST8 14 E3
Nursery Dri. ST8 14 C2
Oakdene Way. ST8 15 D5
Oleton Clo. ST8 15 E5
Orme Rd. ST8 15 D7
Ox-hey Cres. ST8 14 D3
Ox-hey Dri. ST8 14 D3
Palmerston Way. ST8 14 E4
Park La. ST8 15 C6
Pennine Way. ST8 14 E2
Plover Dri. ST8 14 E4
Portland Dri. ST8 14 D2
Potters End. ST8 14 C3
Princess St. ST8 15 D5
Queens Dri. ST8 15 D6
Redwing Dri. ST8 14 E4
Ribble Dri. ST8 14 E3
Rosebery Clo. ST8 14 E4
Royce Av. ST8 15 B7
Rupert St. ST8 14 C4
St Johns Pl. ST8 15 D5
St Johns Rd. ST8 15 C5
Salter St. ST8 15 C5
Sandsdown Clo. ST8 14 C3
Sandy Rd. ST8 14 C2
Sawyer Dri. ST8 14 C3
Severn Clo. ST8 14 E4
Shakespeare Ct. ST8 14 C5
Shaw St. ST8 15 C5
Shepherd St. ST8 15 C5
Silver Clo. ST8 14 C4
Smithy La. ST8 14 D2
Smokies Way. ST8 14 C3
South View. ST8 14 C4
Spedding Way. ST8 14 E4
Springfield Clo. ST8 15 D5
Springfield Rd. ST8 15 D5
Squirrel Hayes Av. ST8 15 E6
Stanley Rd. ST8 14 C2
Stanley St. ST8 14 C4
Station Rd. ST8 14 C3
Stringer St. ST8 14 C4
Style Clo. ST8 15 B7
Swallow Walk. ST8 15 D5
Swift Dri. ST8 14 E4
Sycamore Clo. ST8 14 E2
Tame Clo. ST8 14 D3
Tay Clo. ST8 14 E3
Tern Clo. ST8 14 E4
Thames Dri. ST8 14 D3
Thatcher Gro. ST8 14 B4
The Uplands. ST8 14 E2
Thomas St. ST8 14 D4
Torville Dri. ST8 14 E4
Tower Clo. ST8 15 B6
Tower Hill Rd. ST8 15 A6
Trent Gro. ST8 15 D6
Tunstall Rd. ST8 15 C6
Turnlea Clo. ST8 15 B6
Victoria Row. ST8 15 C8
Villa Clo. ST8 15 C5
Walley St. ST8 14 C4
Warwick St. ST8 15 C5
Washington Clo. ST8 14 C2
Weaver Clo. ST8 14 D3
Wedgwood La. ST8 14 C2
Well La. ST8 14 C2
Well St. ST8 14 C4
Wells Clo. ST8 14 D4
West St. ST8 15 C5
Wharf Rd. ST8 14 C4
Whetstone Rd. ST8 14 C2
Whitbread Dri. ST8 14 E4
William Av. ST8 15 D5
Witham Way. ST8 14 E3
Woodhouse La. ST8 14 D2
Woodland St. ST8 15 D5
Wrexham Clo. ST8 14 D3
York Clo. ST8 14 D2

BLYTHE BRIDGE

Adamthwaite Clo. ST11 16 B2
Adamthwaite Dri. ST11 16 B2
Aldrin Clo. ST3 16 A2
Applewood Cres. ST3 16 A1
Argyll Clo. ST11 16 C3
Ash Grn. ST11 16 A2
Ashwood Gro. ST11 16 E3
Avion Clo. ST3 16 A2
Aynsley Dri. ST11 16 C2
Badger Gro. ST3 16 A2

Bancroft La. ST11 16 D3
Bankhouse Rd. ST11 16 F2
Barlstone Av. ST11 16 D3
Batten Clo. ST3 16 A3
Beckenham Clo. ST3 16 A1
Beechwood Clo. ST11 16 D3
Beverley Cres. ST11 16 E2
Birch Gro. ST11 16 E2
Blanchard Clo. ST3 16 A3
Bleriot Clo. ST3 16 A3
Blythe Bridge Rd. ST11 16 C1
Blythe Clo. ST11 16 B2
Blythe Mount Pk. ST11 16 E2
Blythe Rd. ST11 16 E2
Blythe View. ST11 16 D3
Bogs La. ST11 16 D3
Bonnard Clo. ST3 16 A3
Brabazon Clo. ST3 16 A3
Brammall Dri. ST11 16 C2
Bridgwood Rd. ST11 16 E2
Brook Clo. ST11 16 E2
Brook Gate. ST11 16 E1
Canberra Cres. ST3 16 A3
Catalina Pl. ST3 16 A3
Caverswall Av. ST11 16 A1
Caverswall Old Rd.
 ST11 16 D1
Caverswall Rd. ST11 16 D2
Cayley Pl. ST3 16 A3
Cedar Av. ST11 16 E3
Chapel St. ST11 16 E1
Chartley Clo. ST11 16 C3
Cheadle Rd. ST11 16 D3
Chestnut Cres. ST11 16 C3
Churchill Clo. ST11 16 C3
Churnet Rd. ST11 16 D2
Clematis Av. ST11 16 D4
Crossfield Av. ST11 16 D3
Cypress Gro. ST11 16 E3
Dilhorne Rd. ST11 16 F2
Dolespring Clo. ST11 16 E1
Dove Rd. ST11 16 E2
Draycott Old Rd. ST11 16 E2
East Bank Ride. ST11 16 E1
Edenhurst Av. ST3 16 A1
Elmwood Clo. ST11 16 E3
Elmwood Dri. ST11 16 E3
Faceby Gro. ST3 16 A2
Farman Clo. ST3 16 A2
Farnborough Dri. ST3 16 A3
Ferndale Clo. ST11 16 D3
Field Clo. ST11 16 C3
Fieldway. ST11 16 B2
Freckleton Pl. ST3 16 A2
Glaisher Dri. ST3 16 A2
Glebe Clo. ST11 16 E3
Gosforth Gro. ST3 16 A2
Green Clo. ST11 16 B2
Green La. ST11 16 D3
Greenacres Av. ST3 16 A2
Greenwood Rd. ST11 16 E1
Grindley La. ST11 16 B3
Halifax Clo. ST3 16 A3
Hargreave Clo. ST3 16 A3
Hermes Clo. ST3 16 A3
Highfield Clo. ST11 16 B2
Highland Clo. ST11 16 C3
Hillside Av. ST11 16 D2
Honeysuckle Av. ST11 16 D4
Ivy Clo. ST11 16 D3
Jasmine Clo. ST11 16 D3
Kestrel Av. ST3 16 A3
Laburnum Clo. ST11 16 E3
Lavender Av. ST11 16 D4
Limewood Clo. ST11 16 E3
Lysander Rd. ST3 16 A2
Manifold Rd. ST11 16 D2
Maple Cres. ST11 16 E3
Mayfield Dri. ST11 16 B2
Meadow Clo,
 Blythe Bridge. ST11 16 C3
Meadow Clo,
 Forsbrook. ST11 16 F1
Meadowcroft Gdns. ST11 16 A1
Mickleby Way. ST3 16 A2
Midway Dri. ST11 16 C3
Monyash Clo. ST3 16 A3
Mount Pl. ST11 16 E2
Mount Rd. ST11 16 E3
New Close Av. ST11 16 F1
Oakdene Clo. ST11 16 E3
Orchard Rise. ST11 16 C3
Park End. ST11 16 E1
Park View. ST11 16 C3
Park Way. ST11 16 E2
Penk Rd. ST11 16 E2

Pilsden Pl. ST3 16 A2
Pine Ct. ST11 16 B2
Pinetree Dri. ST11 16 B2
Pinewood Gro. ST11 16 E3
Poplar Clo. ST11 16 D3
Portland Clo. ST11 16 B2
Portland Cres. ST11 16 F1
Ridgway Dri. ST11 16 B2
Roseacre La. ST11 16 D3
Rushton Way. ST11 16 E2
Scarratt Clo. ST11 16 F2
Scarratt Dri. ST11 16 F2
Spring Croft. ST11 16 D3
Spring Gdns. ST11 16 E1
Springfield Av. ST11 16 E2
Springfields. ST11 16 C3
Stallington Gdns. ST11 16 D3
Stallington Rd. ST11 16 C4
Stratford Clo. ST11 16 E2
Sutherland Cres. ST11 16 C3
The Avenue. ST11 16 E3
The Grove. ST11 16 C3
Tissington Pl. ST3 16 A2
Trent Rd. ST11 16 D2
Uttoxeter St. ST3 16 A1
Well St. ST11 16 E2
Wesley St. ST11 16 E3
William Av. ST3 16 A1
William Clo. ST11 16 F2
Willow Way. ST11 16 E1
Woodlands La. ST11 16 F3
York Clo. ST11 16 F2

BURNTWOOD

Acorn Clo. WS7 18 C1
Albion Way. WS7 18 C2
Alden Hurst. WS7 18 B2
Amber Dri. WS7 18 C3
Anglesey Clo. WS7 18 B6
Ankers Clo. WS7 19 F4
Anson Clo. WS7 19 E3
Ash Grove. WS7 18 B5
Ashley Rd. WS7 18 A2
Ashmead Rd. WS7 18 D2
Aspen Gro. WS7 18 C2
Avon Rd. WS7 18 C5
Baker St. WS7 18 B4
Balmoral Way. WS7 18 A1
Bampton Av. WS7 18 D2
Bank Cres. WS7 18 C5
Barn Croft. WS7 18 C6
Baron Clo. WS7 18 B1
Beaudesert Rd. WS7 18 C1
Beech Cres. WS7 18 C4
Beechen Gro. WS7 18 B2
Bells La. WS7 18 C1
Belvedere Clo. WS7 18 B5
Benches Clo. WS7 18 A4
Birch Av. WS7 18 B5
Birch Ter. WS7 18 C1
Blackroot Clo. WS7 19 G6
Blackthorne Av. WS7 18 C6
Blandford Gdns. WS7 19 E4
Bleak House Dri. WS7 18 A2
Blenheim Rd. WS7 18 C2
Blythe Clo. WS7 19 G4
Boney Hay Rd. WS7 18 D2
Boulton Clo. WS7 19 E2
Bracken Clo. WS7 19 E3
Brackenhill. WS7 18 D2
Bramble La. WS7 18 D2
Bridge Cross Rd. WS7 18 B3
Brook End. WS7 18 C6
Brooklyn Rd. WS7 18 C6
Browning Rd. WS7 19 E3
Brunel Clo. WS7 18 D2
Burleigh Cres. WS7 18 D6
Burns Dri. WS7 19 E3
Burntwood Rd. WS7 19 F5
Byron Clo. WS7 18 C1
Californian Gro. WS7 18 B2
Camsey La. WS7 19 G2
Cannel Rd. WS7 18 A4
Cannock Rd. WS7 18 A3
Cannock Rd,
 Burntwood. WS7 18 D3
Canterbury Dri. WS7 19 G3
Carlton Clo. WS7 18 C2
Cedar Clo. WS7 18 C4
Cedar Rd. WS7 18 C4
Chapel St. WS7 18 A2
Chase Rd. WS7 18 C5
Chase Vale. WS7 18 B4

Chaselands. WS7 18 A3
Chaseley Gdns. WS7 19 E3
Chaucer Dri. WS7 18 C1
Chawner Rd. WS7 18 A1
Cherry Clo. WS7 18 C4
Chorley Rd. WS7 18 B1
Church Rd. WS7 19 F3
Church St. WS7 18 A5
Cinder Rd. WS7 18 A3
Clinton Cres. WS7 18 D2
Clive Rd. WS7 18 D3
Columbian Cres. WS7 18 B2
Common Vw. WS7 18 C1
Coppice Clo. WS7 18 B2
Coppy Nook La. WS7 18 D5
Copthorne Av. WS7 18 C6
Corsican Clo. WS7 18 C2
Cottage Clo. WS7 18 B5
Cottage La. WS7 18 B5
Cotton Way. WS7 18 B2
Coulson Clo. WS7 18 A1
Coulter La. WS7 19 G2
Court Dri. WS7 18 D2
Crane Dri. WS7 18 C6
Cranfield Rd. WS7 18 D3
Croft Gdns. WS7 18 D2
Cross St. WS7 18 C2
Cumberland Cres. WS7 18 C2
Dale Dri. WS7 18 C5
Darwin Clo. WS7 19 E3
Deal Av. WS7 18 C2
Deerfold Cres. WS7 18 D3
Derwent Gro. WS7 19 F4
Dewsbury Dri. WS7 19 F4
Dove Clo. WS7 19 F4
Duke Rd. WS7 18 B1
Dunston Dri. WS7 18 C2
Dursley Rd. WS7 18 C3
Earls Dri. WS7 18 B1
Eastgate St. WS7 18 A2
Eastwood Av. WS7 18 D2
Edwards Rd. WS7 18 B5
Elder La. WS7 19 E3
Elmhurst Dri. WS7 18 C6
Elunda Gro. WS7 18 A5
Emmanuel Rd. WS7 18 D3
Fair Lady Dri. WS7 18 A2
Fairford Gdns. WS7 19 E4
Farewell La. WS7 19 G4
Ferndale Clo. WS7 18 D4
Fernleigh Av. WS7 18 C2
Fieldfare. WS7 19 F5
Fieldhouse Rd. WS7 18 C3
Filton Av. WS7 18 D2
Forge Clo. WS7 19 F5
Forge La. WS7 19 H4
Foxcroft Clo. WS7 18 D5
Foxhills Clo. WS7 18 C5
Franklin Clo. WS7 18 D4
Galway Rd. WS7 18 C3
Garrick Rise. WS7 19 E3
Glasscroft. WS7 19 H3
Glenmore Av. WS7 18 D4
Gorseway. WS7 18 D5
Gorsley Lea. WS7 19 E3
Grange Av. WS7 18 D4
Grange Rd. WS7 18 C5
Grantwood Av. WS7 18 C5
Green La. WS7 19 F1
Griffin Clo. WS7 18 A3
Hall La. WS7 19 F6
Halston Rd. WS7 18 D3
Hammerwich Rd. WS7 19 F4
Hamps Clo. WS7 19 F3
Hanney Hay Rd. WS7 18 D6
Hawthorne Cres. WS7 18 C4
Hazelmere Dri. WS7 18 D5
Henley Clo. WS7 18 D5
High St,
 Chase Terrace. WS7 18 A2
High St,
 Chasetown. WS7 18 B4
Highfield Av. WS7 18 D3
Highfield Clo. WS7 18 D3
Highfields. WS7 18 D3
Highfields Rd. WS7 18 B6
Hill La. WS7 18 B1
Hill St. WS7 18 B5
Hillcrest Rise. WS7 18 C4
Hobstone Hill La. WS7 19 G1
Holly Grove La. WS7 18 A1
Hospital Rd. WS7 18 B6
Hudson Dri. WS7 19 E4
Hunslet Rd. WS7 18 D2
Hunter Av. WS7 19 E3

Huntsmans Gate. WS7 18 D2
Ironstone Rd. WS7 18 A1
James Hutchens Ct.
 WS7 18 B5
Jerome Way. WS7 19 E3
Johnson Rd. WS7 18 C2
Jones La. WS7 19 H3
Keble Clo. WS7 19 E3
Keepers Clo. WS7 18 D4
King St. WS7 18 B5
Kingsdown Rd. WS7 18 A1
Knight Rd. WS7 18 B1
Knoll Clo. WS7 18 C5
Laburnum Gro. WS7 18 C4
Larkspur Av. WS7 18 D5
Laurel Dri. WS7 19 E3
Lawnswood Av. WS7 18 B5
Lea Hall Dri. WS7 18 A1
Leafdene Av. WS7 18 C2
Leam Dri. WS7 19 F3
Leander Clo. WS7 18 A1
Lebanon Gro. WS7 18 B2
Leigh Av. WS7 18 D3
Lichfield Rd. WS7 19 F4
Lilac Gro. WS7 18 C3
Lime Gro. WS7 19 E4
Linden Av. WS7 18 C2
Littleton Way. WS7 18 A1
Loftus Cres. WS7 18 C5
Lombardy Gro. WS7 18 C2
Longfellow Rd. WS7 18 C1
Lorne St. WS7 18 A2
Lulworth Rd. WS7 18 C3
Lymington Rd. WS7 18 B1
Macadam Clo. WS7 18 D2
Maidstone Dri. WS7 19 F4
Manifold Clo. WS7 19 F4
Manor Rise. WS7 18 C5
Mansion Dri. WS7 19 F6
Maple Clo. WS7 18 B3
Marton Av. WS7 18 D2
Masefield Clo. WS7 18 C2
Mavor Av. WS7 18 A1
May Clo. WS7 18 C1
May Ter. WS7 19 G4
Meadow Vw. WS7 19 F4
Meadway St. WS7 18 C5
Mease Av. WS7 19 F4
Meg La. WS7 18 D1
Melford Rise. WS7 18 B1
Metcalf La. WS7 19 E2
Millett Av. WS7 18 B6
Morley Rd. WS7 18 D3
Morlings Dri. WS7 18 D2
Moss Bank Av. WS7 18 D4
Mount Rd. WS7 18 B1
Mowbray Croft. WS7 18 A1
Myatt Av. WS7 18 C3
Nailers Clo. WS7 19 F4
Nether La. WS7 19 F2
New Rd. WS7 18 D4
New St,
 Chase Terrace. WS7 18 B2
New St,
 Chasetown. WS7 18 B5
Newcomen Clo. WS7 19 E2
Newgate St. WS7 18 C5
No Name Rd. WS7 18 A3
North St. WS7 18 B1
Norton La. WS7 19 E5
Oak La. WS7 18 C1
Oakdene Rd. WS7 18 C4
Oaken Gdns. WS7 18 C2
Oatfield Clo. WS7 18 C6
Ogley Hay Rd. WS7 18 C1
Ogley Hay Rd. WS7 18 D6
Oregon Gdns. WS7 18 C2
Overhill Rd. WS7 18 D5
Overton La. WS7 19 F6
Padbury La. WS7 19 E1
Paget Dri. WS7 18 A1
Park Av. WS7 18 D5
Park Rd,
 Burntwood. WS7 18 D5
Park Rd,
 Chase Terrace. WS7 18 B2
Parkhill Rd. WS7 18 C2
Paviers Row. WS7 18 C1
Penk Dri. WS7 19 F4
Pine Gro. WS7 18 C5
Pingle La. WS7 19 F5
Plant La. WS7 18 A3
Pooles Way. WS7 19 E3
Poplar Av. WS7 18 C4
Princess Clo. WS7 18 A3

Princess St. WS7 18 A2
Prospect Rd. WS7 18 D4
Queens Dri. WS7 18 C5
Queens St. WS7 18 B5
Radmore Clo. WS7 18 A2
Railway La. WS7 18 B1
Rake Hill. WS7 18 D2
Rake Hill Rd. WS7 19 E2
Redfern Dri. WS7 18 D5
Redwing Clo. WS7 19 F5
Redwood Dri. WS7 18 B2
Ring Rd. WS7 18 A3
Robins Rd. WS7 18 A4
Robinson Rd. WS7 18 B2
Rochester Av. WS7 18 C3
Rose La. WS7 19 E3
Rowan Gro. WS7 18 C3
Rugeley La. WS7 19 F2
Rugeley Rd,
 Burntwood. WS7 19 E1
Rugeley Rd,
 Chase Terrace. WS7 18 B2
Russet Clo. WS7 18 D5
Ryecroft Dri. WS7 18 C2
St Annes Clo. WS7 18 B6
St Benedicts. WS7 19 E4
St Giles Rd. WS7 19 E4
St Lukes Rd. WS7 19 E4
St Marks Rd. WS7 19 E4
St Matthews Av. WS7 19 H2
St Matthews Rd. WS7 19 G3
St Pauls Rd. WS7 19 E4
St Peters Rd. WS7 19 E4
St Stephens Rd. WS7 19 E4
Sanderling Rise. WS7 18 D2
Sandown Clo. WS7 18 B1
Sandringham Clo. WS7 18 A1
Scholars Gate. WS7 19 F4
School Clo. WS7 18 A2
School La. WS7 18 A2
School Walk. WS7 18 A2
Scott Way. WS7 18 C2
Segemoor Av. WS7 18 D5
Severn Dri. WS7 19 F4
Shakespeare Rd. WS7 18 B2
Shaw Dri. WS7 18 C1
Shirelea Clo. WS7 18 D3
Siskin Clo. WS7 19 F5
Slade Av. WS7 18 C2
Smiths Clo. WS7 18 A4
Spencer Dri. WS7 18 B2
Spinney Clo. WS7 18 C1
Spinney La. WS7 18 B1
Spring Hill Rd. WS7 18 C4
Springlestyche La. WS7 19 E1
Squires Gate. WS7 19 E2
Squirrells Hollow. WS7 18 C1
Stamford Cres. WS7 18 C3
Stapleford Gdns. WS7 19 F4
Stockhay La. WS7 19 F5
Stour Clo. WS7 19 F4
Summerfield Rd. WS7 18 C5
Sunnymead Rd. WS7 19 E3
Swanfields. WS7 19 E4
Sycamore Rd. WS7 18 B3
Tame Av. WS7 19 F4
Tean Clo. WS7 19 F4
Telford Clo. WS7 19 E2
Tennyson Av. WS7 18 C1
The Crescent. WS7 18 B1
The Orchard. WS7 18 C5
The Ridgeway. WS7 18 C5
The Roche. WS7 19 H1
Thistledown Av. WS7 18 D4
Thornfield Cres. WS7 18 C2
Thorpe Av. WS7 18 A2
Thorpe Clo. WS7 18 A2
Thorpe St. WS7 18 A3
Travellers Clo. WS7 18 C5
Trent Clo. WS7 18 C5
Trevern Dri. WS7 18 B5
Trevithick Clo. WS7 19 E2
Tudor Clo. WS7 19 E4
Tudor Rd. WS7 19 E4
Union St. WS7 18 B1
Upfield. WS7 19 G3
Victory Av. WS7 18 B3
Viscount Rd. WS7 18 B1
Warren Rd. WS7 18 D5
Water St. WS7 18 B1
Wedgwood Clo. WS7 19 E3
Wentworth Clo. WS7 19 E3
Wesley Clo. WS7 18 B1
*Westbourne Cres,
 Hunter Av. WS7 19 E3
Westwoods Hollow.
 WS7 18 D2

Wharf La. WS7 18 C6
Wheatcroft Clo. WS7 18 D5
Whitehouse Cres. WS7 18 D3
Wilkinson Clo. WS7 18 D2
Willow Av. WS7 19 E4
Windsor Clo. WS7 18 A1
Woodford Cres. WS7 19 E3
Woodhouse La. WS7 19 G4
Woodland Way. WS7 18 D4
Wordsworth Rd. WS7 18 C1

BURSLEM/TUNSTALL

Adelaide St. ST6 17 D6
Aitken St. ST6 17 B6
Alderse Clo. ST6 17 B4
Ambleside Pl. ST6 17 D2
America St. ST6 17 A1
Arthur Cotton Ct. ST6 17 D5
Arthur St. ST6 17 B1
Athelstan St. ST6 17 A1
Auckland St. ST6 17 D6
Audley St. ST6 17 A2
Avondale St. ST6 17 A6
Avonside Av. ST6 17 D1
Baddeley St. ST6 17 D5
Bank St. ST6 17 A1
Baptist St. ST6 17 C4
Barber St. ST6 17 C4
Barton Cres. ST6 17 B4
Beaumont Rd. ST6 17 B2
Beckton Av. ST6 17 C2
Billinge St. ST6 17 C6
Blake St. ST6 17 C6
Bond St. ST6 17 A1
Bournes Bank. ST6 17 D6
*Bournes Bank Sth,
  Baptist St. ST6 17 D6
Bradwell St. ST6 17 A6
Brereton Pl. ST6 17 B5
Brickhouse St. ST6 17 D6
Bridgewater St. ST6 17 A6
Broomhill St. ST6 17 A1
Brownhills Rd. ST6 17 B3
Bulstrode St. ST6 17 B6
Burnhayes Rd. ST6 17 C4
Butterfield Pl. ST6 17 B2
Buttermere Clo. ST6 17 B5
Bycars La. ST6 17 D4
Bycars Rd. ST6 17 D5
Calver St. ST6 17 A2
Canal La. ST6 17 A4
Canal St. ST6 17 A6
Capper St. ST6 17 B2
Card St. ST6 17 D6
Carlton Av. ST6 17 D1
Carson Rd. ST6 17 D3
Caulton St. ST6 17 D4
Challinor St. ST6 17 B2
Chapel La. ST6 17 D6
Chatterley St. ST6 17 C4
Church Sq. ST6 17 B6
Clandon Av. ST6 17 B1
Clay Hills. ST6 17 A2
Clayhanger St. ST6 17 D6
Cleveland St. ST6 17 D6
Cliffe Pl. ST6 17 D2
Clive St. ST6 17 B1
Columbine Walk. ST6 17 A2
Connaught St. ST6 17 A3
Coolidge St. ST6 17 A1
Copes Av. ST6 17 B1
Corbett Walk. ST6 17 A2
Corinth Way. ST6 17 A2
Coronation St. ST6 17 B1
Croft St. ST6 17 C6
Cross Hill. ST6 17 D6
Crossley Rd. ST6 17 D3
Crouch Av. ST6 17 D1
Dain St. ST6 17 C6
Dale St. ST6 17 B6
Dalehall Gdns. ST6 17 B6
Dart Av. ST6 17 D1
Davenport St. ST6 17 A6
Dollys La. ST6 17 D3
Doulton St. ST6 17 D5
Ducal St. ST6 17 B6
Duncalf St. ST6 17 C6
Dunning St. ST6 17 C4
Edge St. ST6 17 C6
Ellgreave St. ST6 17 B6
Ennerdale Clo. ST6 17 B6
Enoch St. ST6 17 D6
Evans St. ST6 17 C4

Fairclough Pl. ST6 17 D2
Farndale St. ST6 17 B2
Federation St. ST6 17 C5
Flamborough Gro. ST6 17 B6
Forster St. ST6 17 A2
Fountain Sq. ST6 17 C6
Fuller St. ST6 17 B1
Furlong La. ST6 17 C6
Furlong Par. ST6 17 C6
Furlong Rd. ST6 17 B1
Furlong View. ST6 17 C6
Gibson St. ST6 17 B3
Glendale St. ST6 17 D6
Globe St. ST6 17 B6
Glyn Pl. ST6 17 D2
Goodfellow St. ST6 17 A1
Greenbank Rd. ST6 17 C2
Greengates St. ST6 17 B1
Greenhead St. ST6 17 C5
Gritton St. ST6 17 B3
Grosvenor Pl. ST6 17 A1
Hall St. ST6 17 C6
Hamil Rd. ST6 17 D5
Hand St. ST6 17 B3
Harewood St. ST6 17 A3
Harper St. ST6 17 B6
Hawes St. ST6 17 A1
Hay Mkt. ST6 17 A2
Haywood Rd. ST6 17 D3
Henry St. ST6 17 A1
Herd St. ST6 17 C4
Heyburn Cres. ST6 17 B5
High St. ST6 17 A1
Holland St. ST6 17 A2
Hoover St. ST6 17 A2
Hose St. ST6 17 A2
Hunt St. ST6 17 B2
Huntilee Rd. ST6 17 C2
INDUSTRIAL ESTATES:
  Longport Enterprise
  Centre. ST6 17 A6
Irene Av. ST6 17 D2
Jackson St. ST6 17 D5
Jacqueline St. ST6 17 A1
Jean Clo. ST6 17 D3
Jefferson St. ST6 17 A1
Jenkins St. ST6 17 D5
Joseph St. ST6 17 C6
Keele St. ST6 17 A1
Kenworthy St. ST6 17 B1
King William St. ST6 17 B2
Knight St. ST6 17 A1
Knightsbridge Way.
  ST6 17 A2
Ladywell Rd. ST6 17 A2
Lambert St. ST6 17 B3
Lascells St. ST6 17 A3
Longport Rd. ST6 17 A6
Longshaw St. ST6 17 A6
Lower Hadderidge. ST6 17 C6
Lucas St. ST6 17 B6
Lyndhurst St. ST6 17 C6
McGough St. ST6 17 A2
Machin St. ST6 17 B1
McKinley St. ST6 17 A1
Maddock St. ST6 17 B6
Madeley St. ST6 17 A1
Madison St. ST6 17 A1
Market Pass. ST6 17 C6
Market Pl. ST6 17 C6
Marshall St. ST6 17 C4
May Av. ST6 17 C2
Mayfair Gdns. ST6 17 A2
Medway Walk. ST6 17 D1
Melfont St. ST6 17 C3
Melstone Av. ST6 17 C2
Metcalf Rd. ST6 17 D2
Mier St. ST6 17 B1
Mill Hayes Rd. ST6 17 B4
Mill Hill Cres. ST6 17 D1
Mitchell St. ST6 17 C4
Moorland Rd. ST6 17 D5
Mott St. ST6 17 B6
Mountford St. ST6 17 D5
Mousley St. ST6 17 B6
Murhall St. ST6 17 C5
Nash Peake St. ST6 17 A2
Navigation Rd. ST6 17 C6
Nephew St. ST6 17 B6
New Hayes Rd. ST6 17 B1
New St. ST6 17 C5
Newcastle St. ST6 17 A6
Newport La. ST6 17 B6
Newport St. ST6 17 B6
Nicholas St. ST6 17 D5
Nile St. ST6 17 D6
Norman Av. ST6 17 D2

Norris Rd. ST6 17 D2
Norton Av. ST6 17 D2
Odell Gro. ST6 17 B4
Old Court St. ST6 17 A2
Orme St. ST6 17 B6
Overhouse St. ST6 17 D5
Owen Gro. ST6 17 D5
Packhorse La. ST6 17 C6
Padlowe St. ST6 17 B5
Paradise St. ST6 17 A2
Parsonage St. ST6 17 A1
Persia Walk. ST6 17 A1
Phoenix St. ST6 17 A2
Piccadilly St. ST6 17 A2
Pierce St. ST6 17 A2
Pinnox St. ST6 17 B3
Pitcairn St. ST6 17 B2
Pitt St East. ST6 17 D6
Plex Street. ST6 17 A2
Port Vale Ct. ST6 17 D5
Port Vale St. ST6 17 B6
Price St. ST6 17 D5
Princess Sq. ST6 17 A6
Princess St. ST6 17 A3
Queen St. ST6 17 C6
Queens Av. ST6 17 C2
Railway St. ST6 17 B3
Rathbone St. ST6 17 B2
Regent Av. ST6 17 C2
Reginald St. ST6 17 D5
Reynolds Rd. ST6 17 D2
Richards St. ST6 17 C2
Riley St Nth. ST6 17 C6
Riley St Sth. ST6 17 C6
Robert St. ST6 17 A1
Robin Croft. ST6 17 D6
Roundwell St. ST6 17 A2
Roylance St. ST6 17 A2
St Aidens St. ST6 17 A1
St Chads St. ST6 17 C2
St Johns Sq. ST6 17 C6
St Pauls St. ST6 17 B6
Salisbury St. ST6 17 B1
Sandra Clo. ST6 17 D3
Sant St. ST6 17 B6
Scotia La. ST6 17 C3
Scotia Rd. ST6 17 B2
Scott Lidgett Rd. ST6 17 A6
Sherwin Rd. ST6 17 D2
Shirley St. ST6 17 B6
Spens St. ST6 17 B1
Stanley St. ST6 17 B1
Station St. ST6 17 A6
Steventon Pl. ST6 17 C6
Stirling St. ST6 17 D6
Stringer Ct. ST6 17 A2
Stubbs St. ST6 17 A6
Summerbank Rd. ST6 17 A1
Sunnyside Av. ST6 17 C2
Swan Sq. ST6 17 D6
The Boulevard. ST6 17 B2
Thornley Rd. ST6 17 D2
Tomlinson St. ST6 17 A6
Tower St. ST6 17 A2
Tried St. ST6 17 B6
Trubshawe St. ST6 17 A6
Tyler Gro. ST6 17 C6
Ullswater Av. ST6 17 B5
Victoria Park Rd. ST6 17 B2
Wain St. ST6 17 D4
Walker St. ST6 17 B3
Wardle St. ST6 17 B2
Washington St. ST6 17 B3
Watergate St. ST6 17 A2
Waveney Walk Nth. ST6 17 D1
Waveney Walk Sth. ST6 17 D1
Wedgwood Pl. ST6 17 D5
Wedgwood St. ST6 17 D5
Wesley St. ST6 17 B2
Westport Rd. ST6 17 B3
Wilkinson St. ST6 17 B3
Wilks St. ST6 17 B1
William Clowes St. ST6 17 C6
Williamson St. ST6 17 B3
Woodbank St. ST6 17 C6
Woodland St. ST6 17 B2
Wycliffe St. ST6 17 B6
Yale St. ST6 17 B6
Zion St. ST6 17 D6

BURTON-UPON-TRENT

Abbey St. DE14 21 G6
Addie Rd. DE13 20 D1
Albert St. DE14 21 E3
Albion Ter. DE14 21 G1
Alfred St. DE14 21 F5
All Saints Rd. DE14 21 E6
Alma St. DE14 21 E6
Anglesey Rd. DE14 21 F2
Arthur St. DE14 21 F2
Ash St. DE14 21 E6
Ashby Rd. DE15 21 H4
Ashford Rd. DE13 20 A1
Astill St. DE15 21 H6
Balfour St. DE14 21 E1
Barley Clo. DE14 21 G1
Bearwood Hill Rd. DE14 21 H4
Becket Clo. DE14 21 E1
Beech St. DE14 21 E6
Belvedere Rd. DE13 20 A1
Belvoir Clo. DE13 20 D2
Belvoir Rd. DE13 20 D2
Blackpool St. DE14 21 F6
Blythefield. DE14 21 G3
Bond St. DE14 21 F6
Borough Rd. DE14 21 E4
Bosworth Dri. DE13 20 D1
Bradmore Rd. DE14 21 E2
Branston Rd. DE14 21 F6
Brizlincote St. DE15 21 H6
Broadway St. DE14 21 E6
Brook St. DE14 21 F4
Burton Bridge. DE14 21 H4
Burton By-Pass. DE14 20 B6
Butler Ct. DE14 20 D4
Byrkley St. DE14 21 E3
Calais Rd. DE13 20 D1
Cambridge St. DE14 20 D6
Canal St. DE14 21 E5
Carlton St. DE13 21 E1
Carver Rd. DE14 21 E2
Casey St. DE14 21 E3
Chaucer Clo. DE14 21 F1
Clarence St. DE14 21 E6
Clay St. DE14 21 H6
Craven St. DE13 21 E1
Cross St. DE14 21 F5
Crossman St. DE14 20 C4
Curtis Way. DE14 20 D3
Curzon St. DE14 21 E4
Curzon St West. DE14 21 E4
Dale St. DE14 21 E5
Dallow Clo. DE14 21 E2
Dallow Cres. DE14 21 E2
Dallow St. DE14 21 E2
Dame Paulet Clo. DE14 21 G5
Denton Rd. DE13 20 C1
Derby Rd. DE14 21 F2
Derby St. DE14 21 E4
Derby St East. DE14 21 F3
Derwent Clo. DE14 21 H4
Dickens Clo. DE14 21 F1
Duke St. DE14 21 F5
Eaton St. DE14 21 G1
Edward St. DE14 21 E3
Electric St. DE14 21 G2
Elm Rd. DE15 21 H5
Elton St. DE14 21 E6
Eoston Av. DE14 20 D1
Eton Clo. DE14 21 G1
Evershed Way. DE14 21 E5
Faversham Rd. DE13 20 C1
Fennel Wk. DE14 20 C1
Field La. DE13 20 C1
Flatts Clo. DE14 21 E1
Fleet St. DE14 21 F6
Forest Rd. DE13 20 A1
Friars Wk. DE14 21 G5
George St. DE14 21 F4
Glensyl Way. DE14 21 G3
Goodman St. DE14 21 F2
Gordon St. DE14 21 E3
Grain Warehouse Yd.
  DE14 21 E4
Grange Clo. DE14 21 E3
Grange St. DE14 20 D4
Green St. DE14 21 F6
Guild St. DE14 21 F4
Halcyon Ct. DE14 20 D3
Halcyon Way. DE14 20 D3
Harbury St. DE13 20 D1
Harlaxton St. DE14 20 D1
Hawkins La. DE14 21 F3
Hay Wk. DE14 21 G5
Haywharf Clo. DE14 21 G4
High St. DE14 21 F5
Highcroft Dri. DE14 20 C3
Horninglow Rd. DE14 21 F1

Horninglow Rd. Nth.
  DE14 21 E1
Horninglow St. DE14 21 F3
Hunter St. DE14 21 F2
Ibstock St. DE13 20 D1
INDUSTRIAL ESTATES:
  Anderstaff Ind Est.
  DE14 21 G2
  Burton Enterprise
  Park. DE14 21 G2
  Clarke Ind Est. DE14 21 G3
  Electric St Ind Est.
  DE14 21 H2
  Falcon Business
  Centre. DE14 21 G2
  Faycross Ind Est.
  DE14 21 G2
  Femwork Ind Est.
  DE14 21 G2
  Hawkins La Ind Est.
  DE14 21 G3
  HCM Ind Est. DE14 21 G3
  Ryknild Ind
  Trading Est. DE14 21 G1
  Trent Ind Est. DE14 21 G1
  Wharf Rd
  Ind Est. DE14 21 G2
  Windsor Ind Est.
  DE14 21 G3
  Yeoman Ind Est.
  DE14 21 G2
James St. DE14 21 F5
Jennings Way. DE14 20 D4
King Edward Pl. DE14 21 E4
King St. DE14 21 E6
Kingsley Rd. DE14 21 F1
Lansdowne Ter. DE14 21 F2
Lichfield St. DE14 21 E5
Little Burton East. DE14 21 F3
Little Burton West. DE14 21 F3
Longmead Rd. DE14 21 E1
Lordswell Rd. DE13 20 B3
Lower Outwoods Rd.
  DE14 20 C2
Lyndham Av. DE14 21 H6
Lyne Clo. DE14 20 D4
Malvern St. DE14 21 H6
Manor Croft. DE14 21 G5
Market Pl. DE14 21 G5
Masefield Cres. DE14 21 F1
Meadow Rd. DE14 21 G4
Meadowside Dri. DE14 21 G4
Meredith Rd. DE14 21 F1
Millers La. DE14 21 E4
Milton St. DE14 21 F5
Modwens Wk. DE14 21 G5
Mona Rd. DE14 20 D2
Moor St. DE14 21 E5
Moores Clo. DE14 21 E1
Mosley St. DE14 21 E6
Napier St. DE14 21 E6
Needwood St. DE14 21 E4
New St. DE14 21 F2
Newton Mews. DE15 21 H4
Newton Rd. DE14 21 H4
Nicholson Way. DE14 20 D6
Norton Rd. DE13 20 D1
Oadby Rise. DE13 20 D1
Oak St. DE14 21 E6
Orchard Pk. DE14 21 F5
Orchard St. DE14 21 F6
Ordish Clo. DE14 21 F5
Ordish St. DE14 21 F5
Osbourne Ct. DE13 20 D1
Outwoods La. DE13 20 A1
Outwoods St. DE13 20 D2
Oxford St. DE14 20 D6
Paget St. DE14 21 E5
Park St. DE14 21 F5
Parker St. DE14 21 F2
Patch Clo. DE13 21 E1
Peel St. DE14 21 E1
Pensgreave Rd. DE13 21 E1
Price Ct. DE14 20 C4
Princess St. DE14 21 E3
Princess Way. DE14 21 G1
Queen St. DE14 21 E6
Rangemore St. DE14 21 E4
Ravens Way. DE14 20 D3
Reservoir Rd. DE14 20 B3
Richmond St. DE14 21 E3
Rosecott Clo. DE14 21 F6
Rosecott Gdns. DE14 21 F6
Rowton St. DE14 21 E1
Ruskin Pl. DE14 21 F1
Russell St. DE14 21 F5
St Georges Rd. DE13 20 C2

St Margarets. DE13 20 C2
St Pauls Sq. DE14 21 E4
St Pauls St West. DE14 20 D3
St Peters Bridge. DE14 21 F6
St Peters Ct. DE15 21 E4
Scalpcliffe Rise. DE15 21 H5
Scalpcliffe Rd. DE15 21 H4
Severn Clo. DE14 21 G4
Shakespeare Rd. DE14 21 F1
Sheffield St. DE14 21 F6
Shelley Av. DE14 21 G1
Shelley Clo. DE14 21 G1
Shobnall Clo. DE14 21 E3
Shobnall Rd. DE13 20 B3
Shobnall St. DE14 20 D4
Sinn Clo. DE13 20 B3
Spring Terrace Rd. DE15 21 H6
Stafford St. DE14 21 F2
Stanley St. DE14 21 E5
Stapenhill Rd. DE15 21 H6
Station St. DE14 21 F4
Swan Ct. DE14 21 H4
Swan Wk. DE14 21 G5
Swannington St. DE13 20 D1
Sydney St. DE14 21 F1
The Carousels. DE14 21 E2
The Cloisters. DE15 21 H6
The Grange. DE14 20 D4
The Maltings. DE14 21 G3
Thornley St. DE14 21 F1
Underhill Wk. DE14 21 F5
Union St. DE14 21 F5
Uxbridge St. DE14 21 E6
Vernon Ter. DE14 21 E3
Victoria Cres. DE14 21 E2
Victoria Rd. DE14 21 F3
Victoria St. DE14 21 E3
Walker St. DE14 21 E6
Warwick St. DE14 21 E1
Waterloo St. DE14 21 E3
Watson St. DE14 21 F6
Waverley La. DE14 20 D4
Welford Rise. DE13 20 C1
Wellington Rd. DE14 20 C6
Wellington St. DE14 21 E4
Wellington St East. DE14 21 E4
Wellington St West. DE14 21 E4
Westfield Rd. DE13 21 E1
Wetmore La. DE14 21 H1
Wetmore Rd. DE14 21 G1
Wharf Rd. DE14 21 G2
Wheatbreach Clo. DE14 21 E2
William St. DE14 21 F2
Wood Ct. DE14 21 F6
Wood St. DE14 21 F6
Wordsworth Clo. DE14 21 F1
Worthington Way. DE14 21 G5
Worthington Wk. DE14 21 G5
Wyggeston St. DE13 21 E1
York St. DE14 21 E3

CANNOCK

Adams Ct. WS11 22 C1
Adamson Clo. WS11 22 A1
Allport St. WS11 22 D1
Allport St. WS11 22 D1
Alton Gro. WS11 22 A2
Ascot Dri. WS11 22 A3
Avon Rd. WS11 22 B3
Back Crofts. WS11 22 D2
Banbury Rd. WS11 22 B2
Barnswood Clo. WS11 22 A2
*Beau Ct,
  Hednesford Rd. WS11 22 D2
Beech Tree La. WS11 22 C2
Beecroft Ct. WS11 22 D1
Beecroft Rd. WS11 22 D1
Belmont Av. WS11 22 B1
Berwick Dri. WS11 22 B3
Bideford Way. WS11 22 A3
Birch Av. WS11 22 B2
Boyden Clo. WS11 22 A1
Brook Vale. WS11 22 E3
Brookfield Dri. WS11 22 D4
Brunswick Rd. WS11 22 D1
Burnham Grn. WS11 22 A2
Calving Hill. WS11 22 D2
Carfax. WS11 22 D3
Carlisle Rd. WS11 22 A3
Caxton St. WS11 22 D2

Chalfont Av. WS11 22 B3
Chaseley Av. WS11 22 B1
Chaseley Croft. WS11 22 B1
Church St. WS11 22 D2
Clifton Av. WS11 22 B1
Coniston Way. WS11 22 D2
Convent Clo. WS11 22 D3
Conway Rd. WS11 22 A3
*Cranford Pl,
  Hednesford Rd. WS11 22 D1
Danilo Rd. WS11 22 C2
Dartmouth Av. WS11 22 B3
Dartmouth Rd. WS11 22 C2
Dee Gro. WS11 22 C3
Delta Way. WS11 22 C4
Derwent Gro. WS11 22 C3
Devon Av. WS11 22 E3
Devon Rd. WS11 22 E2
Don Gro. WS11 22 C3
Dorchester Rd. WS11 22 A2
Downesway. WS11 22 B1
Durnsley Dri. WS11 22 A1
Eastern Way. WS11 22 E4
Ellesmere Rd. WS11 22 A3
Ellis Walk. WS11 22 E3
*Elm Croft,
  Church St. WS11 22 D2
Elms St. WS11 22 B2
Exeter Rd. WS11 22 A2
Fairway. WS11 22 C4
Falcon Clo. WS11 22 B1
Farmount Dri. WS11 22 D2
Fern Dell Clo. WS11 22 B1
Filey Clo. WS11 22 B3
Forrest Av. WS11 22 D3
Girton Rd. WS11 22 D3
Goldthorne Av. WS11 22 E1
Gorsey La. WS11 22 B2
Gowland Dri. WS11 22 A1
Grange Dri. WS11 22 E1
Greenfields. WS11 22 E1
Hall Ct. WS11 22 D2
Hall Ct Cres. WS11 22 D2
Hall Ct La. WS11 22 D2
Hampton Grn. WS11 22 D3
Hampton St. WS11 22 C3
Hannaford Way. WS11 22 E1
Harrison Rd. WS11 22 E2
Hatherton Croft. WS11 22 C3
Hatherton Rd. WS11 22 A2
Hatton Rd. WS11 22 C3
Hawks Green La. WS11 22 F1
Hawksville Dri. WS11 22 E1
Hayes Way. WS11 22 F2
Hazelwood Gro. WS11 22 C2
Hazlemere Gro. WS11 22 A3
Hednesford Rd. WS11 22 D2
Hednesford St. WS11 22 E2
High Bank. WS11 22 D3
High Green. WS11 22 C2
Holder Dri. WS11 22 A1
Hollies Av. WS11 22 E2
Hunter Rd. WS11 22 D2
INDUSTRIAL ESTATES:
  Avon Business Park. WS11 22 B4
  Linkway Retail Park. WS11 22 A4
  Martindale Ind Est. WS11 22 F1
  Mill Park Ind Est. WS11 22 F1
  Orbital Centre. WS11 22 E4
  Progress Business Pk. WS11 22 E4
  Rumer Hill Business Est. WS11 22 E3
Ivy Clo. WS11 22 C3
Keeble Clo. WS11 22 D3
Keeling St. WS11 22 A1
Kendal Ct. WS11 22 A3
*Kenilworth Ct,
  New St. WS11 22 E2
Kilmorie Rd. WS11 22 B1
*Kingston Arc,
  Walsall Rd. WS11 22 D2
Kingswood Av. WS11 22 B3
Laburnum Av. WS11 22 C4
Laburnum Clo. WS11 22 D3
Langdale Dri. WS11 22 B3
Langdale Grn. WS11 22 B3
Leamington Clo. WS11 22 B3
Lichfield St. WS11 22 E2
Lilac Av. WS11 22 C4
Lincoln Dri. WS11 22 E3
Lloyd St. WS11 22 C2

Longford Grn. WS11 22 B3
Longford Rd. WS11 22 A1
Manor Av. WS11 22 C2
Maple Cres. WS11 22 B2
Market Hall St. WS11 22 D2
Market Pl. WS11 22 D2
Marshwood Clo. WS11 22 F1
Martindale. WS11 22 F1
Melchester Wk. WS11 22 E1
Meriden Clo. WS11 22 A2
Merlin Clo. WS11 22 B1
Mill Park. WS11 22 F1
Mill St. WS11 22 D2
Millbrook Clo. WS11 22 F1
Mosswood St. WS11 22 C3
New Penkridge Rd. WS11 22 A1
New St. WS11 22 D4
New St. WS11 22 E2
Newhall St. WS11 22 C2
Nirvana Clo. WS11 22 B1
North St. WS11 22 D4
Oaks Dri. WS11 22 B2
Oakwoods. WS11 22 C3
Old Hednesford Rd. WS11 22 E1
Old Penkridge Rd. WS11 22 B1
Orbital Way. WS11 22 E4
Orchard Av. WS11 22 C4
Oriel Clo. WS11 22 D3
Oxford Grn. WS11 22 F3
Oxford Rd. WS11 22 F3
Park Rd. WS11 22 C1
Park St. WS11 22 D4
Parkside La. WS11 22 A1
Pebblemill Clo. WS11 22 E1
Pebblemill Dri. WS11 22 E1
Pennine Clo. WS11 22 D1
Poplar La. WS11 22 A2
Portland Pl. WS11 22 B3
Price St. WS11 22 D2
Progress Dri. WS11 22 D2
Pye Green Rd. WS11 22 D1
Queen St. WS11 22 C2
Queens Sq. WS11 22 D2
Railway St. WS11 22 E2
Reamington Dri. WS11 22 E2
Repton Clo. WS11 22 B3
Ridings Brook Dri. WS11 22 F1
Ringway. WS11 22 D2
Rockholt Cres. WS11 22 B1
*Rowan Ct,
  Ringway. WS11 22 D2
Rowan Rd. WS11 22 B1
Rumer Hill Rd. WS11 22 E3
St James Rd. WS11 22 B2
St Johns Clo. WS11 22 C3
St Johns Rd. WS11 22 C3
St Lukes Clo. WS11 22 C2
Salcombe Clo. WS11 22 B3
Salop Dri. WS11 22 E3
Sandy La. WS11 22 A1
Sherbrook Rd. WS11 22 B1
Shoal Hill Clo. WS11 22 B1
Skipton Pl. WS11 22 A3
South Clo. WS11 22 B3
Southgate End. WS11 22 B3
Spinney Farm Rd. WS11 22 A3
Spring St. WS11 22 E3
Stafford Rd. WS11 22 C1
Stirling Pl. WS11 22 A3
Stoney Croft. WS11 22 E1
Stoney Lea Rd. WS11 22 E1
Stoneyfields Clo. WS11 22 F1
Strathmore Pl. WS11 22 E1
Sunfield Rd. WS11 22 A2
Surrey Clo. WS11 22 E2
Tame Gro. WS11 22 C3
The Glade. WS11 22 B1
The Green. WS11 22 D2
The Willows. WS11 22 B2
Thirlmere Clo. WS11 22 E1
Trinity Clo. WS11 22 D3
Ullswater Rd. WS11 22 D1
Victoria St. WS11 22 C2
Walhouse St. WS11 22 D3
Walsall Rd. WS11 22 D2
Warwick Clo. WS11 22 E2
Watling St. WS11 22 A4
Waveney Gro. WS11 22 A2
Wellfield Clo. WS11 22 A3
Wellington Dri. WS11 22 A2
Wessex Dri. WS11 22 E1
Whinyates Rise. WS11 22 E3

Whitby Way. WS11 22 B3
Windermere Pl. WS11 22 D1
Wolverhampton Rd. WS11 22 A4
Wolverhampton Rd. WS11 22 C3
Worcester Clo. WS11 22 E3
York Rd. WS11 22 E3

CHEADLE

Alexandre Palace. ST10 23 C3
Allen St. ST10 23 C4
Ash Clo. ST10 23 C4
Ashbounre Rd. ST10 23 C4
Ashtree Hill. ST10 23 A4
Attlee Rd. ST10 23 B5
Avon Gro. ST10 23 C6
Aynslay Clo. ST10 23 A6
Ayr Rd. ST10 23 A4
Baddeley St. ST10 23 B4
Bala Gro. ST10 23 C2
Bank St. ST10 23 B4
Barleycroft. ST10 23 C5
Basset Clo. ST10 23 A4
Beech Clo. ST10 23 D4
Beswick Clo. ST10 23 B6
Bittern Clo. ST10 23 C4
Browning Clo. ST10 23 A5
Byron Clo. ST10 23 A5
Carlos Clo. ST10 23 A4
Carlton Clo. ST10 23 B6
Cecily Ter. ST10 23 C3
Cedar Clo. ST10 23 C4
Chapel St. ST10 23 B4
Charles St. ST10 23 B4
Chasewater Gro. ST10 23 D2
Cheltenham Av. ST10 23 C2
Cherry La. ST10 23 D1
Church St. ST10 23 B3
Churchill Rd. ST10 23 B2
Churnet Gro. ST10 23 C5
Coalfort Clo. ST10 23 A5
Coleridge Dri. ST10 23 A5
Coneygreave Clo. ST10 23 B6
Coniston Dri. ST10 23 C2
Conway Gro. ST10 23 C6
Copeland Clo. ST10 23 B5
Croft Rd. ST10 23 B3
Cross St. ST10 23 B3
Croxden Clo. ST10 23 B6
Dale Clo. ST10 23 C4
Dandillion Av. ST10 23 B6
Dane Gro. ST10 23 C6
Dart Gro. ST10 23 C6
Derwent Dri. ST10 23 C6
Donkey La. ST10 23 B1
Doulton Clo. ST10 23 B6
Dovedale Clo. ST10 23 C1
Draycott Dri. ST10 23 B6
Eaves La. ST10 23 B6
Eden Gro. ST10 23 C6
Elm Dri. ST10 23 C4
Epsom Clo. ST10 23 C2
Foxfield Clo. ST10 23 C1
Friars Clo. ST10 23 B3
*Friars Ct,
  Croft Rd. ST10 23 B3
Froghall Rd. ST10 23 B2
Giles Clo. ST10 23 B4
Glebe Clo. ST10 23 A4
Glebe Rd. ST10 23 A4
Goodwood Av. ST10 23 C3
Graitham Gro. ST10 23 D2
Greenfield Cres. ST10 23 B2
Greenways Dri. ST10 23 B2
Hammersley Hayes Rd. ST10 23 C1
Harbourne Ct. ST10 23 B3
Harbourne Rd. ST10 23 B3
Hardy Clo. ST10 23 A5
Harewood Clo. ST10 23 B2
Hawfinch Rd. ST10 23 C4
Haydock Clo. ST10 23 C2
Hayes Hall Rd. ST10 23 C3
High St. ST10 23 B3
Highfield Av. ST10 23 B2
Highfield Clo. ST10 23 B2
Huntley Clo. ST10 23 C6
INDUSTRIAL ESTATES:
  Harewood Ind Est. ST10 23 A2
Keeling Rd. ST10 23 C3
Kempton Gro. ST10 23 C2

Kestrel La. ST10 23 C4
Kingfisher Cres. ST10 23 C4
Leek Rd. ST10 23 A1
Lid La. ST10 23 A4
Litley Dri. ST10 23 B6
Lommond Gro. ST10 23 C2
Mackenzie Cres. ST10 23 B5
Majors Barn. ST10 23 A4
Mallory Way. ST10 23 C3
Manifold Dri. ST10 23 C6
Mansion Clo. ST10 23 C5
Maple Clo. ST10 23 C4
Masefield Clo. ST10 23 B2
Meadow Dri. ST10 23 B4
Meakin Clo. ST10 23 A5
Mill Gro. ST10 23 C5
Millbrook Way. ST10 23 C5
Millers View. ST10 23 C5
Millhouse Dri. ST10 23 C5
Mills Rd. ST10 23 B4
Millstream Clo. ST10 23 C5
Millwaters. ST10 23 C5
Minton Clo. ST10 23 B5
Monkhouse. ST10 23 B3
Moor La. ST10 23 C3
Moorcroft Clo. ST10 23 A5
Moorland Walk. ST10 23 B3
Moss La. ST10 23 D6
Ness Gro. ST10 23 C2
Newmarket Way. ST10 23 C2
Nursery Clo. ST10 23 A3
Oak St. ST10 23 B4
Oulton Rd. ST10 23 A5
Paragon Clo. ST10 23 A5
Park Av. ST10 23 B5
Park Dri. ST10 23 A2
Park La. ST10 23 A3
Park La Clo. ST10 23 A4
Park Ter. ST10 23 B4
Plant St. ST10 23 B4
Prince George St. ST10 23 B3
Pullman Ct. ST10 23 B5
Queen St. ST10 23 B3
Rawle Clo. ST10 23 A4
Rakeway Rd. ST10 23 C5
Robina Dri. ST10 23 C3
Royal Wk. ST10 23 B4
Rudyard Way. ST10 23 C3
Sandown Clo. ST10 23 C1
Shelley Dri. ST10 23 A5
Shelsley Rd. ST10 23 C3
Silverstone Av. ST10 23 C3
Spode Clo. ST10 23 A5
Stanfield Cres. ST10 23 B6
Station Rd. ST10 23 B5
Sun St. ST10 23 C3
Tamar Gro. ST10 23 C6
Tape St. ST10 23 B3
Tay Clo. ST10 23 C2
Tean Rd. ST10 23 B6
Tennyson Clo. ST10 23 A5
Thames Dri. ST10 23 C6
The Avenue. ST10 23 B4
The Birches. ST10 23 B4
The Bramshaws. ST10 23 C4
The Green. ST10 23 A4
The Paddock. ST10 23 B5
The Terrace. ST10 23 C4
Thorley Dri. ST10 23 C4
Thorpe Rise. ST10 23 C1
Town End. ST10 23 A4
Trent Clo. ST10 23 C6
Tuscan Clo. ST10 23 A5
Ullswater Dri. ST10 23 C3
Victory Cres. ST10 23 B2
Wade Clo. ST10 23 B5
Watt Pl. ST10 23 B4
Weaver Clo. ST10 23 C1
Wedgwood Rd. ST10 23 A5
Well St. ST10 23 B3
Wetherby Clo. ST10 23 C2
Windermere Av. ST10 23 C2
Windy Arbour. ST10 23 B3
Woodhead Yd. ST10 23 B1
Wordsworth Clo. ST10 23 A5
Young St. ST10 23 C4

CHEDDLETON

Ashcombe Rd. ST13 24 B6
Basford La. ST13 24 D1
Basford Vw. ST13 24 B4
Basfordbridge La. ST13 24 B6
Beech Av. ST13 24 B6

Botham Dri. ST13 24 B5
Boucher Rd. ST13 24 A6
Brindley Cres. ST13 24 B6
Brittain Av. ST13 24 C5
Brooklands Way. ST13 24 D1
Burgis Av. ST13 24 B6
Cauldon Av. ST13 24 C5
Cheadle Rd. ST13 24 A6
Cheadle Rd. ST13 24 C3
Cheddleton Heath Rd.
 ST13 24 C3
Cheddleton Park Av.
 ST13 24 C5
Cheddleton Rd. ST13 24 D1
Churchill Av. ST13 24 B6
Churnet Clo. ST13 24 A6
Crony Clo. ST13 24 A6
Dalehouse Rd. ST13 24 A6
East Dri. ST13 24 B3
Grange Rd. ST13 24 B6
Grangefields Clo. ST13 24 B6
Haig Clo. ST13 24 C5
Harrison Way. ST13 24 C4
Hazelhurst Dri. ST13 24 B5
Heathview. ST13 24 C3
High La. ST13 24 C3
Hillside Rd. ST13 24 A6
Hollow La. ST13 24 A5
Holly Av. ST13 24 B6
INDUSTRIAL ESTATES:
 Churnetside
  Business Pk. ST13 24 B4
 Leekbrook Ind Est.
  ST13 24 C1
Kingsley View. ST13 24 C5
Leek Rd. ST13 24 B4
Leekbrook Way. ST13 24 D1
Moorland. ST13 24 B5
Moridge Vw. ST13 24 B6
Oak Av. ST13 24 B6
Ostlers La. ST13 24 A6
Ox Pasture. ST13 24 A5
Park La. ST13 24 A4
Rennie Cres. ST13 24 B5
St Edwards Rd. ST13 24 A6
St Hildas Av. ST13 24 A6
Shaffalong La. ST13 24 A5
Sneyd Clo. ST13 24 A6
Station Rd. ST13 24 B4
Steele Clo. ST13 24 C5
The Avenue. ST13 24 B6
The Croft. ST13 24 B6
The Roche. ST13 24 B6
Villa Rd. ST13 24 B2
Wall La Ter. ST13 24 A3
West Dri. ST13 24 A3
Westwood Clo. ST13 24 A6

CHESLYN HAY/ GREAT WYRLEY

Achilles Clo. WS6 25 C5
Ajax Clo. WS6 25 C6
Alpha Way. WS6 25 D6
Alwyn Clo. WS6 25 C3
Anson Clo. WS6 25 C5
Anson Rd. WS6 25 C5
Anstree Clo. WS6 25 A5
Appledore Clo. WS6 25 D3
Ash La. WS6 25 D3
Barn Croft. WS6 25 D3
Beaumont Clo. WS6 25 C4
Beaumont Dri. WS6 25 C4
Belmont Clo. WS11 25 D2
Bentons La. WS6 25 D5
Berwyn Gro. WS6 25 C4
Bluebell La. WS6 25 D6
Boleyn Clo. WS6 25 A5
Bratch Hollow. WS6 25 D1
Bridge Av. WS6 25 B2
Bridge St. WS11 25 B1
Broad Meadow La.
 WS6 25 D5
Broad St. WS11 25 B1
Brook La. WS6 25 D4
Brook Rd. WS6 25 B2
Brooklands Av. WS6 25 C2
Campians Av. WS6 25 A4
Chapel Sq. WS6 25 B3
Collier Clo. WS6 25 A4
Charles Clo. WS6 25 A5
Chase Av. WS6 25 C4
Cherrington Clo. WS6 25 C2
Cheslyn Dri. WS6 25 A4
Chestnut Clo. WS6 25 A3

Chestnut Dri. WS6 25 C4
Chillington Clo. WS6 25 C6
Cleves Cres. WS6 25 A5
Clover Ridge. WS6 25 A4
Coltsfoot Vw. WS6 25 B4
Coppice La. WS6 25 B3
Coppice La. WS11 25 A2
Cotswold Av. WS6 25 C3
Cranmer Clo. WS6 25 A5
Cross St,
 Cheslyn Hay. WS6 25 A4
Cross St,
 Churchbridge. WS11 25 B1
Dove Hollow. WS6 25 C5
Darges La. WS6 25 C2
Dundalk La. WS6 25 A5
Dunston Clo. WS6 25 B6
Eagle Clo. WS6 25 A4
Eastern Way. WS11 25 C1
Estridge La. WS6 25 D4
Fair Oaks Dri. WS6 25 D6
Fairview Clo. WS6 25 A4
Falcon Clo. WS6 25 A4
Fennel Clo. WS6 25 B3
Field La. WS6 25 C4
Forest Glade. WS6 25 C4
Forest Way. WS6 25 D5
Foxland Av. WS6 25 D3
Frensham Clo. WS6 25 B3
Gemini Dri. WS11 25 C1
Gilpins Croft. WS6 25 A5
Glenthorne Dri. WS6 25 B4
Gorsey La. WS6 25 C6
Hall La. WS6 25 C3
Harrison Clo. WS6 25 A5
Hartwell La. WS6 25 D4
Hatherton St. WS6 25 A4
Hawks Clo. WS6 25 A5
Hawthorne Rd. WS6 25 B2
Hayes View Dri. WS6 25 B2
Hazel La. WS6 25 D4
Hazelwood Clo. WS6 25 B4
High St. WS6 25 A4
Highfields Grange. WS6 25 A6
Highfields Park. WS6 25 A6
Hilton La. WS6 25 D5
Holly La. WS6 25 B6
Hut Hill La. WS6 25 D2
INDUSTRIAL ESTATES:
 Landywood
  Enterprise Pk. WS6 25 C6
 Orbital Retail Centre.
  WS11 25 C1
 The Phoenix Centre.
  WS11 25 B1
 Walkmill Business
  Park. WS11 25 A1
 Wyrley Brook Pk.
  WS11 25 A1
Jacobs Hall La. WS6 25 D6
Johns La. WS6 25 C4
Joness La. WS6 25 D5
Jubilee Clo. WS6 25 C5
Julian Clo. WS6 25 D3
Kempton Dri. WS6 25 C4
Kestrel Way. WS6 25 A5
Kingswood Dri. WS6 25 D2
Lambourne Clo. WS6 25 C4
Landywood Grn. WS6 25 B5
Landywood La. WS6 25 B4
Lapwing Clo. WS6 25 A5
Lea La. WS6 25 D4
Leacroft La. WS11 25 C2
Leveson Av. WS6 25 B4
Lilac Av. WS6 25 D6
Lime Clo. WS6 25 C2
Lingfield Clo. WS6 25 C4
Lingfield Dri. WS6 25 C4
Littlewood La. WS6 25 B2
Littlewood Rd. WS6 25 B3
Lodge La. WS11 25 A2
Love La. WS6 25 D3
Low St. WS6 25 A4
Magna Clo. WS6 25 B3
Manor Av. WS6 25 D3
March Clo. WS6 25 A5
Meadow Gro. WS6 25 D4
Merril Clo. WS6 25 B5
Mill La. WS11 25 A2
Mitre Rd. WS6 25 A4
Moat La. WS6 25 D4
Moons La. WS6 25 B4
Mount Clo. WS6 25 B4
Mount Pleasant. WS6 25 B4
New Horse Rd. WS6 25 B4
New St. WS6 25 D5
Newbury Clo. WS6 25 C4

Norfolk Gr. WS6 25 C6
North St. WS11 25 B1
Norton La. WS6 25 D3
Nuthurst Rd. WS11 25 C2
Oak Av. WS6 25 D5
Oakdene Clo. WS6 25 A5
Oakridge Dri. WS6 25 C4
Old Falls Clo. WS6 25 A4
Old Hall La. WS6 25 C3
Orbital Way. WS11 25 C1
Orchard Clo. WS6 25 B3
Orion Clo. WS6 25 C3
Oxford Clo. WS6 25 C3
Oxley Clo. WS6 25 C5
Paddock La. WS6 25 D3
Park Clo. WS6 25 B3
Park La. WS6 25 D3
Park St,
 Cheslyn Hay. WS6 25 B3
Park St,
 Churchbridge. WS11 25 B1
Peace Clo. WS6 25 B3
Pendrel Clo. WS6 25 C6
Pine Clo. WS6 25 C2
Pinfold La. WS6 25 A4
Pool Meadow. WS6 25 A5
Pool Vw. WS6 25 D2
Poplar Rd. WS6 25 C6
Quarry Rd. WS6 25 B4
Queen St. WS6 25 A4
Quinton Venue. WS6 25 C3
Ramillies Cres. WS6 25 C5
Raven Clo. WS6 25 A5
Robins Clo. WS6 25 A5
Roman Vw. WS11 25 C2
Rosemary Av. WS6 25 A4
Rosemary Rd. WS6 25 A3
Rosewood Pk. WS6 25 A5
St Mark Clo. WS6 25 C3
Sandown Av. WS6 25 B4
Saxon Clo. WS6 25 D5
Seymour Clo. WS6 25 A5
Shanklin Clo. WS6 25 C3
Shaws La. WS6 25 D5
Somerford Clo. WS6 25 B6
South Field Way. WS6 25 D4
Spring Dri. WS6 25 C4
Spring Meadow. WS6 25 D4
Station Av. WS6 25 C2
Station St. WS6 25 B3
Streets La. WS6 25 B6
Sunbeam Dri. WS6 25 C3
Sunset Clo. WS6 25 C3
Sutherland Rd. WS6 25 B4
Swan Clo. WS6 25 A5
Telford Av. WS6 25 C4
Tenniscore Av. WS6 25 B4
The Crescent. WS6 25 D4
The Croft. WS6 25 C4
Tower View Rd. WS6 25 C6
Trevor Av. WS6 25 D3
Triton Clo. WS6 25 C5
Tudor Clo. WS6 25 B3
Tudor Way. WS6 25 A5
Union St. WS11 25 B1
Upper Landywood La.
 WS6 25 B5
Valley Grn. WS6 25 B4
Vine La. WS11 25 A1
Voyager Dri. WS11 25 C1
Walkmill La. WS11 25 A1
Wallace Clo. WS6 25 A6
Walsall Rd,
 Churchbridge. WS11 25 C1
Walsall Rd,
 Gt Wyrley. WS6 25 D6
Wardles La. WS6 25 C4
Watling St. WS6 25 A1
Well La. WS6 25 D6
Wesley Av. WS6 25 A4
Westbourne Av. WS6 25 B3
Weston Dri. WS6 25 B6
Wharwell La. WS6 25 D5
Windsor Rd. WS6 25 B3
Woodgreen. WS6 25 B1
Woodland Dri. WS6 25 B2
Woodman La. WS6 25 B2
Woody Bank. WS6 25 C4
Yemscroft. WS6 25 D6
Zion Clo. WS6 25 A4

CODSALL

Acacia Cres. WV8 26 E2
Acorn Gro. WV8 26 B3

Albert Clo. WV8 26 B2
Alexander Rd. WV8 26 F2
Arps Rd. WV8 26 C2
Ash Clo. WV8 26 E2
Ashley Gdns. WV8 26 C2
Azalea Clo. WV8 26 E3
Bakers Gdns. WV8 26 B1
Bakers Way. WV8 26 B2
Beech Gdns. WV8 26 C4
Belvide Gdns. WV8 26 C1
Bentley Dri. WV8 26 C2
Bilbrook Ct. WV8 26 E2
Bilbrook Gro. WV8 26 E3
Bilbrook Rd. WV8 26 D2
Birches Av. WV8 26 F4
Birches Park Rd. WV8 26 D4
Birches Rd. WV8 26 E3
Blythe Gdns. WV8 26 D2
Broadway. WV8 26 C3
Bromley Gdns. WV8 26 D2
Brook Gro. WV8 26 E3
Brook La. WV8 26 A1
Brookfield Rd. WV8 26 E3
Canford Cres. WV8 26 B2
Carter Av. WV8 26 E2
Cedar Gro. WV8 26 E2
Chadwell Gdns. WV8 26 C2
Chapel La. WV8 26 B2
Charters Av. WV8 26 E4
Cherry Tree Gdns. WV8 26 E2
Cherry Tree La. WV8 26 E2
Chestnut Clo. WV8 26 C3
Chillington Dri. WV8 26 D4
Chillington La. WV8 26 A1
Church Hill. WV8 26 C1
Church La. WV8 26 C1
Church Rd. WV8 26 C1
Clifton Gdns. WV8 26 F3
Codsall Gdns. WV8 26 B2
Cottage Vw. WV8 26 E2
Cranley Dri. WV8 26 C1
Downie Rd. WV8 26 F3
Drury La. WV8 26 C1
Duck La. WV8 26 B3
Elliots La. WV8 26 D2
Elm Gro. WV8 26 D2
Fairfield Dri. WV8 26 B2
Farm Cres. WV8 26 E3
Flemmynge Clo. WV8 26 B2
Florence Rd. WV8 26 F2
Forsythia Gro. WV8 26 D3
Glen Ct. WV8 26 C2
Gorsty Hayes. WV8 26 C2
Green Oak Rd. WV8 26 E3
Greenacre Dri. WV8 26 E4
Gunstone La. WV8 26 A1
Hawthorne La. WV8 26 C4
Hazel Gdns. WV8 26 D2
Heath Farm Rd. WV8 26 E3
Heath Gdns. WV8 26 E3
Heath House La. WV8 26 B4
Histons Dri. WV8 26 B3
Histons Hill. WV8 26 C3
Hollybush La. WV8 26 A3
Holyhead Rd. WV8 26 A4
Homefield Rd. WV8 26 F2
Jasmine Gro. WV8 26 E3
Joeys La. WV8 26 F2
Keepers La. WV8 26 D3
Kingsley Gdns. WV8 26 B3
Kynaston Cres. WV8 26 E4
Lane Grn Av. WV8 26 F4
Lane Grn Ct. WV8 26 E3
Lane Grn Rd. WV8 26 B4
Lansdowne Av. WV8 26 B4
Lime Tree Gdns. WV8 26 E2
Lime Tree Rd. WV8 26 E2
Long Acre. WV8 26 C3
Loveridge Clo. WV8 26 C2
Madeira Av. WV8 26 D4
Magnolia Gro. WV8 26 E3
Malpass Gdns. WV8 26 B1
Manor Clo. WV8 26 E2
Manor Fold. WV8 26 A3
Manor House Pk. WV8 26 B2
Maybury Clo. WV8 26 B2
Meadow Vale. WV8 26 E4
Meadow Way. WV8 26 B3
Middle La. WV8 26 A3
Mill Gro. WV8 26 F2
Mill La. WV8 26 C1
Mill Stream Clo. WV8 26 B3
Moat Brook Av. WV8 26 B1
Moatbrook La. WV8 26 A1
Mount Gdns. WV8 26 C2
Nursery Gdns. WV8 26 C2
Oaken Covert. WV8 26 B3

Oaken Dri. WV8 26 A3
Oaken Gro. WV8 26 B3
Oaken La. WV8 26 A3
Oaken Lanes. WV8 26 B3
Oaken Pk. WV8 26 D4
Oakfield Rd. WV8 26 E3
Oakleigh Dri. WV8 26 D2
Orchard La. WV8 26 E2
Palmers Clo. WV8 26 F4
Palmers Way. WV8 26 F4
Parkes Av. WV8 26 E2
Pendeford Mill La. WV8 26 E2
Pendinas Dri. WV8 26 E3
Pine Wk. WV8 26 C3
Poplars Dri. WV8 26 C4
Primrose Gdns. WV8 26 D3
Princes Dri. WV8 26 D3
Princes Gdns. WV8 26 C3
Queens Gdns. WV8 26 C3
Ravenhill Dri. WV8 26 D2
Red Rock Dri. WV8 26 D2
Reeves Gdns. WV8 26 D2
Ringhills Rd. WV8 26 E3
Roseville Gdns. WV8 26 D1
Sandy La. WV8 26 C3
School Clo. WV8 26 D2
Sherborne Gdns. WV8 26 D2
Shop La. WV8 26 A4
Slade Gdns. WV8 26 D2
Slate La. WV8 26 A1
South View Clo. WV8 26 F4
Stafford La. WV8 26 A4
Station Clo. WV8 26 C2
Station Rd. WV8 26 B2
Stoneleigh Gdns. WV8 26 C1
Strawmoor La. WV8 26 A1
Stretton Gdns. WV8 26 C2
Suckling Green La.
 WV8 26 C4
The Drive. WV8 26 C3
The Paddock. WV8 26 D3
Vaughan Gdns. WV8 26 B3
Walnut Av. WV8 26 E3
Walton Gdns. WV8 26 C2
Ward Rd. WV8 26 C2
Warner Rd. WV8 26 C2
Warwick Dri. WV8 26 B2
Watery La. WV8 26 D1
Watsons Gro. WV8 26 E3
Wayside Acres. WV8 26 C3
Wergs Hall Rd. WV8 26 C4
Wesley Av. WV8 26 E3
Wesley Rd. WV8 26 E3
Wheel Av. WV8 26 C2
Wheeler Clo. WV8 26 C1
Wheelfields. WV8 26 C2
Whitfield Clo. WV8 26 E3
Wilkes Rd. WV8 26 C2
Willow Dri. WV8 26 E3
Windsor Gdns. WV8 26 C3
Withers Rd. WV8 26 E2
Wolverhampton Rd.
 WV8 26 C2
Wood Rd. WV8 26 A1
Woodside Gro. WV8 26 E3
Yew Tree Gdns. WV8 26 D2

HANLEY

Acton St. ST1 27 D3
Addison St. ST6 27 D3
Adkins St. ST6 27 B1
Adventure Pl. ST1 27 C6
Albion Sq. ST1 27 C6
Albion St. ST1 27 C4
Arbour St. ST1 27 C4
Armstrong Grn. ST6 27 B1
Ashbourne Gro. ST1 27 B3
Ashburton St. ST6 27 A1
*Ashmore Walk,
 St Ann St. ST1 27 D5
Avoca St. ST1 27 D3
Bagnall St. ST1 27 C6
Balfour St. ST1 27 D6
Bamford Rd. ST1 27 B3
Barrett Cres. ST6 27 A3
Barrett Dri. ST6 27 A3
Barthomley Rd. ST1 27 D2
Baskerville Rd. ST1 27 D4
Beckford St. ST1 27 D4
Bethell Rd. ST1 27 D1
Bethesda St. ST1 27 C6
Bettany Rd. ST6 27 A1
Bexley St. ST1 27 B4
Birch Ter. ST1 27 C6

60

Birches Head Rd. ST1 27 D3
Bird Cage Walk. ST1 27 B6
Birkett St. ST1 27 B5
Black Horse La. ST1 27 B5
Blackwells Row. ST6 27 B3
Bleak Pl. ST6 27 A1
Botteslow St. ST1 27 D6
Boulton St. ST1 27 D3
Boundary St. ST1 27 B4
Bow St. ST1 27 C4
Bowness St. ST1 27 B3
Brewery St. ST1 27 C4
Brianson Av. ST6 27 C1
Broad St. ST1 27 B6
Brockley Sq. ST1 27 C5
Bromley Ct. ST1 27 A4
Bromley St. ST1 27 A4
Broom St. ST1 27 C4
Broomfield Pl Nth. ST1 27 A6
Broomfield Pl Sth. ST1 27 A6
Brunswick St. ST1 27 C5
Bryan St. ST1 27 C4
Bucknall New Rd. ST1 27 D5
Bucknall Old Rd. ST1 27 D5
Burnley St. ST1 27 D3
Burton Pl. ST1 27 C5
Buxton St. ST1 27 D1
Caldbeck Pl. ST1 27 D5
Cannon St. ST1 27 B6
Cape St. ST1 27 C4
Casewell Rd. ST6 27 C1
Cavendish St. ST1 27 A6
Cecil Av. ST1 27 B4
Century St. ST1 27 A4
Charles St. ST1 27 C6
Cheapside. ST1 27 C6
Chell St. ST1 27 D3
Chelwood St. ST1 27 B4
Chichester Walk. ST1 27 D4
Chorlton Rd. ST1 27 D2
Church Ter. ST1 27 A3
Clough St. ST1 27 A6
Cobridge Rd. ST1 27 A5
Commercial St. ST1 27 D6
Courtway Dri. ST1 27 D1
Crane St. ST1 27 B3
Crep La. ST6 27 B2
Cromwell St. ST1 27 D2
Crossway Rd. ST6 27 C1
Crown St. ST1 27 B6
Crystal St. ST1 27 B2
Dairyfields Way. ST1 27 C1
Dane Walk. ST1 27 D5
Davison St. ST6 27 A1
Denbigh St. ST1 27 A4
Derby St. ST1 27 D6
Derwent St. ST1 27 A3
Dickenson Rd East. ST6 27 C1
Dickinson Rd West. ST6 27 C1
Dilke St. ST1 27 D4
Dobson St. ST6 27 B1
Douglas St. ST1 27 B3
Dover St. ST1 27 D4
Dresden St. ST1 27 D6
Dundas St. ST1 27 D4
Dyke St. ST1 27 D5
Eastbank Rd. ST1 27 A4
Eastwood Rd. ST1 27 D6
Eaton St. ST1 27 D5
Edgware St. ST1 27 A3
Elder Pl. ST6 27 A2
Elder Rd. ST6 27 A3
Eldon St. ST1 27 D3
Ellis St. ST6 27 B1
Elm St. ST6 27 A2
Emery St. ST6 27 A2
Etruria Rd. ST1 27 A5
Etruria Vale Rd. ST1 27 A6
Exmouth Gro. ST6 27 A1
Fairfax St. ST1 27 D3
Festing St. ST1 27 D4
Flintsham Gro. ST1 27 C4
Foundry St. ST1 27 C5
Fraser St. ST6 27 B1
Free Trade St. ST1 27 D4
Furnival St. ST6 27 B2
Garnet St. ST1 27 A6
Garth St. ST1 27 D5
Gibbins St. ST1 27 D3
Gilchrist Ct, Emery St. ST6 27 A2
Gilchrist Pl. ST6 27 A1
Gilman Pl. ST1 27 C5
Gilman St. ST1 27 D3

Gitana St. ST1 27 C5
Glass St. ST1 27 C5
Glover St. ST1 27 D3
Goodson St. ST1 27 D3
Gordon Av. ST1 27 C1
Grafton St. ST1 27 D4
Grange St. ST1 27 A2
Granville Av. ST1 27 D2
Greville St. ST1 27 D4
Greyhound Way. ST1 27 A3
Grove St. ST6 27 A2
Hanley Rd. ST1 27 D1
Hanover St. ST1 27 B4
Harley St. ST1 27 D6
Hassal St. ST1 27 D6
Hawthorn St. ST6 27 A2
Hazelwood Clo. ST6 27 C2
Hillary St. ST6 27 B2
Hillchurch St. ST1 27 C5
Hillcrest St. ST1 27 D5
Hobart St. ST6 27 A1
Holder St. ST1 27 B3
Hope St. ST1 27 B4
Hordley St. ST1 27 D5
Hot La. ST6 27 A1
Howson St. ST1 27 D6
Hughes St. ST6 27 A1
Hulton St. ST1 27 D4
Huntbach St. ST1 27 C5
INDUSTRIAL ESTATES:
Britannia Park Ind Est. ST6 27 B1
Far Green Ind Est. ST1 27 D3
New Forest Ind Est. ST1 27 C4
Jasper St. ST1 27 C6
Jervis St. ST1 27 D4
John Bright St. ST1 27 D4
John St. ST1 27 C6
Josiah Wedgwood St. ST1 27 A6
Keelings Rd. ST1 27 D4
Kelvin Av. ST1 27 D2
Kibworth Gro. ST1 27 C3
King George St. ST1 27 D4
Kingswinford Pl. ST6 27 D1
Kirby St. ST6 27 A2
Lamb St. ST1 27 C5
Langdale Cres. ST1 27 D1
Leek New Rd. ST6 27 A2
Lichfield St. ST1 27 C6
Lincoln St. ST1 27 D6
Lindley St. ST6 27 B1
Linfield Rd. ST1 27 D5
Linoop St. ST1 27 D5
Lockett St. ST1 27 D3
Loftus St. ST1 27 B4
Louvain Av. ST1 27 D1
Lower Bryan St. ST1 27 C3
Lower Foundry St. ST1 27 C5
Lower Mayer St. ST1 27 D4
Lowther St. ST1 27 A4
Ludlow St. ST1 27 D5
Malam St. ST1 27 B4
Market Sq. ST1 27 C5
Marsden St. ST1 27 D5
Marsh St Nth. ST1 27 B5
Marsh St Sth. ST1 27 B5
Martin St. ST6 27 B1
Mawdesley St. ST1 27 A2
Mayer St. ST1 27 C4
Maylea Cres. ST6 27 C1
Meigh St. ST1 27 C5
Melrose Av. ST1 27 D1
Merrick St. ST1 27 D3
Mersey St. ST1 27 B6
Milburn Rd. ST6 27 B2
Milgreen Av. ST1 27 D1
Milton Rd. ST1 27 D1
Moorcroft St. ST1 27 B1
Moore St. ST6 27 A1
Morley St. ST1 27 B6
Moston St. ST1 27 D3
Mount Pleasant. ST1 27 A6
Mount St. ST1 27 D4
Moxley Av. ST1 27 D1
Mulberry St. ST1 27 D6
Mulgrave St. ST1 27 A4
Myatt St. ST1 27 D4
Mynors St. ST1 27 D4
Nelson St. ST1 27 D6
New Hall St. ST1 27 B5
Nile St. ST6 27 A1
North Rd. ST6 27 A1

Northam Rd. ST1 27 D2
Old Hall St. ST1 27 C6
Old Town Rd. ST1 27 C4
Orb St. ST1 27 B6
Orgreave St. ST6 27 A1
Oxford Av. ST1 27 D1
Pall Mall. ST1 27 C6
Parker St. ST1 27 B5
Parliament Row. ST1 27 C5
Parliament Sq. ST1 27 C5
Pavillion Dri. ST1 27 A4
Penarth Gro. ST1 27 B4
Percy St. ST1 27 C5
Perry Clo. ST1 27 D6
Piccadilly. ST1 27 C6
Picton St. ST1 27 D6
Plough St. ST1 27 D4
Podmore St. ST6 27 A1
Portland St. ST1 27 B4
Potteries Way. ST1 27 B4
Powell St. ST1 27 A4
Providence St. ST1 27 D3
Purbeck St. ST1 27 B2
Quadrant Rd. ST1 27 C5
Ranelagh St. ST1 27 C6
Ratton St. ST1 27 A1
Raymond Av. ST1 27 D1
Redman Gro. ST6 27 C1
Remer St. ST6 27 A3
Rhodes St. ST1 27 C1
Rhondda Av. ST6 27 C1
Ringland Clo. ST1 27 D5
Rixdale Clo. ST1 27 C4
Robson St. ST1 27 B6
Rosevean Clo. ST1 27 B4
Rushton Gro. ST1 27 A2
Rushton Rd. ST6 27 A2
Rutland St. ST1 27 D1
St Andrews Cres. ST1 27 D2
St Ann St. ST1 27 D5
*St Ann Walk, St Ann St. ST1 27 D5
St James St. ST1 27 B6
St John St. ST1 27 D4
St Luke St. ST1 27 D6
St Peters Walk. ST6 27 A2
Salcombe Pl. ST1 27 D1
Sampson St. ST1 27 B4
Sandbach Rd. ST6 27 B2
Sandon St. ST1 27 A6
Sceptre St. ST1 27 B6
Sefton St. ST1 27 A3
Severn St. ST1 27 A4
Shaw St. ST1 27 A1
Sheldon St. ST6 27 D1
Sidcot Pl. ST1 27 B6
Slippery La. ST1 27 B2
Sneyd St. ST6 27 C4
Southampton St. ST1 27 B1
Spa St. ST6 27 A3
Stadium Ct. ST1 27 C5
Stafford La. ST1 27 C5
Stafford St. ST1 27 B4
Stansgate Pl. ST1 27 C1
Stanway Av. ST6 27 B6
Statham St. ST1 27 D3
Stedman St. ST1 27 A1
Stokesay Gro. ST6 27 A2
Stonor St. ST6 27 D6
Stubbs La. ST1 27 B1
Sudlow St. ST6 27 C1
Tewson Grn. ST6 27 C1
The Coppice. ST6 27 D4
Tierney St. ST1 27 C5
Tontine St. ST1 27 D1
Tor Rd. ST1 27 C4
Town Rd. ST1 27 C4
Trafalgar St. ST1 27 B5
Trinity St. ST1 27 D4
Turner St. ST1 27 A6
Twemlow St. ST1 27 C4
Union St. ST1 27 D1
Unity Av. ST1 27 D4
Upper Hillchurch St. ST1 27 D5
Upper Huntbach St. ST1 27 A1
Walley Pl. ST1 27 B6
Walley St. ST6 27 C3
Walney Gro. ST1 27 A1
Warburton St. ST6 27 B6
Warner St. ST1 27 A1
Waterloo Rd. ST1 27 D6
Waterloo St. ST1 27 B3
Wayte St. ST1 27 C5
Weaver St. ST1

Well St. ST1 27 D6
Wellington Ct. ST1 27 D5
Wellington Rd. ST1 27 D5
Wellington St. ST1 27 D6
Wellington Ter. ST1 27 D6
Westwood Ct. ST1 27 D5
Whitehaven Dri. ST1 27 B4
Windermere St. ST1 27 A4
Windmill St. ST1 27 D5
Winifred St. ST1 27 A4
Woodall St. ST1 27 B3
Woodward St. ST1 27 D2
York St. ST1 27 B4

HEATH HAYES

Acorn Clo. WS11 39 B5
Almond Clo. WS11 39 B5
Alnwick Clo. WS12 39 D5
Alston Clo. WS12 39 D5
Amber Gro. WS11 39 B4
Ansty Dri. WS12 39 C5
Apple Walk. WS11 39 A5
Appledore Clo. WS12 39 D4
Asquith Dri. WS11 39 B5
Atlee Gro. WS11 39 B5
Attingham Dri. WS11 39 A5
Avenue Rd. WS12 39 C5
Badgers Way. WS12 39 B5
Baldwin Gro. WS11 39 B5
Bank St. WS12 39 D6
Barber Clo. WS12 39 C4
Beacon Way. WS12 39 D4
Birchfields Dri. WS12 39 C6
Blithfield Pl. WS11 39 A5
Boston Clo. WS12 39 D5
Bourne Clo. WS12 39 C5
Brampton Dri. WS12 39 D5
Bristol Clo. WS11 39 A6
Bronte. WS11 39 B5
Brooklyn Rd. WS12 39 B6
Buckingham Pl. WS12 39 B6
Burdock Clo. WS11 39 A4
Callaghan Gro. WS11 39 B5
Cannock Rd. WS12 39 B6
Canterbury Way. WS12 39 A6
Carlton Clo. WS12 39 C5
Chapel St. WS12 39 D6
Chaplain Rd. WS12 39 C5
Charlock Gro. WS11 39 B4
Charterfield Dri. WS12 39 B5
Chester Clo. WS11 39 A6
Chestnut Clo. WS11 39 B5
Chichester Dri. WS12 39 B6
Claygate Rd. WS12 39 D4
Cleeton St. WS12 39 C6
Clover Meadows. WS12 39 B6
Condor Gro. WS12 39 B6
Cromwell Rd. WS12 39 C6
Cross St. WS12 39 D5
Cuckoo Clo. WS11 39 A4
Darwin Clo. WS12 39 C1
Deavall Way. WS11 39 A4
Denbury Clo. WS12 39 C5
Diamond Gro. WS11 39 B4
Dorset Rd. WS12 39 C6
Dugdale Clo. WS12 39 D4
Eagle Gro. WS12 39 B5
Eden Clo. WS12 39 D5
Edgemoor Mdw. WS12 39 B6
Edmonton Clo. WS11 39 A5
Elder Clo. WS11 39 B5
Ely Clo. WS11 39 A6
Fairfield Clo. WS11 39 C5
Firecrest Clo. WS12 39 C5
Foxhill Clo. WS12 39 C5
Gladstone Rd. WS12 39 C6
Gladstone Rd. WS12 39 C6
Gloucester Way. WS12 39 A6
Gorsemoor Rd. WS12 39 B6
Goya Clo. WS11 39 B4
Green Mdws. WS12 39 B5
Greig Ct. WS11 39 B5
Handel Ct. WS11 39 A5
Harebell Clo. WS12 39 C5
Hartlebury Clo. WS12 39 A6
Hawks Grn La. WS11 39 A6
Hayes Way. WS12 39 A5
Heath Way. WS11 39 A5
Heathland Clo. WS12 39 B5
Hednesford Rd. WS12 39 C5
Hemlock Way. WS11 39 A5
Hickery Ct. WS11 39 A5

Highfield Rd. WS12 39 C5
Hill St. WS12 39 B4
Hobart Rd. WS12 39 D5
Hodnet Pl. WS11 39 A5
Holt Cres. WS11 39 A4
Hopton Mdws. WS12 39 B6
Houston Clo. WS12 39 D6
Hudson Clo. WS11 39 A5
Huron Clo. WS11 39 A5
Hyssap Clo. WS11 39 A4
INDUSTRIAL ESTATES:
Chasewood Ind Est. WS12 39 D6
Chaside Ind Est. WS11 39 A4
Ingestre Clo. WS11 39 A6
Jade Gro. WS11 39 B4
Kensington Pl. WS12 39 B6
Kent Pl. WS12 39 D6
Kestrel Clo. WS12 39 B5
Kielder Clo. WS12 39 D5
Knighton Rd. WS12 39 D4
Langholm Dri. WS12 39 C5
Langtree Clo. WS12 39 C6
Lichfield Rd. WS11 39 A6
Lloyd George Gro. WS11 39 B5
Ludlow Clo. WS11 39 B4
Lyndhurst Rd. WS12 39 B4
Marigold Clo. WS11 39 B4
Meadow Way. WS12 39 B6
Melbourne Rd. WS12 39 D5
Michigan Clo. WS11 39 A5
Mill Cres. WS11 39 A5
Millers Vale. WS12 39 C6
Mozart Ct. WS11 39 B5
Newlands Ct. WS12 39 C6
Newlands La. WS12 39 C6
Nicholls Way. WS12 39 D6
Osprey Clo. WS12 39 B6
Otterburn Clo. WS12 39 D5
Peterborough Dri. WS12 39 B6
Picasso Clo. WS11 39 B5
Primrose Mdw. WS11 39 B4
Redbrook Clo. WS12 39 C5
Rembrandt Clo. WS11 39 B5
Rochester Way. WS12 39 B6
Rosebay Mdw. WS11 39 B5
Rothbury Grn. WS12 39 D6
Rutland Clo. WS12 39 D6
St Johns Ct. WS12 39 C6
St Lawrence Dri. WS11 39 A5
St Pauls Clo. WS11 39 A6
Salisbury Dri. WS12 39 A6
Sam Barber Ct. WS12 39 D5
Sapphire Dri. WS11 39 B4
Shirehall Pl. WS11 39 A5
Shugboro Way. WS11 39 A6
Sidon Hill Way. WS11 39 A4
Spindleywood Clo. WS12 39 B6
Spode Clo. WS11 39 B5
Squirrel Clo. WS11 39 B5
Stafford St. WS12 39 D6
The Coppice. WS12 39 D6
Thistledown Dri. WS12 39 B6
Trentham Clo. WS11 39 A5
Truro Pl. WS12 39 B6
Turner Clo. WS11 39 B4
Turquoise Gro. WS11 39 B4
Tutbury Clo. WS11 39 A4
Van Gogh Clo. WS11 39 B5
Weston Clo. WS11 39 A6
Wheatlands Clo. WS11 39 B5
Willowherb Clo. WS11 39 B5
Wilson Clo. WS11 39 B5
Wimblebury Rd. WS12 39 D6
Woodford Way. WS12 39 B5
Woodpecker Way. WS11 39 A4

HUNTINGTON/ HEDNESFORD

Abbey St. WS12 29 E2
Abbots Field. WS12 28 C3
Addison St. WS12 28 C4
Albert St. WS11 28 C5
Albert St. WS12 29 G4
Albion Pl. WS11 28 C5
Almond Rd. WS11 28 B1
Alpine Dri. WS12 29 G5
Amber Gro. WS12 29 G6

Andover Pl. WS11 29 E5
Anglesey Cres. WS11 29 F4
Anglesey St. WS12 29 F4
Anglia Rd. WS12 28 B6
Anne Cres. WS11 29 E5
Apollo Clo. WS11 29 E3
Ardgay Av. WS12 28 D2
Arnotdale Dri. WS12 28 D2
Arran Clo. WS11 29 E6
Arthur St. WS11 28 D5
Ash Gro. WS11 28 D5
Ash Vw. WS12 28 B1
Ashbourne Clo. WS11 29 F5
Ashdale Clo. WS12 28 A2
Ashtree Ct. WS11 28 B5
Bailey Clo. WS11 29 E5
Balmoral Dri. WS12 28 D2
Baltic Clo. WS11 28 C6
Barnard Way. WS11 28 D6
Bath Rd. WS11 28 C3
Bedford Pl. WS12 29 F4
Beech Ct.WS12 29 F1
Beech Gro. WS12 28 B1
Beech Pine Clo. WS12 29 E1
Bell Dri. WS12 29 G1
Belt Rd. WS12 28 C3
Benion Rd. WS12 28 D4
Berry Hill. WS12 29 F5
Bevan Lee Rd. WS12 28 B5
Beverley Hill. WS12 29 G2
Bilberry Bank. WS11 28 C3
Bilberry Clo. WS12 28 A3
Blake Clo. WS11 29 E4
Blewitt St. WS12 29 E2
Bluebell Clo. WS12 29 F3
Bondway. WS12 28 D1
Booth St. WS12 29 F3
Boswell Rd. WS11 28 B5
Bowes Dri. WS11 28 D5
Bracken Clo. WS12 29 G1
Bracken Rd. WS12 28 A3
Bradbury La. WS12 29 E1
Bradford St. WS11 29 E4
Braemar Gdns. WS12 28 D2
Bramble Dri. WS12 29 G1
Brindley Cres. WS12 29 G1
Brindley Heath Rd.
 WS12 29 G2
Broadway. WS12 28 D2
Brooke Rd. WS12 28 D2
Brookland Rd. WS11 29 E5
Broomhill Bank. WS11 28 C5
Broomhill Clo. WS11 28 C5
Brunswick Rd. WS11 28 C6
Buckthorn Clo. WS12 28 D1
Bunyan Pl. WS11 28 C5
Burdock Clo. WS12 29 F6
Burgoyne St. WS11 29 E4
Burleigh Clo. WS12 29 E1
Burns St. WS11 28 D5
Buttermere Clo. WS11 29 E6
Byron Pl. WS11 28 C4
Cambria St. WS11 28 B5
Camelot Clo. WS11 28 D5
Cannock Rd. WS11 28 D6
Cardigan Pl. WS12 29 G4
Cardinal Way. WS12 29 G4
Carmel Clo. WS12 29 G4
Cavans St. WS11 28 C4
Cecil St. WS11 28 D5
Cedar Hill. WS11 28 D6
Celtic Rd. WS11 28 C6
Cemetery Rd. WS11 28 B5
Central Av. WS11 28 D4
Chacery Dri. WS12 29 F1
Chaffinch Clo. WS11 29 E5
Chalicot Dri. WS12 29 G2
Charlemont Clo. WS12 29 G5
Charlock Gro. WS12 29 G6
Charnwood Clo. WS12 29 G5
Chase Wk. WS11 28 A4
Chaseley Av. WS11 28 A6
Chasedale Dri. WS11 29 E6
Chatsworth Dri. WS11 29 F5
Cherry Bank. WS12 29 F3
Cherry Tree Rd. WS12 28 B1
Cheviot Rise. WS12 29 F4
Church Hill. WS12 29 G4
Church St. WS11 29 E5
Clarion Way. WS11 28 C4
Cleveland Dri. WS11 29 E5
Cobden Clo. WS12 29 F4
Cock Sparrow La. WS12 28 A2
Columbian Way. WS11 28 D6
Common La. WS11 29 E6
Common Vw. WS12 29 F1
Common Walk. WS12 28 A4

Conifer Clo. WS12 29 E1
Copperkins Rd. WS12 29 H6
Coppermill Clo. WS12 28 D2
Cornhill. WS12 28 C4
Cornwall Rd. WS12 29 F4
Corsican Dri. WS12 28 D1
Cottage Clo. WS12 29 G4
Crab La. WS11 29 E6
Cross Row. WS11 28 D5
Cuckoo Clo. WS12 29 F6
Cumberland Rd. WS11 29 E5
Curlew Hill. WS11 29 E5
Cygnet Clo. WS12 29 G2
Daisy Bank. WS12 28 D1
Deavall Way. WS11 29 F6
Denmark Rise. WS12 29 H2
Diamond Gro. WS12 29 G6
Dovedale. WS11 29 E4
Downes Way. WS11 28 A6
Dual Way. WS12 28 A1
*Durberville Walk,
 Melbury Way. WS11 28 D6
East Cannock Rd. WS11 29 E6
Eastern Way. WS11 29 E6
Ebenezer St. WS12 29 E2
Edison Clo. WS12 29 G1
Edward St. WS11 28 C4
Elgar Clo. WS11 28 C4
Elizabeth Rd. WS11 28 C3
Elm Gro. WS12 28 B1
Elmwood Clo. WS11 28 C3
Eskrett St. WS12 29 F4
Essex Dri. WS12 29 F4
Exonbury Wk. WS11 28 D6
Fallow Field Rd. WS11 28 C6
Farm Clo. WS12 29 G6
Fern Rd. WS11 28 B4
Field St. WS11 28 D6
Fieldhouse Rd. WS12 28 D2
Fir Clo. WS12 28 B1
Fircroft Clo. WS11 29 E6
Florence St. WS11 29 E2
Forge St. WS12 29 G5
Foster Av. WS11 28 C5
Foxfields Way. WS12 28 B2
Foxglove Wk. WS12 29 G1
Gaelic Rd. WS11 28 B5
Garrick Rd. WS11 28 B5
George St. WS12 29 G4
Glen Clo. WS11 28 C4
Glencoe Dri. WS11 29 E5
Glendawn Clo. WS11 29 E5
Glendene Rd. WS12 29 G2
Gorse Dri. WS12 28 B4
Gorse Way. WS12 29 G1
Grasmere Pl. WS11 29 E6
Gravel La. WS11 28 A3
Gray Rd. WS11 28 C4
Green Slade Gro. WS12 29 G2
Green Heath Rd. WS12 29 E1
Greenwood Pk. WS12 29 F1
Gresham Rd. WS11 28 D6
Grimley Way. WS11 28 D4
Haig Clo. WS11 29 E4
Hamelin St. WS11 28 C6
Hardie Grn. WS11 28 C6
Hartlebury Clo. WS12 29 F6
Hawks Green La. WS11 29 E6
Hawkyard Clo. WS11 29 E5
Hawthorne Rd. WS12 28 B1
Heath Gap Rd. WS11 28 D6
Heath St. WS12 29 E1
Heathbank Dri. WS12 28 A3
Heather Dri. WS12 28 B4
Heather Valley. WS12 29 G3
Hedgerow Clo. WS12 28 D1
Hemlock Way. WS12 29 F6
Hereford Clo. WS12 29 F4
Herondale. WS12 29 F5
Hewston Croft. WS12 29 H5
High Grange. WS11 29 E4
High Mount St. WS11 29 F3
Highfield Ct. WS11 28 A5
Highland Rd. WS12 29 G5
Hill St. WS12 29 G5
Hillside Clo. WS12 29 F6
Hodson Way. WS11 29 F6
Holly La. WS12 28 A2
Holly St. WS11 28 C3
Howard Cres. WS12 29 F2
Huntington Terrace Rd.
 WS11 28 B2
Huntsmans Rise. WS12 28 A1
Hyssop Clo. WS12 29 F6
INDUSTRIAL ESTATES:
 Chaseside Ind Est.
 WS12 29 F6

Hawkes Grn Ind Est.
 WS12 29 E6
Littleton Business Pk.
 WS12 28 A2
James St. WS11 28 D4
John St. WS11 28 D4
Johnson Rd. WS11 28 B5
Keats Av. WS11 28 C4
Kelvin Dri. WS11 29 E6
Kenilworth Dri. WS11 28 B5
Kenmore Av. WS11 28 D2
Kingfisher Dri. WS12 29 F4
Kings Av. WS12 29 G5
Kingsley Av. WS12 29 G2
Kingsway. WS11 29 E4
Kinross Av. WS12 28 D2
Lansbury Dri. WS11 28 C5
Larchwood Dri. WS12 29 E5
Laurel Dri. WS12 29 H5
Leaf Down Ct. WS12 29 G5
Lee Wk. WS11 29 E4
Levetts Hollow. WS12 29 G6
Lichen Clo. WS12 28 A3
Lime Rd. WS12 28 B1
Limepit La. WS12 28 A2
Linden Vw. WS12 29 F5
Ling Rd. WS12 28 A4
Linnet Clo. WS12 28 B2
Linwood Dri. WS12 28 D2
Littleworth Hill. WS12 29 H5
Littleworth Rd. WS12 29 G5
Lomax Rd. WS12 29 E1
Long Croft. WS12 28 A5
Longfellow Pl. WS11 28 C5
Lotus Dri. WS11 28 C3
Lovatt Pl. WS11 28 C4
Lower Rd. WS11 29 F5
Lowland Rd. WS11 28 A4
Lysander Way. WS11 28 C6
McGeough Wk. WS11 29 E4
McGhie St. WS12 29 F3
Maple St. WS12 28 B1
Marcon Pl. WS12 29 G1
Margaret Dri. WS11 28 C3
Marigold Clo. WS12 29 G6
Marina Cres. WS12 29 E3
Market St. WS12 29 F3
Marston Rd. WS12 28 D3
Mary St. WS12 29 F2
Masefield Gro. WS11 28 C5
Matlock Dri. WS11 29 E5
Mavis Rd. WS12 29 G2
Maycroft. WS12 28 D1
Meadow Croft. WS12 28 A5
Meadow Hill Dri. WS11 28 D6
Meadowlark Clo. WS12 29 F5
Meadway Clo. WS12 29 G6
Melbury Way. WS11 28 D6
Melchester Way. WS11 28 D6
Melrose Dri. WS12 28 D2
Mercury Rd. WS11 29 E4
Metcalfe Clo. WS11 29 F2
Midhurst Dri. WS12 29 G1
Midland Rd. WS12 28 A4
Millicent Clo. WS12 29 F2
Millpool Rd. WS12 29 F2
Milton Rd. WS11 28 C5
Mitcham Clo. WS12 28 D2
Montrose Clo. WS11 29 E5
Moore St. WS12 29 G2
Moorland Rd. WS11 28 C4
Moreton St. WS11 28 D4
Moss Clo. WS11 28 B4
Moss Rd. WS11 29 E6
Moss St. WS11 28 D5
Mount Av. WS11 29 F2
Mount Side St. WS12 29 F2
Mount St. WS12 29 F1
Mountain Pine. WS12 29 E1
Mulberry Rd. WS11 28 C6
Muldoon Clo. WS12 29 E4
New St. WS12 29 G4
Newhall Cres. WS11 29 F6
Newhall Gdns. WS11 28 D6
Nightingale Clo. WS12 28 A2
Oak Av. WS12 28 B1
Oakhill Rd. WS11 28 D6
Odin Clo. WS12 28 D3
Old Fallow Rd. WS11 28 C6
Old Hednesford Rd.
 WS11 29 E5
Orion Way. WS11 28 D4
Owen Wk. WS11 29 E4
Partridge Clo. WS12 28 B1
Passfield Av. WS12 29 F2
Pasture Gate. WS11 28 A6

Pattedale Rd. WS11 29 E5
Pear Tree Clo. WS12 28 A1
Pendle Hill. WS12 29 F4
Petersfield. WS11 28 D5
Phillip Gro. WS11 28 C3
Phoenix Rd. WS11 29 E6
Pinewood Av. WS11 28 B5
Platt St. WS11 28 D3
Pope Gro. WS12 28 D2
Poplar Av. WS11 28 D5
Prince St. WS11 28 C3
Princess St. WS11 29 H5
Priory Rd. WS12 29 H5
Pye Green Rd. WS11 28 C6
Queen St. WS11 29 F4
Radnor Rise. WS12 29 F4
Raven Clo,
 Huntington. WS12 28 B2
Raven Clo,
 Littleworth. WS12 29 H5
Rawnsley Rd. WS12 29 G2
Redhill Rd. WS11 28 C5
Redwing Dri. WS12 28 B2
Redwood Dri. WS11 28 D6
Reservoir Rd. WS12 29 H5
Richmond Clo. WS11 29 E4
Rigby Dri. WS11 28 C5
Robin Clo. WS12 28 A2
Rose Hill. WS12 28 D1
Rowan Rd. WS11 28 A6
Rowley Clo. WS12 29 E1
Rugeley Rd. WS12 29 G2
Rydall Clo. WS12 29 E1
St Aidans Rd. WS11 28 C4
St Chads Clo. WS11 29 E5
St Peters Rd. WS12 29 G4
Sandpiper Clo. WS12 29 G2
Sankey Rd. WS11 28 D5
Sapphire Dri. WS12 29 G6
Saturn Rd. WS11 28 D3
Scotia Rd. WS11 28 B6
Shaftsbury Way. WS12 29 F2
Shakespeare Gro. WS11 28 B5
Sharon Way. WS11 29 G5
Shelly Rd. WS11 28 C4
Sheraton Clo. WS12 28 D2
Sherbourne Av. WS12 29 H5
Sherwood Dri. WS11 29 E5
Short St. WS11 28 D6
Sidon Hill Way. WS12 29 F6
Silver Birch Rd. WS12 28 B1
Silver Fir Clo. WS12 29 E1
Simcox St. WS12 29 H4
Skylark Clo. WS12 28 B2
Smalley Clo. WS11 29 E4
Smillie Pl. WS11 28 D5
Snowdon Rd. WS11 28 C3
Somerset Pl. WS11 28 C5
Southbourne Pl. WS11 28 B6
Speedy Clo. WS11 28 C4
Splash La. WS12 29 G5
Springfield Rise. WS12 29 F2
Stafford La. WS11 29 F4
Stafford Rd. WS12 28 A2
Stagborough Way. WS12 29 H5
Stanley Rd. WS11 29 E3
Station Rd. WS12 29 F3
Stevens Dri. WS12 29 G2
Stone Pine Clo. WS12 28 D1
Stratford Way. WS11 29 G2
Stringers Hill. WS12 29 G2
Sunley Dri. WS12 29 G2
Sunrise Hill. WS12 29 F3
Sussex Dri. WS12 29 F4
Swallow Clo. WS12 28 B2
Swallowfields Dri. WS11 28 C3
Sycamore Grn. WS11 28 C3
Sycamore Way. WS12 28 B1
Taplow Pl. WS11 28 D5
*Teddesley Ct,
 Bevan Lee Rd. WS12 28 B5
Telford Gro. WS12 29 E2
The Poplars. WS11 28 C5
The Sidings. WS12 29 G2
Thor Clo. WS11 29 E4
Thornhill Rd. WS12 28 D2
Tranter Cres. WS11 29 F6
Trent Rd. WS11 28 C3
Turquoise Dri. WS12 29 G6
Tutbury Clo. WS12 29 F6
Ulster Clo. WS11 29 E5
Uxbridge St. WS11 29 G5
Valley Rd. WS12 29 G3
Vermont Grn. WS11 28 D6
Victoria St,
 Broomhill. WS11 28 C5

Victoria St,
 Hednesford. WS11 29 F3
View St. WS11 28 D3
Viewfield Av. WS12 28 D2
Walkers Rise. WS12 29 H1
Walnut Clo. WS11 28 D6
Walnut Dri. WS11 28 D6
Ward St. WS11 28 D3
Wardle Pl. WS11 28 C4
Wells Clo. WS11 28 C3
Wesley Pl. WS12 29 G2
West Hill Av. WS12 29 F3
Westbourne Av. WS11 28 B6
Western Rd. WS12 29 F3
Westminster Rd. WS11 28 C3
White Bark Clo. WS12 28 D1
Whitethorn Clo. WS12 29 E1
Whitfield Av. WS12 29 G2
Wilcox Av. WS11 29 F1
William Morris Gro.
 WS11 29 G2
Willow Walk. WS12 28 B1
Winchester Rd. WS11 29 E6
Windrush Rd. WS11 28 C3
Winsor Av. WS12 29 F3
Wood La. WS12 29 G5
Woodford End. WS11 28 D5
Woodland Clo. WS12 29 F1
Woodland Ct. WS12 28 A4
Woodpecker Way.
 WS12 29 F6
Woodside Pl. WS11 28 C4
Woodstock Dri.
 WS12 28 A2
Wootton Clo. WS11 29 F6
Wordsworth Clo. WS11 28 C5
Wrekin Vw. WS12 28 A1
Wrights Av. WS11 28 D4
Wyvern Gro. WS12 29 E3

KIDSGROVE

Acacia Gdns. ST7 31 F1
Acres Nook Rd. ST6 30 D5
Albany St. ST6 31 F5
Alder Clo. ST7 31 E4
Alice St. ST6 31 F5
Ancaster St. ST6 31 G5
Andrew St. ST6 31 G4
Anne Ct. ST7 30 B6
Anne St. ST6 31 G5
Ashenough Rd. ST7 30 B6
Astbury Clo. ST7 31 G1
Attwood St. ST7 31 E2
Aubrey St. ST6 31 F5
Audley Rd. ST7 30 A5
Avon Clo. ST7 31 F2
Back Heathcote St. ST7 30 D2
Banbury St. ST7 30 B3
Barrie Gdns. ST7 30 A4
Bedford Rd. ST7 30 D1
Beech Dri. ST7 30 C4
Beeston Vw. ST7 31 E5
Bevan Av. ST6 30 B6
Birchall Av. ST6 31 F6
Birches Way. ST7 31 F2
Birkdale Dri. ST7 31 G1
Bishops Clo. ST7 30 B4
Boat Horse Rd,
 Kidsgrove. ST7 30 D3
Boat Horse Rd,
 Ravenscliffe. ST6 31 E6
Bosley Gro. ST6 31 G5
Bourne Rd. ST7 30 D2
Brakespeare St. ST6 31 G5
Briarswood. ST7 31 F2
Brieryhurst Rd. ST7 31 F1
Brights Av. ST7 31 F2
Brindley Clo. ST7 30 B3
Broadfield Rd. ST6 31 E5
Browning Gro. ST7 30 A4
Bullocks Ho Rd. ST7 31 H1
Burnaby Rd. ST6 31 F6
Burns Clo. ST7 30 D4
Butt La. ST7 30 B2
Byron Ct. ST7 30 D4
Capper Clo. ST7 31 E2
Cartlich St. ST6 31 G6
Castle View Rd. ST7 31 F1
Cedar Av. ST7 30 B3
Chapel St. ST7 30 B2
Charlotte St. ST6 31 F4
Charnwood. ST7 31 E5
Chatterley Dri. ST7 31 E5

Chester Clo. ST7 30 B5
Chester Rd. ST7 30 B4
Church St. ST7 30 A2
Clough Hall Dri. ST7 30 C5
Clough Hall Rd. ST7 30 C4
Coalpitt Hill. ST7 30 B4
Colclough La. ST6 31 G5
Collinson St. ST6 31 G5
Congleton Rd. ST7 30 B3
Congleton Rd Sth. ST7 30 B1
Coppice Rd. ST7 30 A4
Coronation Cres. ST7 30 C3
Cotton Rd. ST6 31 F5
Covert Gdns. ST7 30 B4
Crown Bank. ST7 30 B5
Crown Bank Cres. ST7 30 B5
Cumberland Clo. ST7 30 C4
Dane Gdns. ST7 31 G2
Dee Clo. ST7 30 B5
Derby Rd. ST7 30 B5
Derwent Cres. ST7 31 G2
Dorset Pl. ST7 31 E1
Dovedale Clo. ST6 31 F5
Drummond St. ST6 31 G5
Edale Clo. ST6 31 F5
Eden Clo. ST7 31 E2
Elgood La. ST6 31 F5
Elizabeth Ct. ST7 30 B6
Elm Clo. ST7 31 E4
Elton Ter. ST6 31 G5
Essex Dri. ST7 30 D2
Everest Rd. ST7 31 F1
Fawfield Rd. ST6 31 F5
Ferney Pl. ST6 31 G5
Fifth Av. ST7 30 C3
First Av. ST7 30 C3
Fourth Av. ST7 30 C3
Fox Gdns. ST7 30 B4
Freedon Dri. ST7 31 H1
Galleys Bank. ST7 31 E1
Garbett St. ST6 31 G5
Gilbert Clo. ST7 31 E2
Gilbert St. ST6 31 F5
Gill Bank Rd. ST7 31 E5
Gill Bank Rd. ST7 31 E3
Glebe St. ST7 30 B2
Gloucester Rd. ST7 30 C2
Golf Links Clo. ST6 31 G4
Gordon Rd. ST6 31 G5
Greenside Clo. ST7 30 D4
Grove Av. ST7 30 C3
Hardings Meadow. ST7 30 C2
Hardingswood Rd. ST7 30 C2
Harecastle Av. ST7 30 B3
Hawthorns Gdns. ST7 30 B4
Hayhead Clo. ST7 31 F2
Hazel Clo. ST7 31 F1
Heath St. ST6 31 G5
Heathcote St. ST7 30 D2
Heathfield Ct, Heath St. ST6 31 G5
Heathside La. ST7 31 F5
Henshall Pl. ST7 31 G6
High St, Goldenhill. ST6 31 F5
High St, Newchapel. ST7 31 H1
High St, Talke Pits. ST7 30 B6
Higher Ash Rd. ST7 30 B3
Highfield Av. ST7 31 E2
Hilary Rd. ST7 31 F1
Hillside Av. ST7 31 E4
Hollins Cres. ST7 30 B3
Hollins Grange. ST7 30 B3
Hollinwood Clo. ST7 30 C4
Hollinwood Rd. ST7 30 C4
Hollywall La. ST6 31 F6
Hurst Clo. ST7 30 B6
...n Rd. ST7 31 G1
INDUSTRIAL ESTATES:
Jamage Ind Est. ST7 30 A6
Nelson Ind Est. ST7 30 A3
Jamage Rd. ST7 30 B6
Jodrell Vw. ST7 31 E4
Joseph St. ST6 31 G5
Keats Gdns. ST7 30 D4
Kidsgrove Bank. ST7 31 F3
Kidsgrove Rd. ST7 31 F4
King St, Kidsgrove. ST7 30 D2
King St, Talke Pits. ST7 30 B6
Kingsley Clo. ST7 30 B6
Kingsley Rd. ST7 30 B6
Kingswood. ST7 31 E3
Kinnersley Av. ST7 30 C4
Kinnersley St. ST7 31 E2
Kite Gro. ST7 31 G1
Laburnum Clo. ST7 30 C4
Lamb St. ST7 30 D2
Lapwing Gro. ST7 31 G1
Larch Clo. ST7 31 E4
Lark Av. ST7 31 G1
Larkfield. ST7 31 E2
Latebrook Clo. ST6 31 F5
Laurel Dri. ST7 31 H1
Lawton Av. ST7 30 B1
Lewisham Dri. ST6 31 F5
Lichfield Rd. ST7 30 B5
Lime Kiln La. ST7 30 C1
Lincoln Rd. ST7 30 D2
Linley Rd. ST7 30 A3
Liverpool Rd. ST7 31 E3
Liverpool Rd East. ST7 30 B1
Liverpool Rd West. ST7 30 A1
Lodge Rd. ST7 30 B6
Long Row. ST7 30 D3
Lower Ash Rd. ST7 30 B4
Lynn Av. ST7 30 A4
Magpie Cres. ST7 31 F2
Maple Av. ST7 30 B3
Market St. ST7 31 E2
Marldon Pl. ST6 31 G6
Marsh Av. ST6 31 H2
Maureen Av. ST6 31 G5
Meadows Rd. ST7 30 D2
Medina Way. ST7 31 E2
Merelake Rd. ST7 30 A4
Merlin Av. ST7 31 G1
Mill Gro. ST7 30 B3
Mill Rise. ST7 30 D3
Millers View. ST7 30 D3
Millstone Av. ST7 30 B2
Milton Cres. ST7 30 A4
Minfield Clo. ST7 31 E4
Mistley Walk. ST6 31 F5
Mitchell Av. ST7 30 B3
Mitchell Dri. ST7 30 B3
Mobberley Rd. ST6 31 F4
Monument Rd. ST7 30 B6
Moreton Clo. ST7 31 E4
Moss Pl. ST7 31 E1
Mount Pleasant. ST7 31 E3
Mount Rd. ST7 31 E2
Murray St. ST6 31 G5
Nabbswood Rd. ST7 31 F2
Napier Gdns. ST7 31 E2
Nelson Bank. ST6 30 D4
Newark Gro. ST6 31 G5
Newcastle Rd. ST7 30 B4
Newchapel Rd. ST7 31 F1
Nursery Clo. ST7 30 B3
Norfolk Rd. ST7 30 D2
Old Butt La. ST7 30 A2
Oldcott Cres. ST7 31 F4
Oldcott Dri. ST7 31 F4
Oldhill Clo. ST7 30 B6
Orchard Cres. ST7 30 B2
Osprey View. ST7 31 G1
Park Av. ST7 30 C4
Park Farm Vw. ST6 31 G5
Park View Rd. ST7 31 E1
Parklands. ST7 31 E2
Peakdale Av. ST6 31 F5
Peckforton Vw. ST7 31 E4
Pennyfields Rd. ST7 31 G2
Perkins St. ST6 31 F5
Pickwick Pl. ST7 30 B2
Pine Clo. ST7 30 A5
Pit La. ST7 30 A6
Poplar Dri. ST7 31 E3
Powy Dri. ST7 31 E2
Premier Gdns. ST7 30 D2
Princess St. ST7 30 B6
Priory Pl. ST7 31 F1
Quarry Ter. ST7 31 E3
Queen St. ST7 30 D2
Queens Gdns. ST7 30 B6
Randel La. ST6 31 F4
Ravenscliffe Rd. ST7 30 D4
Rectory View. ST7 30 B5
Red Lion Clo. ST7 30 B4
Regency Clo. ST7 30 B6
Ridge Rd. ST6 31 G6
Rigby Rd. ST7 31 F1
Rockhouse La. ST7 30 A4
Rodgers St. ST6 31 F4
Rookery Rd. ST7 31 F1
Rowan Clo. ST7 31 E4
Russell Pl. ST6 31 H6
Russell Rd. ST6 31 H6
Rutland Rd. ST7 31 E1
St Andrews Dri. ST7 31 F1
St Johns Wood. ST7 30 D3
St Joseph St. ST7 31 G5
St Martins Rd. ST7 30 B5
St Saviours St. ST7 30 B3
Salop Pl. ST7 31 E1
Sandy Rd. ST6 31 G5
Second Av. ST7 30 C3
Shakespeare Clo. ST7 30 D3
Shannon Dri. ST6 31 F4
Shelford Rd. ST6 31 G6
Shelley Clo. ST7 30 D4
Silvermine Clo. ST7 31 F2
Silverwood. ST7 31 F2
Skellern St. ST7 30 B2
Slacken La. ST7 30 B2
Sneyd Pl. ST6 31 G6
Somerset Av. ST7 30 D2
Sparrowbutts Gro. ST7 31 F2
Spey Dri. ST7 31 F1
Spout Hollow. ST7 30 B6
Springhead Clo. ST7 30 B6
Starling Clo. ST7 31 G1
Station Rd, Kidsgrove. ST7 30 D2
Station Rd, Newchapel. ST7 31 H2
Stonebank Rd. ST7 31 E3
Summerfield. ST7 31 E3
Surrey Rd. ST7 31 E2
Sussex Dri. ST7 30 D1
Swallow Clo. ST7 31 E2
Swallowmore Vw. ST7 30 A4
Swan Bank. ST7 30 A5
Swan Clo. ST7 30 B4
Swift Clo. ST7 31 E2
Sycamore Clo. ST7 30 C4
Tamar Rd. ST7 31 E2
Target Clo. ST7 30 B6
Tawney Clo. ST7 31 F1
Taylor St. ST6 31 G5
Telford Clo. ST7 30 C3
Temperance Pl. ST6 31 G5
Tennyson Av. ST7 30 D4
Tern Av. ST7 31 G2
The Avenue. ST7 30 D3
The Beeches. ST7 30 B4
*The Hollins, Congleton Rd. ST7 30 A3
The Mount. ST7 31 E3
Third Av. ST7 30 C2
Thomas St. ST7 30 B4
Tilewright Clo. ST7 31 E2
Tilstone Clo. ST7 31 E3
Tollgate Clo. ST7 30 A4
Townfield Clo. ST7 30 B2
Trubshaw Ct. ST7 31 G1
Trubshaw Pl. ST7 31 F1
Unity Way. ST7 30 B4
Valentine Rd. ST7 31 E3
Victoria Av. ST7 30 D2
Vine Bank Rd. ST7 31 E2
Walley Dri. ST6 31 G6
Walton Gro. ST7 30 A4
Walton Way. ST7 30 A4
Warwick Clo. ST7 30 D1
Waterloo Gro. ST7 31 E2
Wedgwood Rd. ST7 30 B5
Weetman Clo. ST6 31 F4
Weir Gro. ST7 31 E2
Wellington Rd. ST7 31 E2
Wentworth Dri. ST7 31 G1
Wesley Gdns. ST7 31 E2
West Av. ST7 30 A3
Westmorland Av. ST7 30 C4
Wheelock Way. ST7 31 E2
Whitehall Av. ST7 30 D2
Whitehall Rd. ST7 30 D2
Whitehill Rd. ST7 31 E2
Whiteridge Rd. ST7 31 E2
Whitfield Rd. ST7 31 E2
Wignall Rd. ST6 31 G5
Wild Goose Av. ST7 31 G1
William Rd. ST7 31 E1
Willow Clo. ST7 30 D4
Wilson Way. ST6 31 F5
Windmill Av. ST7 31 E3
Winghay Rd. ST7 31 F2
Woodhall Gdns. ST7 31 F1
Woodlands Av. ST7 30 B2
Woodshutts St. ST7 30 B2
Woodside Av. ST7 30 D3
Woodstock Rd. ST6 31 E5
Woodstock St. ST6 31 F4
Worcester Clo. ST7 30 B5
Wright St. ST7 30 B2
Yew Tree Ter. ST7 30 D4
York Clo. ST7 30 B4

LEEK

Abbey Green Rd. ST13 32 C1
Abbots Rd. ST13 33 G3
Adams Gro. ST13 32 B5
Albert St. ST13 32 D3
Albion St. ST13 33 E4
Alma St. ST13 32 D3
Alsop St. ST13 33 E4
Angle St. ST13 32 D3
Arden Clo. ST13 33 G4
Argles Rd. ST13 33 F2
Arthur St. ST13 33 F3
Ashbourne Rd. ST13 33 E4
Ashcombe Way. ST13 33 E5
Ashdale Rd. ST13 33 G3
Ashenhurst Way. ST13 33 E5
Badnall Clo. ST13 32 D3
Badnall St. ST13 32 D3
Ball Haye Grn. ST13 33 E3
Ball Haye Rd. ST13 33 E3
Ball Haye St. ST13 33 E4
Ball La. ST13 33 E3
Ballington Gdns. ST13 33 E4
Ballington Vw. ST13 33 E5
Bank La. ST13 32 C3
Barnfield Rd. ST13 32 D5
Barngate St. ST13 32 D4
Barracks Way. ST13 32 D3
Bath St. ST13 33 E3
Beatty Rd. ST13 33 F3
Beech Gro. ST13 32 B3
Beggars La. ST13 32 C5
Belle Vue Rd. ST13 32 D3
Birchall Park Av. ST13 33 E6
Boundary Clo. ST13 33 F6
Bourne Pl. ST13 32 B3
Britannia St. ST13 32 D4
Broad St. ST13 32 D5
Brook St. ST13 33 E4
Brunswick St. ST13 33 F3
Burton St. ST13 32 C4
Buxton Rd. ST13 33 E3
Byrom St. ST13 32 D3
Campbell Av. ST13 32 C5
Carlton Ter. ST13 33 F3
Cauldon Clo. ST13 33 E5
Challenor Av. ST13 33 E5
Charnwood Clo. ST13 32 C5
Cheddleton Rd. ST13 33 E5
Chorley St. ST13 32 D4
Church La. ST13 33 E3
Church St. ST13 33 E3
Churnet Vw. ST13 33 F1
City La. ST13 32 A6
Clerk Bank. ST13 32 D3
Compton. ST13 33 E4
Condlyffe Rd. ST13 33 E5
Coopers Clo. ST13 32 B4
Cornhill Gdns. ST13 33 E5
*Cornhill St, Compton. ST13 33 E4
Cross St. ST13 33 F4
Cruso St. ST13 32 D4
Curzon Rise. ST13 32 B4
Daintry St. ST13 32 D4
Dairy Clo. ST13 33 F3
Daisy Bank. ST13 32 D3
Damper Ct. ST13 33 E4
Davenport Clo. ST13 32 B5
*Deansgate, York St. ST13 33 E3
Deebank Av. ST13 33 G3
Derby St. ST13 33 E4
Duke St. ST13 33 E4
Earl St. ST13 33 F3
East St. ST13 33 F4
Eastbourne Clo. ST13 32 C3
Edgehill Rd. ST13 32 C4
Elm Clo. ST13 32 C5
Eversley Av. ST13 33 E4
Fair View Rd. ST13 33 G5
Fernwood Dri. ST13 32 C5
Field St. ST13 33 E4
Ford St. ST13 33 E3
Fountain St. ST13 33 E4
Frith St. ST13 32 D3
Furmston Pl. ST13 33 G2
Fynney St. ST13 33 E4
Garden St. ST13 32 D3
Gaunt St. ST13 32 D3
Geoffrey Av. ST13 32 D4
Gladstone St. ST13 32 D4
Glebeville. ST13 33 E5
Gordon Clo. ST13 32 C5
Grace St. ST13 32 C3
Grange Gdns. ST13 32 D5
Grosvenor St. ST13 33 F4
Grove St. ST13 32 D3
Haig Rd. ST13 33 F2
Hall Av. ST13 33 F2
Hamil Dri. ST13 32 D3
*Haregate Ter, Hall Av. ST13 33 F2
Hargate Rd. ST13 33 F2
Hartington St. ST13 32 D4
Hawksworth Av. ST13 32 C5
Hawksworth Clo. ST13 32 C5
Hayes Clo, Leek. ST13 33 F3
Hayes Clo, Wallbridge Pk. ST13 32 B5
Haywood St. ST13 33 E4
Hazel Gro. ST13 32 C5
Hencroft. ST13 32 D3
High St. ST13 33 E4
High View Rd. ST13 33 G4
Highup Rd. ST13 32 B1
Hill Crest. ST13 32 C3
Hill View. ST13 33 F4
Hillside Dri. ST13 32 C5
Hillswood Av. ST13 32 C3
Horsecroft Cres. ST13 33 G2
Horsecroft Gro. ST13 33 G2
Horton St. ST13 33 E3
Howard Clo. ST13 32 C5
Hugo St. ST13 32 D4
INDUSTRIAL ESTATES:
Barnfields Ind Est. ST13 32 D6
James St. ST13 32 D4
John St. ST13 32 D4
*Jolliffe St, Compton. ST13 33 E4
Jubilee Ter. ST13 32 D3
Junction Rd. ST13 32 D5
Kiln La. ST13 32 C3
King St. ST13 33 E4
Kniveden La. ST13 33 G4
Ladderedge. ST13 32 C6
Ladydale Clo. ST13 33 E5
Lancaster Av. ST13 33 E3
Langford St. ST13 32 D4
Lansdowne Clo. ST13 32 B4
Leonard St. ST13 33 E4
Livingstone St. ST13 33 E4
Locherbie Clo. ST13 33 G4
London St. ST13 33 E4
Lorien Clo. ST13 32 C5
Lowther Pl. ST13 33 G4
Macclesfield Rd. ST13 32 B1
Market Pl. ST13 33 E3
Market St. ST13 33 E3
Mayfield Clo. ST13 32 B4
Melrose Pl. ST13 32 B4
Milk St. ST13 33 F2
Mill St. ST13 32 D3
Milltown Way. ST13 33 F4
Milner Ter. ST13 33 F3
Monyash Dri. ST13 33 F4
Moorfields. ST13 33 F4
Moorhouse St. ST13 33 F4
Moorland Rd. ST13 33 G4
Morley St. ST13 32 D4
Mount Pleasant. ST13 32 D3
*Mount Pleasant Dri, Clerk Bank. ST13 32 D3
Mount Rd. ST13 33 G3
Mountside Gdns. ST13 33 G4
Nab Hill Av. ST13 32 C3
Nabhill Ct. ST13 32 C3
*Naylor Yard, Mt Pleasant. ST13 32 D3
Nelson St. ST13 33 F2
New St. ST13 33 E3
Newcastle Rd. ST13 32 C6
Nicholas Clo. ST13 32 B5
Nicholson Way. ST13 32 C3
North Av. ST13 32 C4
North St. ST13 32 C3
Novi La. ST13 33 F2
Nunn St. ST13 32 D3
Oaklea. ST13 32 B5
Oakwood Rd. ST13 32 C3
Orchard Gdns. ST13 32 C3
Osborne St. ST13 33 F3

Stychbrook Gdns. WS13 34 D2
Summer Gro. WS13 35 E2
Sunbury Av. WS14 35 F4
Swallow Cft. WS13 34 B3
Swan Meadows. WS13 34 C4
Swan Rd. WS13 34 C4
Swinfen Broun Rd. WS13 34 B3
Tamworth Rd. WS14 34 D6
Tamworth St. WS13 34 D4
Tanyard. WS13 34 D3
Terry Clo. WS13 34 A2
The Brambles. WS14 35 E5
The Charters. WS13 34 D3
The Chequers. WS13 34 D3
The Crossing. WS14 35 F4
The Dell. WS13 34 B4
The Dimbles. WS13 34 C1
The Friary. WS13 34 C4
The Garth. WS13 34 C2
The Grange. WS13 34 B2
The Leasowe. WS13 34 C2
The Paddock. WS14 34 D6
The Parchments. WS13 34 D3
The Pines. WS14 35 F4
The Spires. WS14 35 F5
The Squirrels. WS14 35 E4
The Sycamores. WS14 34 C6
The Windings. WS13 34 C3
The Woodlands. WS13 35 E3
Thistle Nook. WS13 34 C2
Thomas Greenway. WS13 34 B2
Titan Way. WS14 35 G4
Town Fields. WS13 34 B4
Town Fields. WS13 34 C4
Tregony Rise. WS14 35 E5
Trenance Clo. WS14 35 E5
Trent Valley. WS13 35 F3
Trent Valley Rd. WS14 35 E4
Truro Clo. WS13 34 D1
Tudor Row, Bore St. WS13 34 C4
Upper St John St. WS14 34 D5
Valley La. WS13 35 E3
Verdi Ct. WS13 34 D2
Vicars Clo. WS13 34 C3
Vulcan Rd. WS13 35 F3
Wade St. WS13 34 C4
Walkers Croft. WS13 34 D2
Walnut Gro. WS14 35 G5
Walsall Rd. WS13 34 A5
Warren Clo. WS14 35 F5
Waverley Wk. WS13 34 C5
Wellington Pl. WS14 34 C6
Wentworth Dri. WS14 35 E6
Western By-Pass. WS13 34 A2
Weston Rd. WS13 34 B2
Wheel La. WS13 34 B3
Wightman Clo. WS14 35 F5
Willow Tree Clo. WS13 34 C2
Willowsmere Dri. WS14 35 F5
Wilmot Clo. WS13 34 B4
Wiltell Rd. WS14 34 D5
Winchester Clo. WS13 34 D1
Windmill Clo. WS13 34 B2
Windmill La. WS13 34 B2
Windsor Ct, Spencer Rd. WS14 34 D5
Winter Clo. WS13 35 E2
Wissage Ct. WS14 35 E4
Wissage Croft, St Chads Rd. WS13 34 D3
Wissage La. WS13 35 E3
Wissage Rd. WS13 35 E3
Wittington Ho, Hobs Rd. WS13 35 F3
Wolsey Rd. WS13 34 B2
Wood Ridings. WS13 34 C2
Woodfields Dri. WS14 35 F6
Woods Croft. WS13 34 C3
Worcester Clo. WS13 34 D1
Wordsworth Clo. WS14 34 D6
Wyrley Clo. WS14 34 C6
ale Clo. WS13 34 C3
ew Tree Av. WS14 35 F4
ork Clo. WS13 35 E1

LONGTON

ddington Way. ST3 36 C2
lbert Av. ST3 36 D5
lbert St. ST3 36 B2
Alberta St. ST3 36 B6
Alexandra Rd. ST3 36 D6
Allensmore Av. ST4 36 A2
Almer St. ST3 36 C4
Amberfield Clo. ST3 36 D4
Amblecote Dri. ST3 36 D4
Amison St. ST3 36 B3
Anchor Pl. ST3 36 B3
Anchor Rd. ST3 36 B4
Anchor Ter. ST3 36 B4
Andover Clo. ST3 36 B1
Annette Rd. ST4 36 A1
Anthony Pl. ST3 36 C3
Argyll Rd. ST3 36 C6
Arundel Way. ST3 36 B1
Asherwood Pl. ST3 36 C4
Ashridge Gro. ST3 36 C1
Ashwood. ST4 36 A2
Auden Pl. ST3 36 C4
Ayshford St. ST3 36 A5
Bambury St. ST3 36 B1
Barbrook Av. ST3 36 D4
Barclay St. ST4 36 A2
Barford St. ST3 36 A4
Barker St. ST3 36 B5
Barleyford Dri. ST3 36 C1
Barlow St. ST3 36 B5
Bartlem St. ST3 36 C2
Baths Pass. ST3 36 A4
Baths Rd. ST3 36 A3
Bathurst St. ST3 36 B4
Battison Cres. ST3 36 A6
Beaufort Rd. ST3 36 B5
Beech St. ST3 36 B4
Beeston St. ST3 36 B2
Belgrave Av. ST3 36 A6
Belgrave Rd. ST3 36 A6
Belsay Clo. ST3 36 A3
Bengry Rd. ST3 36 D6
Bennet Precinct. ST3 36 A4
Bennion St. ST3 36 B5
Berry La. ST3 36 A4
Blantyre St. ST3 36 A6
Bosinney Clo. ST4 36 A2
Branson Av. ST3 36 D4
Brickfield Pl. ST3 36 B1
Bridgewood St. ST3 36 B4
Brightgreen St. ST3 36 C1
Brockford St. ST4 36 A2
Buccleuch Rd. ST3 36 C6
Bywater Gro. ST3 36 C1
Calverley St. ST3 36 C5
Capewell St. ST3 36 B3
Caroline St. ST3 36 A4
Carroll Dri. ST3 36 C3
Carron St. ST4 36 A2
Castledine Gro. ST3 36 C3
Cemetery Av. ST3 36 A6
Cemetery Vw. ST3 36 A5
Chadwick St. ST3 36 B5
Chancery La. ST3 36 A4
Chaplin Rd. ST3 36 B6
Chatfield Pl. ST3 36 C5
Chatterton Pl. ST3 36 C4
Checkley Gro. ST3 36 C1
Chelson St. ST3 36 B5
Chepstow Pl. ST3 36 B1
Church Gdns. ST3 36 A3
Cinderhill La. ST3 36 D5
Clarence Rd. ST3 36 A3
Clayfield Gro. ST4 36 A1
Clewlow Pl. ST3 36 C2
Clivedon Pl. ST3 36 B5
Commerce St. ST3 36 A5
Conrad Clo. ST3 36 C4
Copperstone Gro. ST3 36 D4
Corfe Grn. ST3 36 B1
Corina Way. ST3 36 C3
Cornwall St. ST3 36 B3
Coronation Av. ST3 36 A4
Court No. 1. ST3 36 D6
Cromartie St. ST3 36 B6
Deanscroft Way. ST3 36 D4
Delwood Gro. ST3 36 C1
Denby Av. ST3 36 A2
Dobell Gro. ST3 36 C3
Drayton Rd. ST3 36 A3
Dunrobin St. ST3 36 B6
Dunster Rd. ST3 36 A2
Dylan Rd. ST3 36 C4
Edensor Rd. ST3 36 A5
Edgar Pl. ST3 36 B1
Edgefield Rd. ST3 36 B2
Ely Walk. ST3 36 B3
Erskine St. ST3 36 B6
Eversley Rd. ST3 36 D6
Evesham Way. ST3 36 D4
Farmer St. ST3 36 B5
Farnworth Dri. ST3 36 D4
Fern Pl. ST3 36 A6
Field Pl. ST3 36 B2
Fistral Clo. ST3 36 C4
Flackett St. ST3 36 B3
Fleckney Av. ST3 36 D4
Fleur Gro. ST4 36 A1
Forrister St. ST3 36 B3
Forsythe Rd. ST4 36 A1
Freebridge Clo. ST3 36 D3
Friar St. ST3 36 B3
Furnace Rd. ST3 36 C6
Galsworthy Rd. ST4 36 A1
Gawsworth Clo. ST3 36 C1
George Ct. ST3 36 A4
Glenwood Clo. ST3 36 A3
Goddard St. ST3 36 B4
Gold St. ST3 36 A4
Goldenhill Rd. ST4 36 A3
Goldsmith Pl. ST3 36 C3
Gower St. ST3 36 B5
Grafton Rd. ST3 36 A3
Greendock St. ST3 36 A5
Hackett Clo. ST3 36 B4
Haggett Gro. ST3 36 B6
Haig St. ST3 36 C5
Hamilton Rd. ST3 36 C6
Harber St. ST3 36 B4
Hardsacre Rd. ST3 36 C2
Hathersage Clo. ST3 36 B1
Heath Pass. ST3 36 B5
Heathcote Rd. ST3 36 A4
Heathcote St. ST3 36 A1
Heathdene Clo. ST3 36 A3
Heber St. ST3 36 B3
Helston Av. ST3 36 D4
Hemingway Rd. ST3 36 C4
Hemlock Rd. ST3 36 B3
Hillgreen Rd. ST3 36 C1
Holmesfield Walk. ST3 36 C4
Honiton Walk. ST3 36 C4
Howard St. ST3 36 A6
Hudson Walk. ST3 36 B4
Huxley Pl. ST3 36 C4
Imogen Clo. ST4 36 A1
Jade Ct. ST3 36 C3
Jervison St. ST3 36 C1
Jolyon Clo. ST4 36 A1
June Rd. ST4 36 A1
Kelnore Clo. ST3 36 A3
Kendrick St. ST3 36 C4
Kentmere Clo. ST4 36 A2
Kildare St. ST3 36 B6
King St. ST4 36 A3
Kingcross St. ST3 36 A4
Kirkbridge Clo. ST3 36 C3
Knarsdale Clo. ST3 36 C2
Lamotte Clo. ST4 36 A2
Landon St. ST3 36 B4
Larkin Av. ST3 36 C3
Lawley St. ST3 36 C5
Leaks All. ST3 36 A5
Ledstone Way. ST3 36 D4
Lennox Rd. ST3 36 C6
Leveson St. ST3 36 B6
Lightwood Rd. ST3 36 A5
Lilleshall St. ST3 36 B6
Linnburn Rd. ST3 36 C3
Lloyd St. ST3 36 B6
Locketts La. ST3 36 B6
Loganbeck Gro. ST3 36 D2
Longley Rd. ST3 36 A2
Longsdon Gro. ST3 36 D4
Longview Clo. ST3 36 C2
Loughborough Wk. ST3 36 B3
Loveston Gro. ST3 36 C3
Lower Spring Rd. ST3 36 C5
Ludbrook Rd. ST4 36 A2
Malt La. ST3 36 C5
Mandella Way. ST3 36 B6
Manse Clo. ST3 36 B3
March Rd. ST3 36 A3
Market St. ST3 36 A4
Marlborough Rd. ST3 36 A3
Marlow Clo. ST3 36 C2
Marlow Rd. ST3 36 C2
May Pl. ST4 36 A3
Meir Rd. ST3 36 D6
Meirhay Rd. ST3 36 C5
Melbourne St. ST3 36 C2
Melville Rd. ST3 36 D6
Merton St. ST3 36 B3
Mid Cross St. ST3 36 B3
Millbank St. ST3 36 B4
Monty Pl. ST4 36 A1
Morpeth St. ST3 36 B5
Mossfield Rd. ST3 36 C1
Mossland Rd. ST3 36 B2
Moulton Rd. ST3 36 A4
Naples Clo. ST3 36 D3
Neath Clo. ST3 36 D4
Neath Pl. ST3 36 B1
New Hall Rd. ST3 36 D5
Newmount Rd. ST4 36 A1
Normacot Rd. ST3 36 B5
Normanton Gro. ST3 36 C1
Nyewood Av. ST3 36 C2
Olaf Palm Gro. ST3 36 B6
Oldway Pl. ST3 36 B2
Packett St. ST4 36 A3
Paragon Rd. ST3 36 B4
Park Hall Rd. ST3 36 D2
Park Hall St. ST3 36 B3
Pendine Gro. ST4 36 A1
Pevensey Gro. ST3 36 B1
Pinhoe Pl. ST3 36 D4
Pitlea Pl. ST3 36 B1
Pitsford St. ST3 36 D5
Plant St. ST3 36 B3
Portland Rd. ST3 36 A3
Priestley Dri. ST3 36 C3
Priorfield Clo. ST3 36 A3
Probyn Ct. ST3 36 A6
Queensbury Rd. ST3 36 C6
Rachel Gro. ST4 36 A1
Railway Pas. ST3 36 B4
Railway Ter. ST3 36 C4
Ramshaw Gro. ST3 36 C1
Recreation Rd. ST3 36 D6
Reservoir Rd. ST3 36 D6
Rill St. ST4 36 A3
Robin Hill Gro. ST4 36 A2
Rochester Rd. ST3 36 A2
Rogate Clo. ST4 36 A1
Ronald St. ST3 36 B6
Rosslyn Rd. ST3 36 B5
Rothesay Rd. ST3 36 C6
Rowandale Clo. ST3 36 C2
Roxburghe Av. ST3 36 B6
Royston Walk. ST3 36 B4
Ruskin Clo. ST3 36 C3
Rustington Av. ST3 36 D4
Rutland Rd. ST3 36 A3
St Clair St. ST3 36 B6
St Martins La. ST3 36 A4
St Marys Rd. ST3 36 C2
Saltdean Clo. ST3 36 D6
Sandford St. ST3 36 B2
Sandgate St. ST3 36 C5
Sandwood Cres. ST3 36 B2
Sark Pl. ST3 36 C1
Sedgley Walk. ST3 36 B4
Sefton Rd. ST3 36 D6
Sheaf Pass. ST3 36 B5
Sheldrake Gro. ST4 36 A1
Shenton St. ST3 36 C2
Short Banbury St. ST3 36 C1
Short St. ST3 36 B5
Sitwell Gro. ST3 36 C3
Skye Clo. ST3 36 D4
Smith St. ST3 36 B3
Smithy La. ST3 36 B4
Soames Cres. ST4 36 A1
Solway Gro. ST3 36 D4
Somerton Way. ST3 36 C2
Sorrento Gro. ST3 36 D3
Souldern Way. ST3 36 C3
Speakman St. ST3 36 C6
Speedwall St. ST3 36 B2
Spratslade Dri. ST3 36 A6
Spring Garden Rd. ST3 36 A5
Spring Garden Ter. ST3 36 A5
Spring Rd. ST3 36 D6
Springfield Cres. ST3 36 A5
Stafford St. ST3 36 A4
Stanfield St. ST3 36 C1
Summer Row. ST3 36 A5
Sutherland Av. ST3 36 A6
Sutherland Rd. ST3 36 B4
Swanland Gro. ST3 36 C3
Swithen Dri. ST4 36 A1
Tatton St. ST3 36 B6
The Strand. ST3 36 A4
Thirlmere Gro. ST3 36 D5
Tideswell Rd. ST3 36 B2
Times Sq. ST3 36 A4
Transport La. ST3 36 A4
Trentham Rd. ST3 36 A6
Tunnicliffe Clo. ST3 36 D5
Tuscan St. ST3 36 B3
Tutbury Clo. ST3 36 C3
Upper Cross St. ST3 36 B3
Upper Normacot Rd. ST3 36 C6
Uttoxeter Rd. ST3 36 B4
Vienna Way. ST3 36 D2
Walmer Pl. ST3 36 A2
Walpole St. ST3 36 C2
Warren Pl. ST3 36 C5
Warren St. ST3 36 B5
Warsill Gro. ST3 36 C3
Waterdale Gro. ST3 36 D4
Webberley La. ST3 36 B5
Weston Coyney Rd. ST3 36 C5
Weston St. ST3 36 C1
Westonview Av. ST3 36 C2
Westsprink Cres. ST3 36 D6
Wigmore Pl. ST3 36 B1
Willow Row. ST3 36 A5
Wilmot Gro. ST3 36 B1
Windsor Av. ST3 36 C6
Winterbourne Gro. ST3 36 D4
Woddingdean Clo. ST3 36 C2
Wolstern Rd. ST3 36 C1
Wood St. ST3 36 A3
Worth Clo. ST3 36 C3
Wren Vw. ST3 36 C6
Yarmouth Walk. ST3 36 C2

MADELEY

Agger Hill. CW3 37 F1
Apple Croft. CW3 37 B2
Arbour Clo. CW3 37 B2
Barhill Rd. CW3 37 A4
Beck Rd. CW3 37 C2
Beech Croft. CW3 37 C2
Beresford Dale. CW3 37 B3
Bevan Pl. CW3 37 C3
Birch Dale. CW3 37 B3
Birch Mews. CW3 37 C4
Bower End La. CW3 37 B3
Boysey Wood Rd. CW3 37 B1
Bramble Lea. CW3 37 B3
Castle La. CW3 37 C4
Charles Cotton Dri. CW3 37 B3
Cherry Hill. CW3 37 B3
College Clo. CW3 37 C2
Corrie Clo. CW3 37 C4
Cygnet Clo. CW3 37 E1
Daltry Way. CW3 37 C2
Elkington Rise. CW3 37 C2
Fern Dene. CW3 37 B2
Furnace La. CW3 37 A2
Garners Walk. CW3 37 C2
Grayling Willows. CW3 37 C3
Greenmeadows Rd. CW3 37 C2
Heath Row. CW3 37 E1
Heather Glade. CW3 37 B2
Heighley Castle Way. CW3 37 C1
Heron Clo. CW3 37 C2
Hidden Hill. CW3 37 C1
Hillwood Rd. CW3 37 E1
Holm Oak Dri. CW3 37 C2
Honeywall La. CW3 37 F2
Hungerford La. CW3 37 C4
Izaac Walton Way. CW3 37 B4
John Offley Rd. CW3 37 B3
Keele Rd. CW3 37 D2
Kingfisher Clo. CW3 37 D2
Knightley. CW3 37 C4
Laverock Gro. CW3 37 B4
Leycett La. CW3 37 F1
Lindops La. CW3 37 C2
Lynam Way. CW3 37 C2
Manor La. CW3 37 B4
Merlin Grn. CW3 37 B3
Mill La. CW3 37 C2
Monument View. CW3 37 E2
Morningside. CW3 37 B3
Moss La. CW3 37 B3
Netherset Hey La. CW3 37 C4
New Rd. CW3 37 C2
Newcastle Rd. CW3 37 C3
Park Clo. CW3 37 C1
Parkside. CW3 37 D2
Pastoral Clo. CW3 37 C4
Pear Tree Dri. CW3 37 B3
Plover Field. CW3 37 B3
Poolside. CW3 37 C3

Primrose Dell. CW3 37 B3
Red La. CW3 37 B4
River Lea Mews. CW3 37 B3
Roseberry Dri. CW3 37 C2
Salisbury Clo. CW3 37 C2
Sawpit Yard. CW3 37 D2
Station Rd. CW3 37 C4
The Bridle Path. CW3 37 B2
The Holborn. CW3 37 C4
The Spinney. CW3 37 E1
Thornhill Dri. CW3 37 C4
Vicarage La. CW3 37 C4
Watering Trough Bank. CW3 37 F2
Waterside Clo. CW3 37 E1
Wharf Ter. CW3 37 E1
Woodland Hill. CW3 37 C1
Woodside. CW3 37 C2
Works Dri. CW3 37 E2

NEWCASTLE-UNDER-LYME

Abbots Way. ST5 38 B6
Albany Rd. ST5 38 B2
Albemarle Rd. ST5 38 A1
Andrew Pl. ST5 38 D3
Ashfields New Rd. ST5 38 B2
Baden Rd. ST5 38 B3
Bailey St. ST5 38 B3
Balcombe Clo. ST5 38 B5
Balls Yd. ST5 38 C3
Bankside. ST5 38 D4
Barracks Rd. ST5 38 C4
Beattie Av. ST5 38 C1
Beaumaris Ct. ST5 38 A5
Belgrave Rd. ST5 38 D4
Beresford Cres. ST5 38 A6
Blackfriars Rd. ST5 38 B4
Borough Rd. ST5 38 D3
Brackenberry. ST5 38 C1
Bramfield Dri. ST5 38 C2
Brampton Gdns. ST5 38 D1
Brampton Rd. ST5 38 D2
Brampton Sidings. ST5 38 D2
Bridge St. ST5 38 B3
Brindley St. ST5 38 B3
Broad St. ST5 38 C3
Brook La. ST5 38 C5
Brookside Clo. ST5 38 A5
Brunswick St. ST5 38 C3
Buckleys Row. ST5 38 B4
Buckmaster Av. ST5 38 D6
Castle Hill Rd. ST5 38 B3
*Castle Keep Mews, Silverdale Rd. ST5 38 A3
Castle Ridge. ST5 38 A4
Castle St. ST5 38 D3
Chantry Rd. ST5 38 B6
Charter Rd. ST5 38 B1
Cheapside. ST5 38 C4
Church St. ST5 38 B3
Clarence St. ST5 38 D3
Clayton Rd. ST5 38 C5
Coronation Rd. ST5 38 D4
Corporation St. ST5 38 C2
Croft Rd. ST5 38 C2
Cross May St. ST5 38 B4
Cumberland St. ST5 38 D3
Deansgate. ST5 38 A4
Delamere Gro. ST5 38 C2
Dene Side. ST5 38 A4
Douglas Rd. ST5 38 A1
Drayton St. ST5 38 B4
Duke St. ST5 38 D5
Dunkirk. ST5 38 B3
Dunkirk La. ST5 38 B3
Earl St. ST5 38 D3
Earls Ct. ST5 38 D3
Eleanor Cres. ST5 38 B6
Eleanor Pl. ST5 38 B6
Emery Av. ST5 38 A5
Enderley St. ST5 38 B2
Fairlawns. ST5 38 C1
Fletcher Bank. ST5 38 B3
Florence St. ST5 38 C3
Fogg St. ST5 38 C3
Freehold St. ST5 38 D4
Friars St. ST5 38 C4
Friars Walk. ST5 38 B6
Friarswood Rd. ST5 38 B4
Froghall. ST5 38 B3
Garden St. ST5 38 C4
George St. ST5 38 D3

Goodwin Av. ST5 38 B1
Goose St. ST5 38 C4
Gower St. ST5 38 D3
Granville Av. ST5 38 D2
Greenbook Ct. ST5 38 C1
Greenside. ST5 38 B3
Grosvenor Gdns. ST5 38 D4
Grosvenor Rd. ST5 38 C4
Hall St. ST5 38 B3
Hanover St. ST5 38 C3
Harrison St. ST5 38 D5
Hart Ct. ST5 38 B3
Hassam Av. ST5 38 B1
Hassell St. ST5 38 C4
Hatrell St. ST5 38 C5
Hawkstone Clo. ST5 38 D5
Heath Av. ST5 38 C1
Heath St. ST5 38 C3
Hedley Pl. ST5 38 A4
Hempstalls La. ST5 38 C2
Hick St. ST5 38 C4
Hickman St. ST5 38 B3
High St. ST5 38 C3
Higherland. ST5 38 A4
Highfield Ct. ST5 38 C6
Hill St. ST5 38 B2
Hillside. ST5 38 A5
Holborn. ST5 38 B3
Honeywood. ST5 38 C1
Howard Gro. ST5 38 A6
Howards Pl. ST5 38 A6
Hughes Av. ST5 38 B3
Hyacinth Ct. ST5 38 C1

INDUSTRIAL ESTATES:
Brampton Ind Est. ST5 38 B2
Ironmarket. ST5 38 B2
Jason St. ST5 38 A5
Jenkinson Clo. ST5 38 A5
John O'Gaunts Rd. ST5 38 B3
Kimberley Grange. ST5 38 B1
Kimberley Rd. ST5 38 B1
King St. ST5 38 C3
Knutton La. ST5 38 A2
Lad La. ST5 38 C3
Lancaster Av. ST5 38 D4
Lancaster Rd. ST5 38 D4
Larkspur Gro. ST5 38 C1
Laxey Rd. ST5 38 A1
Leech St. ST5 38 D5
Legge St. ST5 38 A6
Liverpool Rd. ST5 38 B1
London Rd. ST5 38 C4
Lower St. ST5 38 B3
Lyme Valley Rd. ST5 38 C5
Lyme Wood Gro. ST5 38 B5
Lymewood Clo. ST5 38 B5
Marina Dri. ST5 38 D1
Market La. ST5 38 C3
Marsh Par. ST5 38 D3
May Pl. ST5 38 D1
Mayer Av. ST5 38 B1
Mayfield Av. ST5 38 A4
Mellard St. ST5 38 B2
Merrial St. ST5 38 C3
Milford Rd. ST5 38 A5
Mill St. ST5 38 B2
Miller St. ST5 38 D3
Montfort Pl. ST5 38 C6
Moran St. ST5 38 A2
Mount Pleasant. ST5 38 B5
Myott Av. ST5 38 C3
Nelson Pl. ST5 38 C3
North St. ST5 38 D3
Northcote Pl. ST5 38 D3
Occupation St. ST5 38 D5
Orion Ct. ST5 38 A4
Orme Rd. ST5 38 A3
Orton Rd. ST5 38 B1
Paradise St. ST5 38 C4
Parkstone Av. ST5 38 D5
Pembroke Dri. ST5 38 A5
Penarth Pl. ST5 38 A5
Pepper St. ST5 38 C4
Pilkington Av. ST5 38 B6
Pool Dam. ST5 38 B4
Pool Side. ST5 38 B3
Pool St. ST5 38 B4
Poolfield Av. ST5 38 A4
Poplar Gro. ST5 38 D3
Primrose Gro. ST5 38 C1
Princess St. ST5 38 B6
Priory Rd. ST5 38 B3
Prospect Ter. ST5 38 B3
Pump St. ST5 38 B4
Queen St. ST5 38 C3

Queens Ct. ST5 38 C3
Ramsey Rd. ST5 38 A1
Roberts Av. ST5 38 B1
Ronaldsway Dri. ST5 38 A1
Roseacre. ST5 38 A5
Rotterdam. ST5 38 A3
Rye Bank. ST5 38 C3
Rye Bank Cres. ST5 38 C3
Ryecroft. ST5 38 B3
St Andrews Dri. ST5 38 A4
St Anthonys Dri. ST5 38 A6
St Georges Rd. ST5 38 A4
St Martins St. ST5 38 A4
St Marys Dri. ST5 38 A4
St Michaels Rd. ST5 38 B1
St Pauls Rd. ST5 38 A3
Sandy La. ST5 38 D1
School St. ST5 38 B6
Seabridge Rd. ST5 38 D3
Seagrave St. ST5 38 A4
Shaw St. ST5 38 B2
Sidmouth Av. ST5 38 D2
Silverdale Rd. ST5 38 A3
Slaney St. ST5 38 D5
Sneyd Av. ST5 38 A6
Sneyd Cres. ST5 38 A6
Stanier St. ST5 38 B3
Station Walk. ST5 38 C2
Stubbs Gate. ST5 38 C5
Stubbs St. ST5 38 C4
Stubbs Walk. ST5 38 D4
Stubbsfield Rd. ST5 38 D5
Sunny Hollow. ST5 38 D1
The Avenue. ST5 38 D5
The Briars. ST5 38 C1
The Crescent. ST5 38 B6
The Grove. ST5 38 C6
The Hollies. ST5 38 D2
The Midway. ST5 38 B4
The Parkway. ST5 38 B6
Thistleberry Av. ST5 38 A5
Thistleberry Villas. ST5 38 A5
Tulip Gro. ST5 38 C2
Tynwald Grange. ST5 38 A1
Vessey Ter. ST5 38 D4
Vicarage Cres. ST5 38 D5
Victoria Rd. ST5 38 D4
Victoria St. ST5 38 D5
Water St. ST5 38 B4
Webster St. ST5 38 D5
Wedgwood Av. ST5 38 A6
Well St. ST5 38 C4
Wesley St. ST5 38 A4
West Brampton. ST5 38 C3
West St. ST5 38 D4
Westlands Av. ST5 38 A5
Wharf St. ST5 38 D3
Whitfield Av. ST5 38 A5
Whitmore Rd. ST5 38 A6
Wilson St. ST5 38 C2
Wilton St. ST5 38 B1
Woodstock Clo. ST5 38 C1
Wulstan St. ST5 38 C1
York Pl. ST5 38 C3
York St. ST5 38 D3

PENKRIDGE

Abbey Clo. ST19 39 C2
Ablon Ct. ST19 39 C3
Aston Clo. ST19 39 D3
Bartlett Clo. ST19 39 C2
Bedingestone Dri. ST19 39 B1
Bellbrook. ST19 39 B1
Beverley Clo. ST19 39 C3
Bitham Clo. ST19 39 C3
Blount Clo. ST19 39 C3
Boscomoor Ct. ST19 39 B3
Boscomoor La. ST19 39 B3
Boscomoor Rd. ST19 39 B3
Boyden Clo. ST19 39 C3
Bramdean Dri. ST19 39 C2
Bridgewater Clo. ST19 39 C3
Brindley Clo. ST19 39 D3
Broc Clo. ST19 39 C2
Brook Clo. ST19 39 B3
Bungham La. ST19 39 A2
Cannock Rd. ST19 39 C3
Cheadle Clo. ST19 39 C3
Chelford Clo. ST19 39 C3
Chell Clo. ST19 39 C3
Cherrybrook Rd. ST19 39 C1
Chetwynd Clo. ST19 39 C3

Church Rd. ST19 39 B1
Clay St. ST19 39 B2
Commerce Dri. ST19 39 B3
Cooke Clo. ST19 39 B1
Cowley Clo. ST19 39 C3
Crown Bri. ST19 39 B2
Croydon Dri. ST19 39 B2
Dene Clo. ST19 39 C2
Denefield. ST19 39 C2
Druids Way. ST19 39 C3
Edwin Clo. ST19 39 C2
Eggington Dri. ST19 39 C3
Elm Walk. ST19 39 B3
Elmdon Clo. ST19 39 C2
Fallowfield Clo. ST19 39 B2
Filance Clo. ST19 39 C3
Filance La. ST19 39 B2
Francis Clo. ST19 39 B2
Francis Green La. ST19 39 B2
Frederick Rd. ST19 39 C1
Fullmoor Clo. ST19 39 C2
Goods Station La. ST19 39 B1
Grange Clo. ST19 39 B3
Grange Cres. ST19 39 B3
Grange Rd. ST19 39 B3
Greenways. ST19 39 C2
Greville Clo. ST19 39 C3
Grocott Clo. ST19 39 B1
Grosvenor Clo. ST19 39 C1
Haling Clo. ST19 39 B1
Haling Rd. ST19 39 B1
Hatherton Rd. ST19 39 C1
Henney Clo. ST19 39 C3
Holme Rise. ST19 39 C3
Hussey Clo. ST19 39 C3
Kempson Clo. ST19 39 C1
Kentmere Clo. ST19 39 D1
Kingfisher Walk. ST19 39 C3
Knights Clo. ST19 39 C3
Leacroft Rd. ST19 39 C1
Levedale Rd. ST19 39 A1
Lime Walk. ST19 39 B3
Little Marsh Rd. ST19 39 C2
Littleton Cres. ST19 39 C1
Lock Rd. ST19 39 C3
Manorfield Clo. ST19 39 B2
Manston Hill. ST19 39 B3
Market Pl. ST19 39 B2
Market St. ST19 39 B1
Marsh La. ST19 39 C1
Mayfield Av. ST19 39 B2
Micklewood Clo. ST19 39 C3
Mill House Gdns. ST19 39 B1
Moor Hall La. ST19 39 D3
Naggington Dri. ST19 39 C3
New Rd. ST19 39 B2
Newlands Clo. ST19 39 C3
Norman Rd. ST19 39 C2
Norman Rd. ST19 39 C2
Nursery Dri. ST19 39 B1
Oakley Clo. ST19 39 D2
Orchard Clo. ST19 39 C1
Orchard Cres. ST19 39 C1
Otherton Clo. ST19 39 B3
Paget Clo. ST19 39 D3
Pillaton Clo. ST19 39 C3
Pinfold La. ST19 39 A2
Prescott Clo. ST19 39 C1
Preston Vale La. ST19 39 A1
Princefield Av. ST19 39 C3
Rendermore Clo. ST19 39 B3
St Michaels Clo. ST19 39 B2
St Michaels Clo. ST19 39 B2
St Michaels Sq. ST19 39 B2
St Modwena Way. ST19 39 C1
Sapling Clo. ST19 39 C1
Saxon Rd. ST19 39 C2
Shelsey Clo. ST19 39 D2
Sprengers Clo. ST19 39 B1
Stamford Clo. ST19 39 B1
Station Rd. ST19 39 B2
Stone Cross. ST19 39 B1
Streamside Clo. ST19 39 C2
Teddesley Rd. ST19 39 B1
Templars Way. ST19 39 C3
Teveray Dri. ST19 39 C3
The Flaxovens. ST19 39 B1
The Saplings. ST19 39 C1
Tildesley Clo. ST19 39 B2
Uplands Clo. ST19 39 B1
Vale Gdns. ST19 39 B2
Vale Rise. ST19 39 B2
Verdon Clo. ST19 39 C3
Walhouse Dri. ST19 39 C3
Waterbrook Clo. ST19 39 B3
Wheatcroft Clo. ST19 39 B3

Willoughby Clo. ST19 39 C3
Wiscombe Av. ST19 39 C2
Wolgarston Way. ST19 39 D2
Wolverhampton Rd. ST19 39 B3
Woodtherne Clo. ST19 39 B3
Wulfric Clo. ST19 39 C2

RUGELEY

Abbots Wk. WS15 41 F7
Albany Rd. WS15 40 C2
Albion St. WS15 40 D4
Allen Birt Wk. WS15 40 B2
Aneurin Bevan Pl. WS15 40 B2
Anson St. WS15 40 D4
Antler Dri. WS15 40 A3
Arch St. WS15 41 D5
Arden Clo. WS15 40 B3
Armishaw Pl. WS15 41 F7
Armitage La. WS15 41 D5
Armitage Rd. WS15 41 D5
Arthur Evans Clo. WS15 41 E7
Arthur St. WS15 40 C2
Arthur Wood Pl. WS15 40 C2
Ashleigh Rd. WS15 41 D6
Ashtree Bank. WS15 41 F7
Attlee Cres. WS15 41 D5
Averill Dri. WS15 40 B3
Avondale Gdns. WS15 40 A3
Bank Top. WS15 41 F7
Barn Clo. WS15 41 F7
Batesway. WS15 41 F8
Bayswater Rd. WS15 40 B3
Bedford Way. WS15 41 C7
Beeches La. WS15 41 E6
Beechmere Rise. WS15 40 A3
Bees La. WS15 40 B4
Bilberry Clo. WS15 40 B4
Birch La. WS15 41 E7
Birchtree La. WS15 41 C6
Bishops Grange. WS15 40 D3
Blithbury Rd. WS15 40 E2
Bond La. WS15 41 E5
Bow St. WS15 40 D4
Bower La. WS15 40 A2
Bracken Way. WS15 40 B3
Bramble Way. WS15 40 B4
Brereton Lodge. WS15 41 F7
Brereton Manor Ct. WS15 41 F8
Brereton Rd. WS15 41 D5
Brewery Rd. WS15 40 D4
Briar Clo. WS15 40 A4
Brick-Kiln Way. WS15 41 E8
Bridle Wk. WS15 40 A3
Brindley Bank Rd. WS15 40 C2
Brinkburn Clo. WS15 40 A4
Brook Sq. WS15 40 D4
*Brookside, Albion St. WS15 40 D4
*Browns Way, Green La. WS15 40 C4
Bryans La. WS15 40 D4
Burnfield Dri. WS15 40 B3
Burnthill La. WS15 41 C8
Bush Dri. WS15 40 C4
Byron Pl. WS15 40 B2
Cambrian La. WS15 40 B2
Campbell Clo. WS15 40 A3
Canaway Wk. WS15 40 A3
Cardigan Av. WS15 41 C6
Catkin Wk. WS15 40 B3
Cedar Cres. WS15 41 E8
Chadsfield Rd. WS15 40 C3
Chadwick. WS15 41 D5
Charnwood Clo. WS15 40 A3
Chase Side Dri. WS 40 B4
Chaseley Clo. WS15 40 A4
Cherry Tree Rd. WS15 41 D7
Chetwynd Clo. WS15 41 C7
Cheviot Dri. WS15 40 B2
Chieveley Clo. WS15 40 A4
Church Clo. WS15 41 A5
Church Cft Gdns. WS15 40 D7
Church La. WS15 40 A3
Church St. WS15 40 C4
Coach House La. WS15 40 C4
Coalpit La. WS15 41 E8
Coalway Rd. WS15 41 F7
Colton Rd. WS15 40 D7
Common La. WS15 41 B4
Coppice La. WS15 41 C6
Coppive Rd. WS15 41 C6
Cornwall Ct. WS15 40 C4

Coulthwaite Way. WS15 41 D6
Cowlishaw Way. WS15 41 E6
Crabtree Way. WS15 40 A3
Crestwood Rise. WS15 40 A2
Crocketts Nook. WS15 40 B2
Cross Rd. WS15 41 C5
*Crossley Stone,
 Sheep Fair. WS15 40 C4
Curzon Pl. WS15 41 D6
Daffodil Wk. WS15 40 A3
Davy Pl. WS15 41 C7
Daywell Rise. WS15 40 D3
Deacon Way. WS15 40 D3
Deafield Way. WS15 40 A3
Deanery Clo. WS15 40 D3
Deerleap Way. WS15 40 B4
Devall Clo. WS15 41 C6
Devonshire Dri. WS15 41 B7
Durham Dri. WS15 41 B7
Dyton Dri. WS15 40 A3
East Butts Rd. WS15 40 A4
Edwards Dri. WS15 40 C4
*Elmore Ct,
 Elmore La. WS15 40 D4
Elmore La. WS15 40 D4
Essex Dri. WS15 41 B7
Fairmount Way. WS15 40 B4
Farm Clo. WS15 40 A3
Ferncombe Dri. WS15 40 A3
Fernwood Dri. WS15 40 B3
Field Pl. WS15 41 A5
Finches Hill. WS15 40 A2
Flaxley Rd. WS15 41 C6
Forge Mews. WS15 40 D4
Forge Rd. WS15 40 D4
Fortescue La. WS15 40 C3
Foxglove Clo. WS15 40 B4
Frank Gee Clo. WS15 40 C4
Frank Rogers Wk.
 WS15 40 B3
Garden Dri. WS15 41 E6
Garden Vw. WS15 41 E6
Garrick Rose. WS15 41 F7
George Brealey Clo.
 WS15 41 E5
Glenhaven. WS15 40 B3
Gorse La. WS15 41 D7
Gorse Rd. WS15 41 D6
Gorseburn Way. WS15 40 A3
Green La. WS15 40 B3
Greenacres. WS15 41 C6
Greenfields Dri. WS15 40 B4
Grindcobbe Gro. WS15 40 C2
Hagley Dri. WS15 40 C4
Hagley Park Gdns.
 WS15 41 C5
Hagley Rd. WS15 40 B4
Hardy Cres. WS15 41 C6
Harley Clo. WS15 41 D7
Harley Rd. WS15 40 D3
Harney Ct. WS15 40 B2
Haseley Rd. WS15 40 A4
Hawthorne Way. WS15 41 E6
Heath Rd. WS15 41 E6
Heather Clo. WS15 41 D7
Hednesford Rd. WS15 41 A8
Heron St. WS15 41 C6
High Falls. WS15 41 C6
High Ridge. WS15 40 A2
Highland Way. WS15 40 A2
Hill St. WS15 41 C5
Hillary Cres. WS15 41 C7
Hillside Clo. WS15 41 F7
Hilltop. WS15 41 D6
Hillway Clo. WS15 40 B4
Hislop Rd. WS15 41 C6
Hobbs Vw. WS15 41 F7
Holly Lodge Clo. WS15 41 C5
Holy Oake Pl. WS15 40 B2
Horns Croft. WS15 41 A5
Horse Fair. WS15 41 D5
Horseshoe Dri. WS15 40 A3
Huntsmans Wk. WS15 40 B4
Hurstbourne Clo. WS15 40 B4
Hutchinson Clo. WS15 40 A3

INDUSTRIAL ESTATES:
Lea Hall Enterprise Pk.
 WS15 41 F6
Redbrook La Ind Est.
 WS15 41 D7
Riverside Ind Est.
 WS15 40 E3
The Levels Ind Est.
 WS15 41 E8
Ingleside. WS15 40 B3
James Warner Clo.
 WS15 40 C4

Jeffery Clo. WS15 40 B2
John Ball Ct. WS15 40 B2
John Till Clo. WS15 40 C3
Johnson Ct. WS15 40 C3
Jones La. WS15 41 A5
Joseph Dix Dri. WS15 40 C3
Jubilee St. WS15 40 B3
Kelly Av. WS15 41 D6
Kelvedon Way. WS15 40 A4
Keystone Rd. WS15 41 D5
Kimberley Way. WS15 41 E7
King St. WS15 40 E4
Landdowne Way. WS15 40 A3
Landor Cres. WS15 41 C6
Landsbury Rd. WS15 41 C6
Lanehead Wk. WS15 40 A3
Lanrick Gdns. WS15 40 D3
Larch Rd. WS15 41 E6
Leasowe Rd. WS15 41 E7
Leathermill La. WS15 40 D4
Lees Clo. WS15 41 F7
Leyland Dri. WS15 40 D3
Lichfield St. WS15 41 D5
Lion St. WS15 40 E4
Little Orchard. WS15 40 C3
Lodge Rd. WS15 41 F7
Love La. WS15 40 E4
Lovett Clo. WS15 40 B2
Lower Brook St. WS15 40 D4
Mckie Way. WS15 41 E6
Main Rd. WS15 41 E6
March Banks. WS15 40 B4
Marden Clo. WS15 41 D7
Market Sq. WS15 40 D4
Market St. WS15 40 D4
Mayflower Dri. WS15 40 B4
Mersey Clo. WS15 40 C2
Mill La. WS15 40 D4
Millington St. WS15 40 D3
Moorland Clo. WS15 40 B4
Moss Grn. WS15 40 B3
Mossley. WS15 41 E5
Mount Rd. WS15 40 A3
Myatt Way. WS15 41 E6
Newman Gro. WS15 41 D6
Nursery Rd. WS15 41 E8
Oakleigh Dri. WS15 41 F7
Oaktree Rd. WS15 41 E6
Old Chancel Rd. WS15 40 C3
Old Eaton Rd. WS15 40 C2
Orchard Clo. WS15 40 C2
Overland Clo. WS15 41 E7
Overpool Clo. WS15 40 B4
Owen Clo. WS15 40 C3
Park Hall Clo. WS15 40 C2
Park Vw Ter. WS15 40 B4
Peakes Rd. WS15 40 A3
Penk Dri North. WS15 40 A2
Penk Dri South. WS15 40 A3
Penkridge Bank Rd.
 WS15 41 A5
Phoenix Clo. WS15 40 D4
Pine Vw. WS15 40 A2
Plovers Rise. WS15 40 B3
Pool Meadow Clo.
 WS15 40 B4
Portobello. WS15 40 C2
Post Office La. WS15 41 A5
Power Station Rd.
 WS15 40 D3
Priory Rd. WS15 41 F7
Pump La. WS15 40 A2
Quarry Clo. WS15 41 A5
Queen St. WS15 40 E4
Queensway. WS15 41 C6
Rangers Wk. WS15 40 A4
Ravenhill Clo. WS15 41 D6
Ravenslea Rd. WS15 41 E7
Redbrook La. WS15 41 E7
*Redmond Clo,
 Dayton Clo. WS15 40 A3
Riders Way. WS15 40 A4
Rishworth Av. WS15 40 D3
Rose Way. WS15 40 B2
Rowley Clo. WS15 41 E7
Rutherglen Clo. WS15 40 A3
Rutland Av. WS15 41 E7
St Anthonys Clo. WS15 40 D4
St Augustines Rd.
 WS15 41 C7
St Edwards Grn. WS15 41 C6
St Johns Clo. WS15 41 A5
St Michaels Dri. WS15 41 E7
St Michaels La. WS15 41 E7
St Pauls Rd. WS15 41 D5

Sandy La. WS15 41 C6
Sankey Cres. WS15 41 C6
Sarah Challinor Clo.
 WS15 41 C5
*Scholars Gate,
 Seabrook Rd. WS15 41 F7
Seabrook Rd. WS15 41 F7
Setterfield Way. WS15 41 D6
Shaftsbury Rd. WS15 40 A4
Sharnbrook Dri. WS15 40 B3
Sheep Fair. WS15 40 C4
Sheringham Dri. WS15 40 A3
Shrewsbury Mall. WS15 40 D4
Shugborough Rd. WS15 40 B2
Slitting Mill Rd. WS15 41 A6
Somerset Av. WS15 41 C7
Speechly Dri. WS15 40 C3
Springfields Rd. WS15 40 B2
Springhill Av. WS15 41 E6
Springhill Ter. WS15 41 E7
Spruce Av. WS15 40 A2
Stag Clo. WS15 40 A3
Station Rd. WS15 40 D3
Stile Clo. WS15 41 D7
Stile Cop Rd. WS15 41 B7
Surrey Clo. WS15 41 B7
Sutton Clo. WS15 41 D6
Swallow Clo. WS15 40 C3
Swan Clo. WS15 41 F8
Sycamore Cres. WS15 41 F7
Talbot Rd. WS15 41 E7
Talbot St. WS15 41 D5
Tannery Clo. WS15 40 E4
Taylors La. WS15 40 D4
The Beeches. WS15 40 B2
The Green. WS15 41 E7
The Laurels. WS15 41 D6
The Oaklands. WS15 40 A4
The Rise. WS15 41 E7
The Slade. WS15 41 E8
The Stables. WS15 40 C4
The Willows. WS15 41 F8
Thistle Clo. WS15 40 A3
Thompson Rd. WS15 41 F7
Thorn Clo. WS15 41 E6
Tithebarn Rd. WS15 40 C3
Toy Clo. WS15 40 B3
Trentview Clo. WS15 41 E6
Tunnicliffe Dri. WS15 40 C3
Upfield Way. WS15 40 B3
Uplands Gdns. WS15 41 C7
Upper Brook St. WS15 40 D4
Upper Cross Rd. WS15 41 C5
Upton Pl. WS15 40 C5
Vicars Croft. WS15 40 D3
Walnut Ct. WS15 41 F7
Wat Tyler Clo. WS15 40 C2
Waterside. WS15 41 E7
Watfield Clo. WS15 41 F8
Watkiss Dri. WS15 40 C2
Watson Clo. WS15 40 C2
Waverley Gdns. WS15 40 A3
Weatherall Clo. WS15 40 B3
Wellington Dri. WS15 40 D4
Western Springs Rd.
 WS15 40 C2
Western View. WS15 40 B3
Wharf Rd. WS15 41 D5
Whitgreave La. WS15 41 C6
Whitworth La. WS15 41 E6
William Morris Ct. WS15 40 B2
Winstanley Pl. WS15 40 C2
Wolseley Rd. WS15 40 A1
Woodcock Rd. WS15 40 A4
Woodhayes Lawns.
 WS15 40 A4
Woodthorne Clo. WS15 40 B3
Woodview. WS15 41 E7
Yew Tree Rd. WS15 41 E6

STAFFORD

Abbots Walk. ST16 43 E5
Albert Ter. ST16 43 E5
Aldbury Clo. ST16 43 E1
Alder Gro. ST17 44 C4
Aldershaw Clo. ST16 42 D1
Aldrin Clo. ST16 43 H5
Alexandra Rd. ST17 45 F2
Allendale. ST16 42 C2
Alliance St. ST16 42 D4
Allotment La. ST17 44 D2
Alstone Clo. ST16 42 B3
Amblefield Way. ST16 42 D1

Ampleforth Dri. ST17 45 H3
Ardingley Av. ST17 45 H3
Armstrong Av. ST16 43 H5
Ashdale Dri. ST16 42 D1
Ashley Clo. ST16 42 B5
Ashridge Walk. ST16 43 E1
Aspen Croft. ST17 44 C4
Aston Ter. ST16 43 E3
Astonfields Rd. ST16 43 E4
Astoria St. ST16 45 F5
Attlee Cres. ST17 44 D4
Auden Way. ST17 44 C3
Austin Friars. ST17 45 E2
Averil Rd. ST17 44 D4
Avon Rise. ST16 43 H6
Back Browning St. ST16 43 E5
Bagots Oak. ST17 44 C4
Barker Clo. ST16 42 D1
Barlaston Clo. ST16 42 D1
Barley Ct. ST16 42 B5
Barn Bank La. ST17 44 D6
Barnet Rd. ST17 44 D5
Baxter Grn. ST16 42 C6
Baxter Rd. ST17 44 D4
Beaconside. ST16 42 D1
Beaconside Clo. ST16 43 G4
Beaumont Gdns. ST17 44 C3
Bedford Av. ST16 43 G6
Beechcroft Av. ST17 44 D2
Beechway. ST16 42 D3
Beeston Ridge. ST17 44 C4
Bell Clo. ST16 43 F5
Bellasis St. ST16 43 E4
Benenden Clo. ST17 44 C5
Berry Rd. ST16 42 B2
Bertelin Rd. ST16 43 G3
Betjeman Way. ST17 44 C5
Beton Way. ST16 43 E1
Beverley Dri. ST16 42 C1
Bigwood La. ST18 44 A6
Billington Bank. ST18 44 A4
Binyon Ct. ST17 44 C4
Birch Gro. ST17 44 C4
Blackberry La. ST16 42 D6
Blakiston St. ST16 43 E5
Blythe Rd. ST17 45 F6
Boardman Cres. ST16 44 D1
Boningale Way. ST17 44 B3
Bonington Cres. ST16 44 C1
Boon Gro. ST17 45 F6
Border Way. ST17 45 F5
Bracken Clo. ST17 44 C5
Brackenfield Way. ST16 43 E1
Bradbury Rise. ST16 42 B5
Bradshaw Av. ST16 43 E1
Bramall La. ST16 44 D4
Bridge St. ST16 45 E1
Brindley Clo. ST16 43 F1
Brisbane St. ST17 44 C3
Broad Eye. ST16 43 E6
Broad Meadow Croft.
 ST16 42 B5
Broad St. ST16 43 E6
Bromstead Cres. ST16 42 B3
Brook Ct. ST17 45 E4
Brook Glen Dri. ST17 45 E4
Brook Glen Rd. ST17 45 E4
Broughton Clo. ST16 42 D2
Browning St. ST16 43 E5
Brundle Av. ST16 44 C1
Brunel Clo. ST16 42 C3
Brunswick Ter. ST16 45 E2
Buckland Rd. ST16 42 D1
Burcham Clo. ST16 42 C3
Burlington Dri. ST16 44 B3
Burnett Ct. ST16 42 B5
Burns Av. ST17 44 C3
Bursley Clo. ST17 44 D5
Burton Bank La. ST17 44 D6
Burton Manor Rd. ST17 44 D6
Burton Sq. ST17 45 E5
Busbys Bldg. ST16 43 E5
Byron Clo. ST17 44 C3
Cairns Dri. ST16 43 H5
Cambridge St. ST16 43 G6
Cameo St. ST16 42 B2
Cape Av. ST17 44 C4
Carder Av. ST17 44 C2
Carisbrooke Dri. ST16 44 C1
Carling Clo. ST16 42 D1
Carlton Sq. ST17 44 B3
Carson Way. ST17 44 C1
Carver Rd. ST16 42 F3
Castle Acre. ST17 44 C5
Castle Bank. ST17 44 A3
Castle St. ST16 44 D6
Castle Way. ST16 44 D2

Castledene Dri. ST16 44 C2
Castlefields. ST16 44 D1
Caulden Rd. ST16 42 D3
Charles Cotton St. ST16 42 D3
Charnley Rd. ST16 43 F4
Charterhouse Av. ST17 45 H3
Chartley Clo. ST16 42 D1
Chaucer Rd. ST17 44 C3
Chebsey Dri. ST16 42 B3
Chell Rd. ST16 43 E6
Chelsea Way. ST17 44 D2
Chesham Rd. ST16 43 G4
Christie Av. ST16 44 C1
Christopher Ter. ST17 45 G2
Church Clo. ST17 45 F6
Churchill Way. ST17 45 E6
Clare Rd. ST16 42 D3
Claremont Gro. ST17 44 B3
Clarendon Dri. ST17 44 B3
Clement Clo. ST16 43 G5
Cleveland Walk. ST17 44 B3
Clifton Clo. ST16 43 H6
Clifton Dri. ST16 43 H6
Co-operative St. ST16 43 E4
Coghlan Dri. ST17 44 D4
Cole Dri. ST16 44 C1
Coleridge Dri. ST17 44 C4
Common Rd. ST16 43 E1
Common Walk. ST16 43 E4
Compton Clo. ST17 45 G2
Conway Rd. ST16 42 B5
Cope St. ST16 45 F1
Copper Glade. ST16 43 H6
Coronation Rd. ST16 43 G4
Corporation St. ST16 43 E5
Corran Rd. ST17 44 D5
County Rd. ST16 43 E5
Coventry Ct. ST16 42 B5
Cowan Dri. ST16 43 G6
Cowley Clo. ST17 44 C3
Crab La. ST16 42 B2
Crabbery St. ST16 43 E6
Craddock Rd. ST16 42 C3
Cramer St. ST17 45 F2
Cranberry Clo. ST16 42 B3
Cranbrook Walk. ST17 44 B3
Crescent Rd. ST16 45 E2
Creswell Dri. ST18 42 A2
Creswell Farm Dri. ST16 42 B3
Creswell Rd. ST18 42 A1
Crinan Gro. ST17 44 D5
Crispin Clo. ST16 42 D2
Crooked Bridge Rd.
 ST16 43 E5
Cross St. ST16 43 E5
Crossway. ST17 45 G1
Cull Av. ST16 43 H6
Danby Crest. ST17 44 B3
Darnford Clo. ST16 42 D1
Dart Av. ST17 44 B4
Dartmouth St. ST16 45 G1
Davies Clo. ST16 43 G6
Deanshill Clo. ST16 44 D2
Dearnsdale Clo. ST16 42 B2
Delamere La. ST17 44 B4
Dell Clo. ST16 42 C2
Denstone Av. ST17 45 H3
Denver Fold. ST17 44 B3
Denzil Grn. ST17 44 B3
Derby St. ST16 45 E1
Devon Way. ST17 44 D6
Dexter Rise. ST17 44 C6
Dickson Rd. ST16 43 G5
Dorrington Dri. ST16 43 E4
Douglas Rd. ST16 43 G5
Douglas Rd West. ST16 43 G5
Dove Clo. ST17 45 F6
Downderrry Clo. ST17 44 B4
Downfield Gro. ST16 42 D1
Doxey. ST16 42 A6
Doxey Fields. ST16 42 B6
Doxey Rd. ST16 42 D6
Dreieich Clo. ST16 43 F5
Drummond Rd. ST16 43 E4
Dryburgh St. ST16 44 C5
Dryden Cres. ST17 44 C3
Dunster Clo. ST17 44 B4
Earl St. ST16 45 E1
Easby Clo. ST17 44 C4
Eastgate St. ST16 43 E6
Eastlands. ST16 45 E3
Eastlands. ST17 45 E3
Eastlands Gro. ST17 45 F3
Eccleshall Rd. ST16 43 F4
Edison Rd. ST16 43 F4

Edmund Av. ST17 44 C3
Edwards Dri. ST16 44 C1
Edwin Clo. ST17 44 C3
Elford Clo. ST16 42 D1
Eliot Way. ST17 44 C3
Ellington Av. ST16 43 H5
Elmhurst Clo. ST16 42 D1
Elsdon Rd. ST17 44 D5
Elworthy Clo. ST16 43 G4
Embry Av. ST16 45 G5
Espleys Yd. ST16 45 E1
Eton Clo. ST17 45 H3
Exeter St. ST17 45 F3
Fairfield Ct. ST17 43 F4
Fairoak Av. ST16 42 D2
Fairway. ST16 45 G1
Fancy Walk. ST16 43 E5
Faraday Rd. ST16 43 F5
Felden Clo. ST16 43 E1
Fellfield Way. ST16 43 E1
Fern Dri. ST16 42 B5
Fernleigh Gdns. ST16 42 A5
Fernwood. ST16 42 D2
Field Pl. ST16 42 E3
First Av. ST16 42 C2
Fonthil Rd. ST16 43 F3
Foregate St. ST16 43 E5
Freemen St. ST16 43 F4
Frew Clo. ST16 43 H6
Friar St. ST16 43 E5
Friars Rd. ST16 43 E1
Friars Ter. ST17 43 E2
Frinton Gro. ST17 43 G3
Furness Gro. ST17 44 C5
Gaol Rd. ST16 43 E5
Gaolgate St. ST16 43 E6
Garden Pl. ST17 45 F2
Garden St. ST17 45 F2
Garrod Sq. ST16 43 H5
Garth Clo. ST17 45 F6
George Bailey Ct. ST17 44 C1
George St. ST16 43 E5
Gillingham Cres. ST16 44 C1
Glebe Av. ST16 42 D3
Glebelands. ST17 45 F6
Globe Av. ST17 45 F5
Glover St. ST16 43 E6
Gordon Av. ST16 42 D2
Gorsebrook Leys. ST16 42 A4
Gough Clo. ST17 42 C2
Grassmere Hollow. ST16 42 A5
Gray Walk. ST17 44 C4
Greengate St. ST16 45 E1
Greensome Clo. ST16 42 B5
Greensome Ct. ST16 42 A5
Greensome Cres. ST16 42 A5
Greensome La. ST16 42 A5
Greenway. ST16 45 G1
Greenways. ST18 44 C6
Greenwood Gro. ST17 44 D4
Greyfriars St. ST16 43 E5
Greyfriars Pl. ST16 43 E5
Greyfriars Way. ST16 42 D5
Grissom Clo. ST16 43 H5
Gunnel Clo. ST16 44 C1
Hall Clo. ST17 45 G4
Hambridge Clo. ST17 44 D5
Harcourt Way. ST16 42 C2
Hardy Rd. ST17 44 C3
Hargreaves La. ST17 44 D2
Harmony Grn. ST17 44 C4
Harris Rd. ST17 43 H5
Harrowby St. ST16 45 H1
Hartwell Gro. ST16 42 B3
Hatherton St. ST16 45 G1
Hawke Rd. ST17 42 C3
Hawksmoor Rd. ST16 45 E4
Hawthorn Way. ST17 45 G2
Hazel Gro. ST16 45 E4
Hazleton Grn. ST17 45 E5
Hearn Ct. ST17 45 E5
Heath Dri. ST17 42 C2
Heenan Gro. ST17 45 F6
Helen Sharman Dri. ST16 43 H5
Helford Gro. ST17 44 C4
Henry St. ST16 43 F4
Herbert Rd. ST17 45 E3
Hesketh Rd. ST17 45 E5
High Park. ST17 44 C2
Highfield Gro. ST17 44 D4
Highlands. ST17 44 D4
Hill Crest. ST17 44 D4
Hillcote Hollow. ST16 42 B3
Hillfarm Clo. ST17 45 F6

Hinton Clo. ST17 45 G6
Holmcroft Rd. ST16 42 C3
Holmes Clo. ST16 44 C1
Homestead Ct. ST16 43 E2
Hopton Ct. ST16 43 E4
Hopton La. ST17 43 H1
Hopton St. ST16 43 F4
Howard Rd. ST17 45 F5
Hurlingham Rd. ST16 42 C2
Hyde Ct. ST17 45 E4
Hyde Lea Bank. ST18 44 D6

INDUSTRIAL ESTATES:
Astonfields Ind Est. ST16 43 F3
Astonfields Rd Business Pk. ST16 43 F3
Carver Rd Business Pk. ST16 43 F3
Dorrington Ind Pk. ST16 43 E4
Palmbourne Ind Pk. ST16 44 D1
St Albans Rd Ind Est. ST16 43 F2
Tollgate Ind Pk. ST16 43 F1

Ingestre Rd. ST17 45 F2
Inglewood. ST17 44 D2
Isabel Clo. ST17 44 C3
Izaak Walton Clo. ST16 42 D4
Izaak Walton St. ST16 42 D4
Jacobs Croft. ST16 42 D2
Jerningham St. ST16 42 D6
John Amery Dri. ST17 45 E5
John Donne St. ST16 42 D3
John St. ST16 43 G6
Jones Clo. ST17 44 D4
Jubilee Ct. ST16 43 F5
Keats Av. ST17 44 C4
Keld Av. ST17 44 B4
Kendal Clo. ST17 44 B4
Kennedy Way. ST16 42 C2
Kent Way. ST17 45 H4
Kentish Clo. ST17 44 B4
Kentmere Clo. ST17 44 B4
Kenworthy Rd. ST16 43 E3
Keswick Gro. ST17 44 B4
Kimberley Way. ST17 44 B4
Kingsley Clo. ST17 45 E4
Kingsley Rd. ST17 45 E4
Kingston Gro. ST16 43 H6
Kingsway. ST16 44 D1
Kirkstall Av. ST17 44 C4
Knight Av. ST16 43 G5
Lammascote Rd. ST16 45 F1
Lancaster Rd. ST17 45 G4
Lancing Av. ST17 45 H3
Lansbury Clo. ST17 45 E3
Lapley Av. ST16 42 B3
Lara Clo. ST16 44 C1
Larkin Clo. ST17 44 C5
Laurel Gro. ST17 45 F4
Lawn Rd. ST17 44 D3
Lawnsfield Walk. ST16 42 D1
Lawrence St. ST17 45 F3
Lea Cres. ST17 45 E4
Lea Gro. ST16 42 D2
Leigh Clo. ST17 45 F6
Lethbridge Gdns. ST17 44 B4
Levedale Rd. ST16 42 B3
Lexington Grn. ST17 44 B4
Liberty Park. ST17 44 B3
Lichfield Rd. ST16 45 F2
Lilac Gro. ST17 45 F5
Lilleshall Way. ST16 44 C4
Limetree Av. ST16 43 E4
Lincoln Meadows. ST17 44 B4
Lindon Clo. ST17 44 B4
Lineker Clo. ST17 44 C1
Linksfield Gro. ST16 42 D1
Lister Rd. ST16 43 F5
Lloyd St. ST16 44 D5
Longshore Clo. ST17 44 D5
Lovatt St. ST16 43 E4
Lovelace Clo. ST17 44 D3
Loynton Clo. ST16 42 B3
Lyric Clo. ST17 45 G6
Lyttleton Ct. ST16 45 G6
Malcolm Rd. ST16 45 E6
Mallard Av. ST17 45 H4
Malvern Clo. ST17 45 H3
Manor Farm Cres. ST17 45 E6
Manor Grn. ST17 45 D5
Manor Sq. ST17 45 F5
Mansel Clo. ST16 45 F4
Maple Gro. ST17 45 F4
Market Sq. ST16 43 E6

Market St. ST16 43 E6
Marlowe Rd. ST17 44 C3
Marsh Ct. ST16 43 E4
Marsh St. ST16 43 E5
Marsland Clo. ST16 42 B5
Marsland Rd. ST16 42 B5
Marston Ct. ST16 43 E4
Marston Dri. ST16 43 E4
Marston Ho. ST16 43 E4
Marston Rd. ST16 43 E5
Marsworth Way. ST16 42 D1
Martin Dri. ST16 44 C1
Martin St. ST16 43 E6
Mary Rand Clo. ST17 45 E4
Masefield Dri. ST17 44 C3
Matthews Rd. ST17 44 D5
Mayock Cres. ST17 44 C1
Meadow Ct. ST17 45 G4
Meadow Rd. ST17 45 G4
Meadowbank Wk. ST16 42 D1
Meakin St. ST17 42 C3
Melbourne Cres. ST16 43 H5
Melrose Av. ST17 44 C4
Merrey Rd. ST17 45 E5
Merrivale Rd. ST17 45 F4
Meyrick Rd. ST17 45 F2
Mill Bank. ST16 45 E1
Mill St. ST16 45 E1
Milton Gro. ST17 44 C4
Moorfields. ST16 42 D3
Morton Rd. ST17 45 E5
Mosspit. ST17 45 F6
Mossvale Gro. ST16 42 A5
Mount Edge. ST16 43 H1
Mount St. ST16 44 C3
Mountville Dri. ST17 44 C3
Mynors St. ST16 43 G6
Nash Av. ST16 42 C3
Nelson Way. ST16 45 E6
New Garden St. ST17 45 F2
New St. ST16 43 E5
Newall Av. ST16 43 H5
Newland Av. ST16 42 D2
Newport Rd. ST17 44 B3
Newton Rd. ST16 43 G4
Norfolk Way. ST17 44 D5
North Av. ST16 42 D3
North Castle St. ST16 42 D6
North Pl. ST16 43 E6
North Walls. ST16 43 E6
Nursery La. ST16 42 D5
Oak Tree Clo. ST16 44 B4
Oaklands Dri. ST17 44 D5
Orchard St. ST17 45 F2
Orwell Dri. ST17 44 B4
Oulton Way. ST16 42 B3
Owen Walk. ST17 44 C5
Oxford Gdns. ST16 44 C5
Oxleathers Ct. ST16 44 C4
Paddock Clo. ST16 42 C2
Pantulf Clo. ST16 44 C3
Park Av. ST17 45 E4
Park Cres. ST17 45 E3
Park St. ST17 45 E2
Parkers Croft Rd. ST17 45 F2
Parkfields. ST17 44 D4
Parkside Av. ST16 42 D1
Peach Av. ST17 45 F5
Peel St. ST16 44 D1
Peel Ter. ST16 43 E4
Penkvale Rd. ST17 45 F6
Pennycroft Bungalows. ST16 43 G6
Perrin Clo. ST17 45 F5
Peter James Ct. ST17 43 H4
Pike Clo. ST16 43 H4
Pintail Clo. ST17 45 H5
Pitstone Clo. ST16 43 E1
Pitt St. ST16 42 D3
Plant Av. ST17 45 F5
Pope Gdns. ST17 44 C5
Poplar Way. ST17 45 E6
Portal Rd. ST16 43 H4
Prescott Av. ST16 43 G5
Prestwood Ct. ST17 45 F2
Princes St. ST16 43 E4
Princess Pl. ST16 43 E4
Prospect Rd. ST16 43 F5
Pulteney Dri. ST16 42 C3
Queensville. ST17 45 H3
Queensville Av. ST17 45 G2
Queensville Bri. ST17 45 G2
Queensway. ST16 43 E6
Radford Bank. ST17 45 H4
Railway St. ST16 44 D1
Ralph Ct. ST17 44 C3

Rambleford Way. ST16 42 D1
Read Av. ST16 43 G5
Reason Rd. ST17 45 F6
Rectory Ct. ST17 44 D2
Red Lion St. ST16 43 E6
Redgrave Dri. ST16 44 C1
Redhill. ST16 42 C2
Redhill Gorse. ST16 42 C1
Repton Clo. ST17 45 H3
Reva Rd. ST17 45 F4
Richards Av. ST16 43 G6
Richmond Clo. ST17 44 D3
Rickerscote Av. ST16 45 G5
Rickerscote Hall La. ST17 45 G6
Rickerscote Rd. ST17 45 F6
Rising Brook. ST17 45 E4
Riversmeade Way. ST16 42 A5
Riverway. ST16 45 G2
Roedean Av. ST17 45 H3
Romford Rd. ST16 43 F3
Rose Hill. ST16 44 C1
Rotherwood Dri. ST17 44 D3
Rouse Clo. ST16 44 C1
Rowley Av. ST17 44 D3
Rowley Bank. ST17 45 E3
Rowley Bank Gdns. ST17 45 E3
Rowley Gro. ST17 45 E3
Rowley Hall Clo. ST17 44 D3
Rowley Hall Dri. ST17 44 D3
Rowley St. ST16 43 E5
Rye Ct. ST16 42 A5
Sabine St. ST17 45 F3
St Albans Rd. ST16 43 E3
St Andrews Rd. ST17 44 D4
St Davids Rd. ST17 44 D4
St Georges Rd. ST17 45 G2
St Johns Rd. ST17 45 E3
St Johns Walk. ST16 45 G6
St Leonards Av. ST17 45 G2
St Patricks St. ST16 43 E5
St Peters Clo. ST17 45 F6
St Peters Gdns. ST17 45 F6
St Thomas St. ST16 43 G6
Salisbury Dri. ST16 43 H5
Salisbury Rd. ST16 43 H5
Salmond Av. ST16 43 H5
Salt Av. ST17 45 F2
Salt Rd. ST17 45 F2
Salter St. ST16 43 E6
Sandon Mews. ST16 43 F4
Sandon Rd. ST16 43 E5
Sandown Croft. ST17 44 D2
Sandyford St. ST16 43 E5
Sash St. ST16 43 E5
Sayers Rd. ST16 42 C2
School Clo. ST16 43 F5
School La. ST17 45 F6
School Lane Clo. ST17 45 G6
Searle Av. ST16 44 C1
Second Av. ST16 42 C2
Shakespeare Rd. ST17 44 C3
Shallowford Mews. ST16 42 D4
Shannon Rd. ST17 44 D5
Shaw Gdns. ST17 44 C4
Shebdon Clo. ST16 42 B3
Shelley Clo. ST16 43 G5
Shelmore Clo. ST16 42 C2
Shenley Gro. ST17 44 D5
Sheridan St. ST16 43 G5
Sherwood Av. ST17 45 E4
Shrewsbury Rd. ST17 45 F2
Sidney Av. ST17 45 F3
Siemens Rd. ST17 45 F3
Silkmore Cres. ST17 45 G4
Silkmore La. ST17 45 G5
Simpson Clo. ST16 42 C3
Slessor Rd. ST16 43 G5
Smallman St. ST16 43 G5
Snows Yd. ST16 43 E5
Somerset Rd. ST17 44 C5
Somerville Sq. ST17 45 F6
South St. ST16 45 E1
South Walls. ST16 45 F1
Southfields Clo. ST17 45 E6
Southfields Rd. ST17 45 E6
Spencer Ct. ST17 44 C4
Spode Av. ST16 43 H1
Springfield Dri. ST16 43 G5
Springvale Rise. ST17 42 D1
Stafford St. ST16 43 G4
Stanway Ct. ST16 43 G4
Station Rd. ST16 45 E1
Steadman Cres. ST17 45 E6

Stevenson Dri. ST17 44 C4
Stone Rd. ST16 42 D1
Stone Rd. ST17 45 F6
Stretton Av. ST16 42 B3
Stychfields. ST17 45 F3
Sundown Dri. ST17 45 F3
Surrey Rd. ST17 44 C4
Sutton Dri. ST16 42 B5
Swan Clo. ST16 44 C1
Swinburne Clo. ST17 44 C4
Sycamore La. ST17 44 C4
Talbot Rd. ST17 45 F2
Tamar Gro. ST17 44 B4
Taplin Clo. ST16 42 D2
Taylor Walk. ST17 44 C4
Tedder Rd. ST16 43 H5
Telegraph St. ST17 45 E2
Telford Dri. ST16 43 F2
Tenby Dri. ST16 43 F3
Tennyson Rd. ST17 44 C3
Tenterbanks. ST16 45 E1
Thackery Walk. ST17 44 D4
Thames Way. ST17 45 F4
The Birches. ST17 45 F4
The Brandons. ST17 45 G6
The Close. ST16 44 C2
The Close. ST17 45 F6
The Crescent. ST16 42 C6
The Drive. ST16 42 B6
The Glade. ST17 45 H3
The Green. ST17 45 E6
The Haybarn. ST16 43 G3
The Lawn. ST17 45 F6
The Oval. ST16 45 F1
The Rockeries. ST17 45 G6
The Russetts. ST17 45 F5
Thirlmere Way. ST17 44 C5
Thomas Av. ST16 44 C1
Thompson Clo. ST17 44 C4
Thornyfields La. ST16 43 E4
Tillington St. ST16 43 E4
Tipping St. ST16 45 E1
Tithe Barn Ct. ST16 43 G5
Tithe Barn Rd. ST16 43 G6
Tixall Rd. ST16 43 G6
Tollgate Dri. ST16 43 F1
Torridge Dri. ST17 44 C4
Trenchard Av. ST16 43 G5
Trent Clo. ST16 45 F6
Trevelyans Grn. ST16 42 C2
Trinity Gorse. ST16 42 C2
Trinity Rise. ST16 42 C2
Tudor Rise. ST16 42 C2
Tudor Way. ST17 42 C3
Tullis Clo. ST16 44 C1
Turney Gro. ST17 44 D4
Turnhill Clo. ST17 44 D5
Underwood Clo. ST16 42 D1
Uplands Rd. ST17 44 C4
Upmeadows Dri. ST16 42 D1
Vaughan Way. ST17 44 C2
Verulam Ct. ST16 43 F3
Verulam Rd. ST16 43 E2
Vicarage Way. ST17 45 E1
Victoria Rd. ST16 45 E1
Victoria Sq. ST16 45 E1
Victoria St. ST16 45 E1
Victoria Ter. ST16 43 E4
Walden Av. ST16 42 D3
Warrens La. ST16 42 B3
Warwick Rd. ST17 45 H4
Water St. ST16 45 E1
Wayfield Dri. ST16 42 D1
Weaver Dri. ST17 44 B4
West Clo. ST16 45 G1
West Way. ST17 44 C3
Westbury Hayes. ST17 44 C4
Westhead Av. ST16 43 G6
Weston Rd. ST16 43 G6
Whimster Sq. ST17 44 B4
Whitby Clo. ST17 44 B4
Whitgreave Ct. ST16 43 E4
Whittingham Dri. ST17 44 B4
Wilkes Wood. ST16 42 A1
Williams Clo. ST16 44 C1
Willow Moor. ST17 45 E6
Windsor Rd. ST17 45 H4
Wogan St. ST16 43 E5
Wolverhampton Rd. ST17 45 E2
Wood Cres. ST16 42 D2
Woodlands Clo. ST16 42 C5
Woodlands Rd. ST16 42 C5
Wootton Dri. ST16 42 B3
Wordsworth Av. ST16 44 C3
Wright St. ST16 43 E5

Yarlet Croft. ST16 43 E4
York Rd. ST17 45 H4
Young Av. ST16 42 D3

STOKE-UPON-TRENT

Albany Gro. ST4 46 A4
Albany Rd. ST4 46 A5
Albert St. ST4 46 A3
Allen St. ST4 46 C4
*Aqueduct St,
 Glebe St. ST4 47 F5
Aquinas St. ST4 47 E5
Argyle St. ST1 47 E1
Ashford St. ST4 47 F3
Ashlands Av. ST4 46 B4
Ashlands Cres. ST4 46 B5
Ashlands Gro. ST4 46 B5
Ashlands Rd. ST4 46 B5
Ashley St. ST1 47 F1
Ashwell Rd. ST4 46 A4
Austin St. ST1 47 H2
Avenue Rd. ST4 47 F3
Aynesley Rd. ST4 47 E3
Bailey St. ST4 46 C2
Balliol St. ST4 46 D5
Balloon St. ST4 46 A3
Bamber St. ST4 47 E5
Bank House Dri. ST5 46 B2
Basford Park Rd. ST5 46 A1
Bath St. ST4 47 E6
Bath Ter. ST4 47 E6
Beaumaris Clo. ST4 46 A4
Bedford Rd. ST1 47 F2
Bedford St. ST1 47 E2
Belford Pl. ST4 46 C3
Belmont Rd. ST1 46 D1
Beresford St. ST4 47 F3
Berkeley St. ST1 47 H1
Bernard St. ST1 47 H1
Berry Hill Rd. ST4 47 H3
Berry St. ST4 47 E5
Bethesda Rd. ST1 47 G2
Bethesda St. ST1 47 G1
Bilton St. ST4 47 E6
Boon Av. ST4 46 D6
Booth St. ST4 47 E6
Boothen Rd. ST4 47 F6
Boswell St. ST4 46 C2
Botteslow St. ST1 47 H1
Boughey Rd. ST4 47 G4
Boundary St. ST4 46 A3
Bower St. ST1 47 G2
Bowstead St. ST4 47 F6
Brickkiln La. ST4 46 C2
Brighton St. ST4 46 D5
Britton St. ST4 46 C3
Broad St. ST1 47 F1
Brook Pl. ST4 46 C2
Brook St. ST4 47 F5
Broughton Rd. ST5 46 A2
Brunswick Pl. ST1 47 G1
Buller St. ST1 47 H2
Butler St. ST4 47 F6
Byron St. ST4 47 G2
Caledonia Rd. ST1 47 E2
Campion Av. ST5 46 A1
Cannon St. ST1 47 F1
Cardiff Gro. ST1 47 G1
Carlton Rd. ST4 47 G4
Cartlidge St. ST4 46 A3
Castlefield St. ST1 47 E2
*Cauldon Pl. ST4 47 F2
Cauldon Rd. ST4 47 F2
Cavour St. ST1. ST4 46 C1
Cemetery Rd. ST1 47 E2
Chamberlain St. ST1 47 F2
Charlton St. ST4 47 E4
Chatham St. ST1 47 F2
Church St. ST4 47 E5
City Rd. ST4 47 G6
Clare St. ST4 46 A2
Claridge Rd. ST4 46 B3
Clarke St. ST1 47 E1
Cleveland Rd. ST1 47 G2
Cliff Vale Pl. ST4 46 D3
Clyde St. ST1 47 H1
College Rd. ST4 47 F1
Collingwood Gro. ST4 46 C4
Collis Av. ST4 46 A3
Compton St. ST1 47 E1
Consort St. ST4 47 E5

Convent Clo. ST4 47 E4
Convent Ct. ST4 47 E4
Conway St. ST4 47 G4
Cooper Av. ST5 46 B1
Cooper St. ST1 47 F1
Copeland St. ST4 47 F5
Cornes St. ST1 47 H2
Cornwallis St. ST4 47 F6
Coronation Rd. ST4 46 B4
Coteshealth St. ST1 47 H2
Cottons Row. ST4 46 A5
Couldon Rd. ST4 47 F3
Cranmer St. ST4 47 F5
Crescent Gro. ST4 46 B3
Cresty St. ST4 46 D6
Croston St. ST1 47 F2
*Crowther St. ST4 47 F4
Cumming St. ST4 46 B3
Curzon St. ST5 46 A1
Cutts St. ST1 47 F2
Darnley St. ST4 47 G4
Davis St. ST1 47 E2
Dean Pl. ST1 47 H2
Dominic St. ST4 46 D4
Doncaster La. ST4 46 D6
Downey St. ST1 47 G1
Downing Av. ST5 46 A1
Dundee Rd. ST1 46 D1
Eardley St. ST4 46 D6
East Cres. ST5 46 A1
Easthead Walk. ST1 47 E1
Eastwood Pl. ST1 47 G1
Eastwood Rd. ST1 47 H1
Egerton St. ST4 46 B4
Egerton St. ST4 47 H3
Elenora St. ST4 47 E5
Elgin St. ST4 47 E3
Elliott St. ST4 46 A2
Elm St. ST5 46 A1
Elsing St. ST4 47 H6
Ephraim St. ST1 47 G1
Epworth St. ST4 47 E6
Errill Clo. ST4 47 G6
Etruria Locks. ST1 46 D1
Etruria Old Rd. ST1 46 C1
Etruria Rd. ST4 46 A2
Etruria Vale Rd. ST1 47 E1
Etruria Way. ST1 46 B1
Etruscan St. ST1 46 C1
Faraday Pl. ST4 46 B5
Featherstone Gro. ST4 46 D5
Fleming Rd. ST4 47 E6
Fletcher St. ST1 47 F1
Floyd St. ST4 47 E5
Ford St. ST4 46 B3
Fosbrook Pl. ST4 46 A4
Foulson St. ST4 47 E6
Franklin Rd. ST4 46 C6
Franklyn St. ST1 47 H1
Frederick Av. ST4 46 D5
Garden Pl. ST4 46 B5
Garden St. ST4 46 C6
Garfield St. ST1 47 E1
Garibaldi St. ST1 46 D1
Garner St. ST1 46 C1
Geen St. ST4 47 E5
George St. ST4 46 A3
Gerrard St. ST4 47 E5
Gifford Pl. ST4 46 C6
Gill Walk. ST1 47 F1
Gladstone St. ST4 46 B2
Glebe Ct. ST4 47 F5
Glebe St. ST4 47 F5
Granby Walk. ST4 46 D6
Grant St. ST4 47 G6
Great Rothwell St. ST4 46 D6
Greatbatch Av. ST4 46 D6
Grice Rd. ST4 46 B4
Grindley Pl. ST4 46 C6
Grove Pl. ST1 47 F1
Guildford St. ST4 47 G4
Hallahan Gro. ST4 46 D4
Hampton St. ST1 47 H2
Hancock St. ST4 47 G5
Harcourt St. ST4 47 F2
Harding Rd. ST1 47 G2
Hardinge St. ST4 47 H6
Harris St. ST4 46 D5
Harthill St. ST4 47 G5
Hartshill Rd. ST4 46 A3
Havelock Pl. ST4 47 E2
Haydon St. ST1 46 B2
Haywood St. ST4 47 E3
Hazelhurst St. ST1 47 H1
Heathcote Av. ST1 47 E5
Herbert St. ST4 47 H6

Hide St. ST4 47 E6
Higson Av. ST4 47 E5
Hill St. ST4 47 E5
Hillside Walk. ST4 46 A4
Hilltop Av. ST5 46 B1
Hilton Rd. ST4 46 A5
Honeywall. ST4 46 D6
Hornby Row. ST4 47 E6
Horton St. ST4 46 A3
Houghton St. ST1 47 G1
Howard Pl. ST1 47 F2
Howson St. ST1 47 H1
Hulme St. ST4 46 C4
Humbert St. ST1 46 D1
Hunters Way. ST4 46 D6
Huntley Av. ST4 46 D6
Imperial Ct. ST4 47 H1

INDUSTRIAL ESTATES:
Etruria Trading Est.
 ST4 46 B1
Stoke Business Pk.
 ST4 47 F6
Inglis St. ST4 47 G5
Irene Av. ST4 46 A1
James Brindley Clo. ST1 47 G1
Jasper St. ST1 47 G1
Joanhurst Cres. ST1 47 E1
John St. ST4 46 A3
Jordan St. ST1 47 E1
Jubilee St. ST4 47 E1
Kenilworth Gro. ST5 46 B1
Kimberley Rd. ST1 46 D1
Kildown Clo. ST1 47 E1
Kings Croft. ST4 46 A3
Kings Pl. ST4 46 A2
Kings Ter. ST4 46 A2
Kingsfield Oval. ST4 46 A2
Kingsfield Rd. ST4 46 A3
Kingsway. ST4 47 F5
Kingswell Rd. ST4 46 A3
Kirkham St. ST4 47 E6
Kirkland La. ST4 46 D4
Knowle St. ST4 47 E4
Ladysmith Rd. ST4 46 D1
Lancaster Av. ST4 46 A4
Lancaster Cres. ST4 46 A5
Lancaster Rd. ST4 46 A4
Lanehead Rd. ST1 46 D1
Langley St. ST4 46 A2
Lansdowne Rd. ST4 46 B3
Lawrence St. ST1 47 F2
Leason St. ST4 47 F5
Leek Rd. ST4 47 G4
Leese St. ST4 47 E5
Leonard Av. ST4 46 A4
Lewis St. ST4 47 E5
Lichfield St. ST1 47 G1
Lindsay St. ST1 47 F1
Linley Rd. ST4 46 B4
Lion St. ST4 46 D6
Lionel Gro. ST4 46 B6
Liverpool Rd. ST4 47 E5
Lockwood St. ST4 46 A3
Lodge Rd. ST4 46 B5
Lomas St. ST1 47 E2
London Rd. ST4 46 A6
London Rd. ST4 47 E6
Longfield Rd. ST4 46 B5
Lonsdale St. ST4 47 F6
Lordship La. ST4 47 G6
Lovatt St. ST4 47 E5
Lowe St. ST4 47 F6
Lower Bedford St.
 ST1 47 E2
Lower Cres. ST4 46 B4
Lower Oxford Rd.
 ST5 46 B1
Lukes Land Av. ST4 46 B6
Lyham St. ST4 47 E5
Lytton St. ST4 47 F5
Maclagan St. ST4 47 F6
Manor St. ST4 46 D6
Margill Clo. ST4 47 F1
Matlock St. ST1 47 G2
Mawson Gro. ST4 47 G3
Maxwell St. ST4 46 B5
May Av. ST5 46 A1
Meliden Way. ST4 46 C6
Milton St. ST1 47 E1
Minton St. ST4 46 C4
Mount Av. ST4 46 D5
Mount Pleasant,
 Hanley. ST1 47 E1
Mount Pleasant,
 Newcastle. ST4 46 A3
Nelson Rd. ST4 46 B4

Newcastle La. ST4 46 B6
Newcastle Rd. ST4 46 A6
Newlands St. ST4 47 E3
Newton St. ST4 46 B2
Norfolk St. ST1 47 F2
Norman Gro. ST5 46 A1
North St. ST4 46 D3
Northcote St. ST4 47 E3
Oak St. ST5 46 A1
Ogden St. ST1 47 G1
Old Mill St. ST4 47 G6
Oldham St. ST1 47 H2
Oliver Rd. ST4 46 B6
Oriel St. ST4 46 D5
Osborne Rd. ST4 46 B4
Oxford Cres. ST4 47 E5
Oxford Rd. ST5 46 A1
Oxford St. ST4 46 D4
Palmers Grn. ST4 46 A4
Palmers Way. ST4 46 A4
Palmerston St. ST4 47 H2
Park Ho St. ST1 47 F1
Parkside Dri. ST5 46 A1
Parkside Gro. ST5 46 A1
Paxton St. ST1 47 H1
Pelham St. ST1 47 H1
Penkhull Ct. ST4 47 E1
Penkhull New Rd. ST4 46 D6
Penkhull Ter. ST4 46 D6
Potteries Way. ST1 47 F1
Pretoria Rd. ST1 46 D1
Princes Rd. ST4 46 C4
Pump St. ST4 47 E5
Pyenest St. ST1 47 E2
Quarry Av. ST4 46 D4
Quarry Rd. ST4 46 D5
Queen Anne St 47 F4
Queens Rd. ST4 46 C5
Queensway. ST5 46 B1
Radford Rd. ST4 46 C3
Raymond St. ST1 47 F1
Rebecca St. ST4 47 E5
Rectory Pass. ST1 47 F1
Rectory Rd. ST1 47 E2
Rectory St. ST1 47 E1
Red Lion Pass. ST1 47 F1
Regent Rd. ST4 47 G2
Registry St. ST4 46 D1
Richmond Gro. ST5 46 B1
Richmond St. ST4 46 D4
Richmond Ter. ST1 47 F2
Ridgeway Rd. ST4 47 G3
Riseley Rd. ST4 46 B4
Robson St. ST1 47 F1
Rogerstone Av. ST4 46 B6
Rope St. ST4 46 A3
Rosebuck St. ST4 47 G5
Rutherford Pl. ST4 46 B5
Sackville St. ST4 46 B2
Sage Clo. ST1 47 G1
St Andrews Sq. ST4 47 E5
St Christopher Av. ST4 46 B6
St Marks St. ST1 47 F1
St Marks St. ST1 47 F1
St Peters Clo. ST4 47 F5
St Thomas Pl. ST4 46 D6
Salem St. ST1 46 D1
Salisbury Av. ST1 47 F2
Scrivener Rd. ST4 46 C2
Seaford St. ST4 47 F3
Selwyn St. ST4 47 F6
Seven Arches Way. ST4 47 G5
Shackson Clo. ST1 47 F2
Shallowford Ct. ST1 47 E1
Sharman Clo. ST4 46 C5
Sheaf St. ST1 47 F1
Shearer St. ST1 47 E2
Shelton Farm Rd. ST1 47 E1
Shelton New Rd. ST4 46 A3
Shelton Old Rd. ST4 47 E4
Shirley Rd. ST1 47 F2
Showan Av. ST5 46 A1
Sillitoe Pl. ST4 46 D6
Simon Pl. ST4 47 E3
Simonbury Av. ST4 46 B6
Simpson St. ST1 47 H2
Slippery La. ST1 47 F1
Smithfield Ct. ST1 47 G1
Snow Hill. ST1 47 F2
Somerville Rd. ST5 46 B1
South Wolfe St. ST4 47 E6
Spark St. ST4 47 F4
Spencer Rd. ST4 47 F4
Spoutfield Rd. ST4 46 C3
Spring St. ST4 46 A3
Spring Ter. ST4 47 E6

Spur St. ST1 47 H2
Squires View. ST4 47 G5
Stamer St. ST4 47 F6
Standard St. ST4 47 H6
Stanhope St. ST1 47 E1
Stanley Gro. ST5 46 A2
Stanley Rd,
 Basford. ST5 46 B1
Stanley Rd,
 Hartshill. ST4 46 B4
Station Rd. ST4 47 F4
Steel St. ST4 46 C4
Stoke Old Rd. ST4 46 A3
Stoke Rd. ST1 47 F2
Stone St. ST4 46 D5
Stonehaven St. ST4 47 H2
Stoneleyfields Ct. ST4 46 A2
Stuart Rd. ST1 47 H2
Stubbs La. ST1 47 H1
Sturgess St. ST4 47 E6
Sun St. ST1 47 E1
Swan St. ST4 47 E5
Sydney St. ST5 46 B1
Talbot St. ST4 47 H1
Tavistock Pl. ST4 46 B3
The Avenue,
 Basford. ST5 46 A1
The Avenue,
 Newcastle. ST4 46 A5
The Green. ST4 46 B4
The Parkway. ST4 47 G2
Thornburrow Dri. ST4 46 B5
Thorndyke St. ST1 47 E2
Thornton Rd. ST4 47 F4
Tilson Av. ST4 46 D6
Timmis St. ST4 47 E1
Tolkein Way. ST4 46 D4
Trade St. ST4 47 E5
Trafalgar Rd. ST4 46 B4
Trent Way. ST1 47 H2
Tyndall Pl. ST4 46 B5
Upper Cres. ST4 46 B4
Vale St. ST4 47 E5
Vernon Rd. ST4 47 F4
Vicarage Rd. ST4 46 C4
Victoria Av. ST1 47 F2
Victoria Rd. ST1 47 H2
Victoria Sq. ST1 47 F1
Victoria St. ST4 46 A2
Wadham St. ST4 46 D5
Walklate Av. ST5 46 A1
Wallesley St. ST1 47 F2
Walleys Dri. ST4 46 A1
Warrington Rd. ST4 47 H3
Warwick St. ST1 47 E1
Watford St. ST4 47 G4
Watson St. ST4 46 D5
Wayfield Gro. ST4 46 A4
Welch St. ST4 47 F6
Weller St. ST4 46 C4
West Av,
 Basford. ST5 46 A2
West Av, Stoke. ST4 46 D5
West Bank. ST4 46 D6
Westhead Walk. ST1 47 E1
Westland St. ST4 46 D5
Westmill St. ST1 47 H2
Whalley Av. ST4 46 C6
Wharf Pl. ST4 47 F5
Whitmore St. ST1 47 E1
Wilfred Pl. ST4 46 C4
Winton Sq. ST4 47 F4
Wintonfield St. ST4 47 G5
Wolfe St. ST4 47 E6
Wood Ter. ST1 47 F1
Woodhouse St. ST4 47 F6
Yates St. ST1 47 F1
York St. ST4 46 A3
Younger St. ST4 47 H6
Yoxall Av. ST4 46 C4

STONE

Abbey St. ST15 49 D5
Adies Alley. ST15 49 C5
Airdale Gro. ST15 48 D3
Airdale St. ST15 48 D4
Airdale Spinney. ST15 48 D3
Albert St. ST15 48 C3
Alexandra St. ST15 48 C3
Alma St. ST15 48 C4
Altona Clo. ST15 49 E5
Ambleside Clo. ST15 49 F5
Arthur St. ST15 48 C3

Ash Rd. ST15 49 D5
Ashdale Clo. ST15 49 D6
Ashford Gro. ST15 49 F6
Aston Chase. ST15 49 F6
*Aston Lodge Parkway,
Saddler Av. ST15 49 F6
Augustine Clo. ST15 49 F5
Austin Clo. ST15 49 C6
Avon Gro. ST15 49 D7
Back Radford. ST15 48 C4
Bakewell Dri. ST15 49 F7
Balmoral Clo. ST15 49 B6
Bankside. ST15 49 B6
Barnfield Clo. ST15 49 B6
Beacon Rise. ST15 49 C7
Beacon Rd. ST15 49 C7
*Beech Ct,
Church St. ST15 49 D5
Beechwood Dri. ST15 49 D6
Berkeley St. ST15 48 C3
Birch Rd. ST15 49 D5
Birchfield Clo. ST15 49 B7
Blackies La. ST15 49 F6
Bostock Clo. ST15 49 F7
Boundary Clo. ST15 49 B8
Bowers Ct. ST15 49 F5
Brandon Walk. ST15 49 C6
Bridge Cres. ST15 49 D6
Bromfield Ct. ST15 48 C4
Brookfield Ct. ST15 49 F5
Brookside La. ST15 49 B5
Broomfield Clo. ST15 49 D7
Brooms Rd. ST15 49 D8
Bushberry Clo. ST15 49 B6
Caernarvon Av. ST15 49 F7
Canal Rd. ST15 48 B3
*Canalside Mews,
The Moorings. ST15 49 C5
Canons Clo. ST15 49 C6
Castle Ct. ST15 49 F7
Cedar Park. ST15 49 D5
Cedars Dri. ST15 49 D7
Centre Rd. ST15 48 B3
Cherry Orchard. ST15 49 E5
Cherry Tree Clo. ST15 49 B8
Christchurch Way. ST15 48 C4
Church Clo. ST15 48 E2
Church La. ST15 48 E2
Church St. ST15 49 D5
Churchill Rd. ST15 49 B5
Claremont Clo. ST15 49 D5
Clinton Gdns. ST15 49 C6
*Collingwood Ct,
Lichfield St. ST15 49 D5
Common La. ST15 49 B7
Coniston Clo. ST15 49 F5
Convent La. ST15 48 E1
Coombe Park Rd. ST15 49 B8
Cooper Clo. ST15 49 F5
Copeland Dri. ST15 49 F7
Coppice Clo. ST15 48 D4
Coppice Gdns. ST15 48 D4
Coppice Rd. ST15 48 D4
Cranmore Gro. ST15 49 F5
Crestwood Dri. ST15 49 B7
Croft Rd. ST15 49 B6
Crompton Dri. ST15 49 D5
Cross St. ST15 48 C4
Crown St. ST15 49 C5
De Wint Rd. ST15 49 E6
Derwent Av. ST15 49 F5
Diamond Way. ST15 49 D8
Dominic Ct. ST15 48 C4
Downing Gdns. ST15 49 C6
Dutton Way. ST15 49 B7
East Clo. ST15 49 B5
Eccleshall Rd. ST15 49 A7
Edward St. ST15 48 C3
Elm Rd. ST15 49 D5
Emerald Way. ST15 49 D8
Ernald Gdns. ST15 49 C6
Essex Dri. ST15 49 B7
Fallowfield Ct. ST15 49 E6
*Farrier Clo,
Saddler Av. ST15 49 F6
Fenhurst Clo. ST15 49 E6
Fernie Clo. ST15 49 F7
Field Ter. ST15 48 C4
Fieldhouse Ct. ST15 48 B3
Fieldsway. ST15 49 B5
Fillybrook Clo. ST15 49 B5
Flax Croft. ST15 49 E5
Ford Clo. ST15 49 D6
Forrester Rd. ST15 49 D6
Foxwood Clo. ST15 49 B7
Frazer Clo. ST15 49 B8

Friars Av. ST15 49 C6
George La. ST15 49 F6
Glamis Clo. ST15 49 F7
Goodill Clo. ST15 49 B7
Gower Rd. ST15 49 E6
Grange Rd. ST15 49 E6.
Granville Sq. ST15 48 C4
Granville Ter. ST15 48 C4
Green Clo. ST15 49 C6
Greenway Av. ST15 49 D6
Griffiths Way. ST15 49 F6
Grove Rd. ST15 49 B5
Haddon Pl. ST15 49 F5
Hallahan Clo. ST15 49 F7
Harrow Pl. ST15 49 F7
Hawley Clo. ST15 49 F8
Hawthorn Av. ST15 49 B7
Heath Gdns. ST15 49 C7
Heathfields Av. ST15 49 D6
High St. ST15 48 C4
Highgrove. ST15 49 F7
Highlands. ST15 49 B7
Hill Cres. ST15 49 C7
Hill Dri. ST15 49 C7
Holly Gro. ST15 49 E5
Holyrood Clo. ST15 49 F7
Hoskings Clo. ST15 49 E5
INDUSTRIAL ESTATES:
Stone Business Pk.
ST15 49 D8
Walton Ind Est. ST15 49 C7
Jervis Rd. ST15 49 B8
Johnson Gro. ST15 49 F6
Jordan Way. ST15 49 E5
*Keepers Cottage,
The Moorings. ST15 49 C5
Kensington Clo. ST15 49 F7
Kent Gro. ST15 49 B3
Kibblestone Rd. ST15 48 E1
Kings Av. ST15 48 C4
Kingsland Clo. ST15 49 F5
Kingsland Ct. ST15 49 F5
Kingsland Rd. ST15 49 F5
Kingston Dri. ST15 49 D7
Lamb La. ST15 49 B6
*Lander Clo,
Saddler Av. ST15 49 F6
Lansdowne Clo. ST15 49 B8
Larchfields. ST15 49 D7
Lea Rd. ST15 49 B7
*Leacroft,
Saddler Av. ST15 49 F6
Lichfield Gdns. ST15 49 D5
Lichfield St. ST15 49 D5
Limedale Ct. ST15 48 B4
*Lockside Ct,
The Moorings. ST15 49 C5
Longfield Av. ST15 49 B8
Longhope Dri. ST15 49 B6
Longton Rd. ST15 48 C4
Lotus Ct. ST15 48 C4
Lyndhurst Gro. ST15 49 F6
Malory Clo. ST15 49 D7
Manor Ct. ST15 49 B6
Manor Rise. ST15 49 B6
Maple Gdns. ST15 49 D7
Margaret St. ST15 49 D7
Marlborough Rd. ST15 49 B7
Meadow Way. ST15 49 B7
Meadowbrook Ct. ST15 49 F7
Meaford Av. ST15 48 A2
Meaford Rd. ST15 49 F7
Meakin Clo. ST15 49 C6
Melrose Av. ST15 49 F7
Mercer Av. ST15 49 F5
Mill St. ST15 48 C4
Mill Walk Av. ST15 49 E6
*Millhouse Gdns,
The Moorings. ST15 49 C5
Moorland Clo. ST15 49 D7
Mount Av. ST15 48 B2
Mount Cres. ST15 48 C3
Mount Pleasant Clo.
ST15 49 F6
Mount Rd. ST15 48 A2
Nannygoat La. ST15 48 D4
Newcastle Rd. ST15 48 B3
Newcastle St. ST15 48 C4
Newlands Clo. ST15 49 B7
Newman Clo. ST15 49 F5
Nicholls La. ST15 48 D2
Northesk St. ST15 48 C4
Oak Rd. ST15 49 D5
Old Rectory Rd. ST15 49 B5
Old Rd. ST15 48 C3

Old Road Clo. ST15 48 C3
Oldfield Dri. ST15 49 F7
Opal Way. ST15 49 C8
Orchard Clo. ST15 49 C6
Oulton Rd. ST15 48 C3
Park Av. ST15 49 B5
Parkhouse Dri. ST15 49 E6
Parkway. ST15 49 E6
Pearson Dri. ST15 49 F5
Pembroke Dri. ST15 49 F5
*Phillips Clo,
Saddler Av. ST15 49 F6
Pingle La. ST15 49 E5
Pirehill La. ST15 49 C8
Poplar St. ST15 49 B6
Princes St. ST15 49 C3
Priory Rd. ST15 49 D5
Priory Walk. ST15 49 E6
Queens Sq. ST15 48 C3
Radford Clo. ST15 48 D4
Radford St. ST15 48 C4
Rectory Clo. ST15 49 D5
Redfern Rd. ST15 49 B7
Redhill Gdns. ST15 48 D4
Redhill Rd. ST15 48 D4
Redwood Av. ST15 49 D7
Regent St. ST15 48 C4
Ridge Croft. ST15 49 E5
Ridgemont Ct. ST15 49 F6
River Way. ST15 49 D5
Rock Cres. ST15 48 E1
Rowan Clo. ST15 49 D7
Ruffin Ct. ST15 49 F5
Runnymede. ST15 49 D6
Saddler Av. ST15 49 F6
St Chads Clo. ST15 49 F6
St Georges Rd. ST15 49 F6
St Johns Av. ST15 48 E2
St Michaels Clo. ST15 49 D5
St Michaels Ct. ST15 48 D4
St Michaels Mount.
ST15 49 D5
St Vincent Rd. ST15 49 B5
Saxifrage Dri. ST15 49 F7
Shardlow Clo. ST15 49 E7
Shepley Clo. ST15 49 B6
Sheridan Way. ST15 49 F6
Sidings Rd. ST15 48 B3
Simeon Way. ST15 49 C7
Spring Gdns. ST15 49 C7
Springwood Dri. ST15 49 C5
Stafford Clo. ST15 49 C5
Stafford Rd. ST15 49 C5
Stafford St. ST15 49 C5
Staines Ct. ST15 49 F6
Station App. ST15 48 B3
Station Rd. ST15 48 C4
Stone By-Pass. ST15 48 B3
Stonefield Ct. ST15 48 B3
Stonefield Mews. ST15 48 B4
Stonefield Sq. ST15 48 C4
Stuart Clo. ST15 49 B7
Stuart Clo Nth. ST15 49 B7
*Stubbs Dri,
Saddler Av. ST15 49 F6
Sunningdale. ST15 49 C6
Sutherland St. ST15 49 E6
Sycamore Rd. ST15 49 D5
Tannery Walk. ST15 49 C6
The Avenue. ST15 48 C4
The Crescent. ST15 48 D4
The Fillybrooks. ST15 48 A2
The Glen. ST15 49 D6
The Hempbutts. ST15 49 E7
The Lindens. ST15 49 E7
The Moorings. ST15 49 D5
The Redlands. ST15 49 E6
The Willows. ST15 49 D7
Thomas Av. ST15 49 E7
Tilling Dri. ST15 49 C6
Trent Rd. ST15 49 A4
Tudor Clo. ST15 49 B7
Tunley St. ST15 48 C4
Tyler Gro. ST15 49 B6
Ullswater Dri. ST15 49 F5
Uttoxeter Rd. ST15 49 F7
Valley Rd. ST15 49 D6
Vanity Clo. ST15 48 E1
Vanity La. ST15 48 E1
Vicars Clo. ST15 49 B7
Victor St. ST15 48 C3
Victoria St. ST15 48 C3
Walton Grange. ST15 49 C6
Walton Way. ST15 49 C6
Warm Croft. ST15 49 E6
Wash Dale La. ST15 48 A1

Watersmeet Ct. ST15 49 E7
Weavers La. ST15 49 E6
Wesley Dri. ST15 49 F7
West Clo. ST15 49 B6
*Wharf Lodge,
The Moorings. ST15 49 C5
Whitebridge La. ST15 48 B3
Whitemill La. ST15 49 B6
Willow Rd. ST15 49 D6
Willow Walk. ST15 49 D5
Windsor Clo. ST15 49 B8
Wood Cres. ST15 49 C7
Wood La. ST15 49 C7
Woodlands Av. ST15 49 B5
Woodlands Clo. ST15 49 B5
Wulfad Ct. ST15 49 E5
Yarnfield La. ST15 48 A4
York St. ST15 48 C3

TAMWORTH

Abbey Rd. B79 52 B2
Abelia. B77 52 D2
Adonis. B79 51 F2
Adonis Clo. B79 51 F2
Albert Rd. B79 51 E4
Albion St. B79 51 E4
Aldergate. B79 51 E4
Alders La. B79 50 B3
Alexandra Mews. B79 51 F4
Alfred St. B79 50 D4
Allard. B77 52 C3
Allen St. B77 52 A5
Allens Mead. B77 52 A4
Alvis Clo. B79 51 F4
Alwyn. B77 53 C6
Amber Clo. B77 52 F2
Amington Rd. B77 52 A1
Anchor Clo. B77 52 C2
Anders. B79 50 D3
Angelica. B77 52 D2
Anker Dri. B79 51 E5
Anker Vw. B77 51 F6
Apollo. B79 50 C3
Appian Clo. B77 53 A6
Arbor Clo. B77 52 B2
Arden Clo. B77 51 H4
Arden Rd. B77 53 D8
Argyle Av. B77 52 B1
Argyle St. B77 52 C2
Ariane. B79 50 B2
Arion Clo. B77 51 G4
Arkall Clo. B79 51 F2
Armstrong. B79 50 C3
Arnold Clo. B79 50 D3
Arundel. B77 53 A6
Ash Gro. B77 53 D8
Ashby Rd. B79 51 E3
Ashdale Rd. B77 51 H4
Ashland Clo. B79 51 F2
Ashleigh Dri. B79 53 C5
Athelstan Way. B79 50 C2
Avill. B77 53 E8
Avon. B77 53 E8
Bailey Av. B77 53 D8
Balfour. B79 50 C3
Balfour. B77 50 D5
Bamburgh. B77 53 A6
Bamford St. B77 52 B2
Bancroft. B77 52 B2
Barbara St. B79 50 D4
Barcliff Av. B77 52 C2
Barlow Clo. B77 52 C1
Barnbridge. B77 52 A4
Basin La. B77 52 C1
Beauchamp Rd. B77 53 D8
Beech Av. B77 52 C2
Beech Rd. B79 50 D1
Beech Rd. B79 50 D1
Beechwood Cres. B77 52 D1
Belgrave Rd. B77 53 B5
Belmont Rd. B77 53 C7
Belsize. B77 52 E4
Belvedere Clo. B79 51 F2
Belvior. B77 53 A6
Benson Vw. B79 51 F1
Bentley Way. B79 50 C2
Beyer Clo. B77 53 C5
Birds Bush Rd. B77 53 C5
Bitterscote Dri. B78 50 D6
Blackwood Rd. B77 53 A6
Blenheim Clo. B77 53 B6
Bloomfield Way. B79 50 C1
Blythe St. B77 52 A2

Bolebridge St. B79 51 F5
Bonehill Rd. B78 50 B6
Borman. B79 51 E2
Borough Rd. B78 51 E2
Bowling Green Av.
B77 53 C7
Bradford St. B79 50 C4
Braham. B79 50 A3
Brain St. B77 52 E3
Bramber. B77 52 B4
Brambling. B77 53 E6
Bream. B77 53 B6
Brendon. B77 52 F4
Brent. B77 53 B6
Briar. B77 52 E2
Bridge St. B77 51 H4
Bridgewater St. B77 51 G4
Bright Cres. B77 51 H3
Brindley Dri. B77 51 H3
Broadsmeath. B77 52 B4
Bronte. B79 50 D3
Brook Av. B77 53 D6
Brookside Way. B77 53 D7
Brookweed. B77 52 E2
Browning Clo. B79 50 C1
Browns La. B79 51 E1
Brownsholme. B79 50 A3
Brunel Clo. B79 51 E3
Buckingham Rd. B79 50 A3
Burns Rd. B79 50 D3
Burton Clo. B79 51 F2
Byland. B77 52 B2
Byron Rd. B79 50 D1
Cadogan Rd. B77 53 B8
Calder. B77 52 F4
Cale Clo. B77 52 A4
Caledonian. B77 52 D3
Callis Wk. B77 53 D7
Cambrian. B77 52 D4
Camden Dri. B77 53 C6
Camhouses. B77 52 F4
Campbell Clo. B77 50 C1
Campion Dri. B77 51 F6
Canning Rd. B77 52 C2
Caradoc. B77 52 E3
Carey. B77 53 E8
Carlcroft. B77 52 F4
Carlton Cres. B79 50 C1
Carnoustie. B77 52 F1
Castle Clo. B77 52 C2
Castle Rd. B77 53 D8
Castle Vw. B77 51 F6
Castlehall. B77 52 E3
Cavendish. B79 50 B2
Cedar Dri. B79 50 D1
Celandine. B77 51 F6
Centurian Way. B77 53 F7
Chalfield. B79 50 A2
Chapelon. B77 52 E4
Chapelon Dri. B77 52 E4
Chartwell. B79 50 A2
Chatsworth. B79 50 A2
Cherry St. B79 51 E4
Cherry Tree Wk. B79 50 D1
Chesterton Way. B79 50 D3
Chestnut Av. B79 51 E2
Chestwood. B77 52 E1
Chillingham. B77 53 A6
Chub. B77 53 B6
Church La. B77 51 E4
Church St. B79 51 E4
Claremont Rd. B79 50 C1
Claymore. B77 53 B6
Cleeve. B77 52 B2
Clematis. B77 52 D2
Clifford Clo. B77 52 C2
Clifford St. B77 52 C2
Clifton Av. B79 50 D1
Coach House Rise. B77 53 C6
Cobia. B77 53 B6
Cole Hill. B79 51 E2
Coleridge Clo. B79 50 D3
College La. B79 51 E4
Collett. B77 52 E4
Comberford Rd. B79 50 D1
Compton Rd. B79 50 C2
Coniston. B77 53 E6
Copes Dri. B79 51 E2
Cornel. B77 52 D2
Coronation St. B79 51 E4
Corporation St. B79 51 E4
Coton La. B79 50 A2
Cottage Farm Rd. B77 53 B6
Cowley. B77 52 C3
Craven. B77 52 E4
Cringlebrook. B77 53 E8

Croft St. B79 51 E3
Cromwell Rd. B79 50 B1
Cross St, Kettlebrook. B77 51 F6
Cross St, Tamworth. B79 51 E4
Crossfell. B77 52 E4
Crowden Rd. B77 52 E4
Curlew. B77 53 E6
Dace. B77 53 B6
Danelagh Clo. B79 50 C2
Dart. B77 53 E8
Davis Rd. B77 52 D1
Deeley. B77 52 E4
Deltic. B77 52 D4
Dennis. B77 52 C3
Dent St. B79 51 F4
Derwent. B77 52 B4
Devereux Ho. B79 50 D4
Dorado. B77 53 B7
Dormer Av. B77 51 G4
Dosthill Rd. B77 53 B6
Draycott Cres. B77 52 A4
Dryden Rd. B79 50 D2
Dumolos La. B77 52 C2
Dunedin. B77 52 E4
Dunstall La. B78 50 A4
Dunster. B77 53 A6
Eagle Dri. B77 52 F2
Ealingham. B77 52 F4
East St. B77 53 B8
East Vw. B77 52 C2
Edale. B77 52 F4
Edgar Clo. B79 50 C2
Ediths Clo. B79 51 E4
Edward St. B79 50 D4
Elizabeth Dri. B79 50 D3
Ellerbeck. B77 52 F4
Engine La. B77 52 E3
Eringden. B77 52 F4
Ethelfleda Rd. B77 53 D8
Exley. B77 52 B4
Fairview Clo. B77 52 D1
Fairway. B77 53 C8
Falcon. B77 53 E7
Falna Cres. B79 50 C2
Faringdon. B77 52 D4
Farm CLo. B79 51 F2
Fazeley Rd. B78 51 E6
Felspar Rd. B77 52 E3
Fenn St. B77 53 B5
Ferrers Rd. B77 52 B1
Field Farm La. B77 52 B4
Firtree Clo. B79 50 B1
Flora Clo. B79 51 F2
Florendine St. B77 52 D1
Fontenaye Rd. B79 50 B1
Forties. B77 53 B6
Fossdale Rd. B77 53 E5
Foxglove. B77 52 E2
Freasley La. B77 53 E7
Freville Clo. B79 50 D3
Furness. B77 52 B3
Gagarin. B79 50 C4
Galena Clo. B77 52 F3
Garrigill. B77 53 E5
Gawsnorth. B79 50 A2
Gayle. B77 52 E4
George St. B79 51 E5
Gerard. B79 50 B2
Gillway La. B79 50 D1
Glascote La. B77 53 D6
Glascote Rd. B77 52 A2
Gleneagles. B77 52 F1
Glyndebourne. B79 50 A2
Godolphin. B79 50 A2
Gofton. B77 53 E5
Goldcrest. B77 53 E8
Goldsborough. B77 53 E5
Goldsmith Pl. B79 50 D2
Goostry Clo. B77 51 G4
Goostry Rd. B77 51 G4
Gorsy Bank Rd. B77 53 D8
Grange Clo. B77 53 A5
Granville. B77 52 D5
Grassholme. B77 53 E5
Grayling. B77 53 B7
Grayston Av. B77 52 C2
Great Mead. B77 52 A4
Greenhart. B77 52 E2
Greenhill Clo. B77 53 A8
Greenlea. B77 53 E5
Gresley. B77 52 D4
Grindsbrook. B77 53 E5
Gurnard. B77 53 B7
Guys Clo. B79 50 C2
Hadrians Clo. B77 53 A5
Halford St. B79 50 D4
Haltonlea. B77 53 E5
Hamble. B77 52 B3
Hampton Clo. B79 51 F2
Hanbury Rd. B77 52 D1
Hanlith. B77 53 E5
Harcourt Ho. B79 50 D5
Harebell. B77 52 E1
Hartleyburn. B77 53 E5
Hastings Clo. B77 53 D7
Hawfinch. B77 53 D8
Hawkside. B77 53 E5
Hawksworth. B77 52 D4
Hawthorne Av. B79 50 D1
Hayle. B77 52 B4
Hayworth Clo. B79 50 C1
Hazel Garth. B77 53 E5
Heath St. B79 51 F4
Hebden. B77 53 F5
Hedging La. B77 53 B8
Helmingham. B79 50 A2
Helston Clo. B79 51 F1
Henley Clo. B79 51 F3
Hesleden. B77 53 E5
High St. B77 53 A8
Highcliffe Rd. B77 53 B5
Highfield Av. B77 52 D1
Hill Top Av. B79 51 E1
Hillcrest Clo. B79 51 E3
Hilman. B77 52 C3
Hockley Rd. B77 53 C8
Hodge La. B77 52 F1
Holly Clo. B79 51 E2
Holsworth Clo. B77 52 B4
Holwick. B77 53 F5
Honeybourne. B77 52 B3
Hopleys Clo. B77 52 C2
Hornbeam. B77 52 E1
Hospital St. B79 51 E4
Houting. B77 53 B8
Hoylake. B77 52 F1
INDUSTRIAL ESTATES:
Amington Ind Est. B77 52 F3
Beauchamp Ind Pk. B77 53 B5
Centurian Pk Ind Est. B77 53 F7
Hedging La Ind Est. B77 53 C8
Lichfield Rd Ind Est. B79 50 C4
Tame Valley Ind Est. B77 53 C7
Ventura Shopping Centre. B79 50 D6
Ingram Pit La. B77 52 E1
Iris Clo. B79 51 F3
Irwell. B77 52 C4
Ivatt. B77 52 D3
Ivyhouse Wk. B77 53 D7
Jaguar. B77 52 C3
Jasmine Rd. B77 52 E1
Jason Clo. B77 51 G4
Jenson. B77 52 C3
Jervis Rd. B77 53 D8
John Dory. B77 53 B7
John St. B77 52 B2
Johns St. B79 51 E4
Jonkel Av. B77 53 D8
Jowett. B77 52 B3
June Cres. B77 51 H4
Juniper. B77 52 E1
Keats Clo. B79 50 C1
Kenilworth Rd. B77 52 C1
Kennedy Clo. B77 53 A5
Kennet. B77 52 B4
Kentwell. B79 50 A2
Kepler. B79 50 B2
Kerria Rd. B77 52 E1
Kestrel. B77 53 E7
Kettlebrook Rd. B77 52 A2
Kilbye Clo. B77 53 D8
Kimberley. B77 53 D6
King St. B79 51 E4
Kingfisher. B77 53 E7
Kingsley Clo. B79 50 D3
Kingston Clo. B79 51 F2
Kipling Rise. B79 50 C1
Kirtley. B77 52 C4
Kurtus. B77 53 B7
Laburnum Av. B79 51 E1
Lagonda. B77 52 B3
Lagrange. B79 50 B3
Lakeland Dri. B77 53 E6
Lakenheath. B79 51 F2
Lamprey. B77 53 B7
Lanchester Clo. B79 50 C2
Landsberg. B79 50 C3
Lansdowne Cres. B77 53 B5
Lapwing. B77 53 E7
Launceston Clo. B77 52 B4
Lavender Rd. B77 52 C1
Lawrence Ct. B79 50 D3
Leedham Av. B77 51 G4
Leisure Wk. B77 53 D7
Leyland Rd. B77 52 C3
Liberty Rd. B77 53 D8
Libra Clo. B79 50 C2
Lichfield Rd. B79 50 A2
Lichfield St. B79 50 D4
Lilac Rd. B79 50 D1
Linden Clo. B77 52 D1
Lindera. B77 52 E1
Lindisfarne. B77 52 B3
Lintly. B77 53 F5
Little Church La. B79 51 E4
Littlecote. B79 50 B2
Litton. B77 53 F5
Lomita Clo. B77 53 B5
Lomond Clo. B79 50 C1
Longfellow Wk. B79 50 C1
Longfield Clo. B77 52 C1
Longlands Dri. B77 52 D2
Longleat. B79 50 B2
Lorton. B79 50 A2
Lothersdale. B77 53 F5
Lotus. B77 52 B3
Lovell. B79 50 C3
Lovers Wk. B78 50 D5
Lower Gungate. B79 51 E4
Lower Pk. B77 52 A4
Lud La. B79 50 D4
Ludgate. B79 50 D3
Lyneham Clo. B79 51 E1
Macgregor Cres. B77 52 D2
Madox Clo. B79 50 B1
Madrona. B77 52 F1
Magnolia. B77 52 E1
Magnus. B77 53 C7
Maitland. B77 52 D3
Malham Rd. B77 53 F5
Manor Rd. B77 52 A1
Manston Vw. B79 51 F1
Manta Rd. B77 53 B7
Mariner. B79 50 B2
Market St. B79 51 E4
Marlborough Way. B77 52 B4
Marlin. B77 53 B7
Marlow Rd. B77 51 G4
Marmion St. B79 51 E4
Marshall St. B77 51 G4
Masefield Dri. B79 50 D2
Masefield Rd. B79 50 D1
Meadow Pk. B79 50 C4
Meadow St. B77 51 F5
Mealey. B77 52 C3
Medina. B77 52 C4
Medway. B77 52 B4
Melford. B79 50 B3
Mercia Clo. B79 50 B2
Mercian Way. B77 52 F1
Merganser. B77 53 E7
Metfield Clo. B79 51 F1
Mica Clo. B77 52 F3
Mildenhall. B79 51 E1
Mill La. B79 51 E4
Milton Av. B79 50 D2
Minerva Clo. B77 51 G4
Monks Way. B77 52 D1
Moor La. B77 51 G4
Moor St. B79 50 D4
Moorgate. B79 50 D4
Morpeth. B77 53 A6
Mount Pleasant. B77 53 A5
Muirfield. B77 52 F1
Napier. B77 52 C3
Neander. B79 50 C3
Nemesia. B77 52 F2
Nevill St. B79 50 D4
Neville St. B77 52 B2
New Rd. B77 53 D7
New St, Glascote. B77 52 C2
New St, Mt Pleasant. B77 53 A5
Newstead. B79 50 B3
Nightingale. B77 53 E7
Ninefoot La. B77 53 C5
Ninian Way. B77 53 B8
Norman Clo. B79 50 C2
Norton Clo. B79 51 F2
Nymet. B77 53 C5
Offa Dri. B79 51 E4
Offa St. B79 51 E4
Old Cotton La. B79 50 B1
Old Hedging La. B77 53 B8
Orchard Clo. B77 53 A8
Orchard St, Kettlebrook. B77 51 F6
Orchard St, Tamworth. B79 51 E4
Osbourne. B79 50 A2
Osprey. B77 53 E7
Ottery. B77 53 E8
Overwoods Rd. B77 53 D7
Parbury. B77 53 B8
Park Farm Rd. B77 52 A4
Park Rd. B77 53 A8
Park St. B79 50 D4
Parkfield Av. B77 53 A5
Parkfield Clo. B77 53 A5
Parkfield Cres. B77 53 A5
Parkside. B77 53 C5
Parson St. B77 53 C6
Peeble Clo. B77 52 F2
Peel Ho. B79 50 D4
Peelers Way. B78 51 F6
Pennine Way. B77 52 F4
Pennymoor Rd. B77 53 F6
Perrycrofts Cres. B79 51 F2
Pine Clo. B79 51 E1
Plantation La. B78 50 A6
Primley. B77 53 D8
Priory Clo. B79 50 D2
Prospect St. B79 50 D4
Pullman Clo. B77 52 E3
Purbrook. B77 53 C5
Queensway. B79 50 D1
Quince. B77 52 F2
Rainscar. B77 53 F6
Ravenstone. B77 53 F5
Raygill. B77 53 F5
Redhill Clo. B79 50 D2
Redlake. B77 53 C5
Redwell Clo. B77 51 G4
Redwing. B77 53 E7
Reedmace. B77 51 F6
Rene Rd. B77 51 G4
Ribblesdale. B77 53 F6
Richmond Clo. B79 50 D4
Ridgeway Rise. B77 52 E1
Ridgewood Rise. B77 52 E1
Ripley. B77 52 C3
River Dri. B78 50 D5
Riverfield Gro. B77 51 G4
Roach. B77 53 B7
Robert Clo. B79 50 C2
Robinson Clo. B79 50 B2
Roman Ct. B77 53 C6
Roman Way. B79 50 B2
Romney. B77 53 D5
Rosemary Rd. B77 52 C1
Rosewood Clo. B77 52 B1
Rosewood Ct. B77 52 B2
Rosy Cross. B79 51 E4
Rothay. B77 53 D5
Rufford. B79 50 B3
Ryton. B77 53 D5
Saffron. B77 52 F2
St Andrews. B77 52 F2
St Austell Clo. B79 50 D3
St Christophers Dri. B77 52 A5
St Georges Way. B77 52 C2
St Ives Clo. B79 51 E3
St Margarets Rd. B79 51 E2
St Marys Way. B77 52 C1
St Peters Clo. B77 52 A4
Salters La. B79 51 E3
Sandpiper. B77 53 E8
Sandy Way. B77 52 E3
Saxon Clo. B77 53 D7
Saxon Dri. B77 51 F5
Saxon Mill La. B79 51 F4
Scammerton. B77 53 E6
Scampton Way. B79 51 F1
School La. B77 53 A8
School St. B77 52 B2
Scimitar Clo. B79 50 B2
Scott Rd. B77 52 C1
Seaton. B77 53 D5
Sefton Rd. B77 53 B8
Selker Dri. B77 51 H4
Shakespeare Clo. B79 50 D3
Shannon. B77 53 D5
Sharpe St. B77 52 E1
Sheepcote La. B77 52 D2
Shelley Rd. B79 50 D2
Shelton St. B77 53 D6
Sherbrooke Av. B77 53 C7
Shirley Wk. B79 50 C2
Signal Wk. B77 52 E3
Silica Rd. B77 52 F3
Silver Link Rd. B77 52 C3
Silver St. B79 51 E4
Skidmore Av. B77 53 A8
Skipness. B77 51 H4
Slingsby. B77 53 A6
Smithy La. B77 53 D6
Solway Clo. B79 50 D2
Sorbus. B77 52 F1
Sorrel. B77 52 F1
Spenser Av. B79 50 D3
Spinning School La. B79 51 E4
Spruce. B77 52 F1
Standedge. B77 53 E6
Stanhope Ho. B79 50 D5
Steere Av. B79 51 E2
Stephenson Clo. B77 52 E3
Stevenson Rd. B79 50 D3
Stonehaven. B77 51 H4
Stonepit. B77 52 A4
Stoneydelph La. B77 53 E6
Stour. B77 53 E8
Stretton St. B77 52 C2
Strode Ho. B79 50 D4
Sudeley. B77 53 A6
Summerfield Rd. B77 52 B1
Sunbeam. B77 52 C3
Sunningdale. B77 52 F1
Sunset Clo. B79 50 D4
Swallowfield. B79 50 B3
Swanmote. B79 50 C4
Swift. B77 52 C3
Swindale. B77 53 F6
Sycamore. B77 53 C6
Sykesmoor. B77 53 F6
Talbot. B77 52 C3
Talland Av. B77 51 H4
Tamar Rd. B77 53 E8
Tame Dri. B78 50 D4
Tame St. B77 51 F6
Tamworth Rd, Dosthill. B77 53 A8
Tamworth Rd, Glascote. B77 52 C1
Tamworth Rd, Kettlebrook. B77 52 A3
Tanhill. B77 53 F6
Tansy. B77 52 A3
Tarrant. B77 53 C5
Tavistock Clo. B79 51 F2
Teign. B77 53 E8
Telford Rd. B79 50 C1
Tempest St. B79 50 D4
Tennyson Av. B79 50 D3
Thackeray Dri. B79 50 D2
The Dell. B79 51 E3
The Ridings. B77 51 H4
Thomas Guy Way. B78 50 C6
Thomas St. B77 52 B2
Thoresby. B79 50 B3
Thornby Av. B77 53 C5
Thurne. B77 53 C6
Thurso. B77 51 H4
Tilia Rd. B77 52 E1
Tinkers Green Rd. B77 53 D7
Tolman Dri. B77 52 A2
Tolson Clo. B77 53 A8
Torbay. B77 51 H4
Torc Av. B77 52 C2
Torridge. B77 53 E8
Torside. B77 53 F6
Townsend Ho. B79 50 D5
Townwall Ct. B77 53 D7
Treasure Clo. B77 52 C1
Trefoil. B77 52 E1
Triumph. B77 52 C3
Trojan. B77 52 C3
Troon. B77 52 F2
Tudor Clo. B77 52 D2
Tudor Cres. B77 52 D2
Tutbury. B77 53 A6
Tutehill. B77 53 F6
Two Gates. B77 53 B6
Union Clo. B77 52 A3
Upper Gungate. B79 51 E3
Valley La. B77 53 C6
Vanguard. B77 53 B7
Ventura Park Rd. B78 50 D6
Victoria Rd. B79 51 E4

Wainrigg. B77	53 F6	
Wansbeck. B77	53 C6	
Wardle St. B79	50 D4	
Warwick Rd. B77	52 C1	
Watling St. B77	53 A5	
Waveney. B77	53 C5	
Welford Rd. B77	53 A8	
Wellers Bourne. B79	51 E1	
Wembury. B77	51 H4	
Wenlock. B77	52 B2	
Wesley Way. B77	52 C1	
West St, Kettlebrook. B77	51 F6	
West St, Tamworth. B79	51 F4	
Weymouth Ho. B79	50 D4	
Whitesands Clo. B77	51 H4	
Whiting. B77	53 B7	
Whitley Av. B77	51 H3	
Wigford Rd. B77	53 A8	
Wigginton Rd. B79	51 E2	
Willington Rd. B79	51 E2	
Willoughby Rd. B79	50 C2	
Wilnecote La. B77	52 A3	
Windmill Clo. B79	50 D1	
Windsor Rd. B79	51 F2	
Witney Clo. B79	50 C2	
Woburn. B77	51 G6	
Wolseley. B77	52 C3	
Woodcroft Av. B79	51 E3	
Woodhouse La. B77	52 E1	
Woodhurst Clo. B77	52 D1	
Woodland Rd. B77	52 D3	
Wordsworth Av. B79	50 D3	
Wynyates. B79	50 B3	
Wyvern. B77	52 C3	
Yeovilton. B79	51 F1	

UTTOXETER

Alexandra Cres. ST14	54 D3	
Alleyne Pl. ST14	54 B2	
Applewood Clo. ST14	54 C2	
Ash Clo. ST14	54 C2	
Ashbourne Rd. ST14	54 D1	
Ashleigh Dri. ST14	54 A1	
Avocet Clo. ST14	54 E4	
Badgery Clo. ST14	54 C1	
Back La. ST14	54 E3	
Back Westlands Rd. ST14	54 C4	
Balance Hill. ST14	54 E4	
Balance St. ST14	54 D3	
Bank Clo. ST14	54 E4	
Batemans Way. ST14	54 E2	
Beech Clo. ST14	54 C3	
Beechdale. ST14	54 C2	
Benteley Rd. ST14	54 B2	
Blackbird Clo. ST14	54 E4	
Bradley St. ST14	54 E3	
Brambling Clo. ST14	54 D4	
Bramshall Rd. ST14	54 A3	
Bridge Rd. ST14	54 F4	
Bridge St. ST14	54 E3	
Brookside Rd. ST14	54 E3	
Bunting Clo. ST14	54 D4	
Burton Ter. ST14	54 E2	
Byrds Clo. ST14	54 B2	
Byrds La. ST14	54 B2	
Carter St. ST14	54 D3	
Cedar Clo. ST14	54 B2	
Chaffinch Dri. ST14	54 E4	
Cheadle Rd. ST14	54 D2	
Chestnut Dri. ST14	54 B2	
Church St. ST14	54 E3	
Clarkes Clo. ST14	54 D2	
Cockstubbles Rd. ST14	54 D2	
Collin St. ST14	54 D3	
Colne Mt. ST14	54 D3	
Copes Way. ST14	54 B1	

Croft Gro. ST14	54 D2	
Cross Rd. ST14	54 C2	
Curlew Clo. ST14	54 D4	
Davies Dri. ST14	54 B1	
Derby Rd. ST14	54 E2	
Dove Bank. ST14	54 E3	
Dove Fields. ST14	54 F3	
Dove Wk. ST14	54 F2	
Eagle Clo. ST14	54 D4	
Eaton St. ST14	54 E2	
Elmwood Gro. ST14	54 B1	
Fairfield Rd. ST14	54 D3	
Fennel Clo. ST14	54 D4	
Foxglove Av. ST14	54 D4	
Gardner Pl. ST14	54 C1	
Gas St. ST14	54 D4	
George Elliot Clo. ST14	54 E4	
Grange Rd. ST14	54 C1	
Green Way. ST14	54 D2	
Greenacres Dri. ST14	54 C3	
Greenfield Dri. ST14	54 C3	
Grenville Clo. ST14	54 B2	
Hall Rd. ST14	54 B2	
Hallam Rd. ST14	54 B2	
Harvey Pl. ST14	54 D2	
Hawthornden Av. ST14	54 B2	
Hawthornden Clo. ST14	54 B2	
Hawthornden Gdns. ST14	54 B2	
Hawthornden Manor. ST14	54 C3	
Heath Cross. ST14	54 C2	
Heath Rd. ST14	54 C2	
Heathfields. ST14	54 D3	
Heaths Dri. ST14	54 D2	
Heron Dri. ST14	54 D4	
High St. ST14	54 D2	
Highwood Rd. ST14	54 E4	
Hill Clo. ST14	54 B2	
Hockley Rd. ST14	54 D4	
Holly Rd. ST14	54 C3	
Howitt Cres. ST14	54 D1	
Ivy Clo. ST14	54 C2	
James St. ST14	54 D3	
John St. ST14	54 D3	
Johnson Rd. ST14	54 D1	
Kestrel Clo. ST14	54 D4	
Kimberley Dri. ST14	54 B1	
Kingfisher Way. ST14	54 D4	
Lambert Rd. ST14	54 B2	
Lark Rise. ST14	54 D4	
Leighton Clo. ST14	54 E4	
Leighton Rd. ST14	54 E4	
Lightfoot Rd. ST14	54 B2	
Mallard Clo. ST14	54 E4	
Manor Clo. ST14	54 D3	
Manor Rd. ST14	54 D2	
Market Pl. ST14	54 E3	
Market St. ST14	54 E3	
Marlborough Way. ST14	54 B2	
Mellor Rd. ST14	54 D2	
Merlin Clo. ST14	54 E4	
Milverton Dri. ST14	54 A2	
Moor Gro. ST14	54 C2	
Mosley Dri. ST14	54 C2	
New Rd. ST14	54 B1	
New St. ST14	54 E2	
Northfield Clo. ST14	54 C1	
Oak Clo. ST14	54 B2	
Oldfield Rd. ST14	54 C2	
Orchard Clo. ST14	54 D1	
Park Av. ST14	54 D1	
Park St. ST14	54 D1	
Partridge Dri. ST14	54 E4	
Parva Ct. ST14	54 B1	
Pennycroft La. ST14	54 E2	
Pennycroft Rd. ST14	54 B1	
Picknall La. ST14	54 C3	
Pine Wk. ST14	54 B2	
Pinfold St. ST14	54 E3	
Poplar Clo. ST14	54 B2	

Primrose Way. ST14	54 D2	
Princess Rd. ST14	54 C2	
Queen St. ST14	54 E3	
Redfern Rd. ST14	54 C1	
Robin Clo. ST14	54 D4	
Rosemary Dri. ST14	54 D4	
St Marys Cres. ST14	54 D2	
Sandpiper Cloi. ST14	54 D4	
School Rd. ST14	54 B2	
Shipton Dri. ST14	54 B2	
Short St. ST14	54 D3	
Silver St. ST14	54 E3	
Skylark Clo. ST14	54 E4	
Slade Fields. ST14	54 D4	
Smithfield Rd. ST14	54 D3	
South View. ST14	54 D4	
Springfield Rd. ST14	54 D3	
Stafford Rd. ST14	54 C4	
Stanley Cres. ST14	54 C1	
Station Rd. ST14	54 E3	
Stone Rd. ST14	54 C3	
Stoneyford Ter. ST14	54 E4	
Summerfield Dri. ST14	54 C3	
Sunnyside Rd. ST14	54 D4	
Swallow Clo. ST14	54 D4	
Swift Clo. ST14	54 D4	
Sycamore Clo. ST14	54 B2	
The Hollow. ST14	54 E4	
The Hornbeams. ST14	54 C2	
The Lawns. ST14	54 C1	
The Meadows. ST14	54 C1	
The Picknals. ST14	54 D3	
Timber La. ST14	54 D4	
Torrance Gro. ST14	54 B1	
Trinity Rd. ST14	54 D4	
Tunnicliffe Way. ST14	54 B1	
Uttoxeter By-Pass. ST14	54 B1	
Walkmill Clo. ST14	54 D2	
Weaver Rd. ST14	54 C1	
West Hill. ST14	54 E4	
West Way. ST14	54 B2	
Westlands Rd. ST14	54 D4	
Westward Clo. ST14	54 D4	
Windsor Rd. ST14	54 C2	
Wood La. ST14	54 F4	
Wood Leighton Gro. ST14	54 E4	
Wood Leighton Rd. ST14	54 E4	

WOMBOURNE

Anbery Dri. WV5	55 C4	
Apse Clo. WV5	55 C2	
Bankside. WV5	55 C2	
Battlefield La. WV5	55 F2	
Beggars Bush La. WV5	55 E3	
Billy Buns La. WV5	55 E1	
Birch Coppice. WV5	55 B3	
Birch Hill Av. WV5	55 C3	
Blakely Heath Dri. WV5	55 D3	
Bloomfield Clo. WV5	55 B3	
Boss Gate Clo. WV5	55 D4	
Botteham La. WV5	55 C4	
Bramber Dri. WV5	55 D2	
Bratch Common Rd. WV5	55 C2	
Bratch Hollow. WV5	55 D1	
Bratch La. WV5	55 C1	
Bratch Park. WV5	55 C1	
Brickbridge La. WV5	55 B4	
Bridge Clo. WV5	55 D2	
Bridgewater Dri. WV5	55 D1	
Bridgnorth Av. WV5	55 C4	
Bridgnorth Rd. WV5	55 A3	
Brindle Clo. WV5	55 B3	
Brook Rd. WV5	55 C3	
Brook Seleys Leys. WV5	55 B3	

Bull La. WV5	55 E1	
Bullmeadow La. WV5	55 E1	
Bumblehole Mdws. WV5	55 C2	
Calvin Clo. WV5	55 D4	
Campion Clo. WV5	55 C2	
Cannon Rd. WV5	55 D2	
Cedars Av. WV5	55 E3	
Chapel Clo. WV5	55 D4	
Chapel La. WV5	55 A4	
Chapel St. WV5	55 D4	
Chartwell Rd. WV5	55 C4	
Chestnut. WV5	55 A4	
Church Rd. WV5	55 A4	
Church Rd. WV5	55 E2	
Churchward Gro. WV5	55 D1	
Churchwell Ct. WV5	55 E2	
Clap Gate Gro. WV5	55 B3	
Clap Gate Rd. WV5	55 C2	
Clee View Rd. WV5	55 C4	
Common Rd. WV5	55 D3	
Copper Beech Dri. WV5	55 E3	
Corns Gro. WV5	55 C4	
Crane Hollow. WV5	55 B3	
Cranwell Green. WV5	55 C4	
Dean Rd. WV5	55 B3	
Deep Dales. WV5	55 B3	
Dickenson Rd. WV5	55 D4	
Dingle Rd. WV5	55 D3	
Elder Gro. WV5	55 C3	
Elm Tree Clo. WV5	55 D3	
Foley Gro. WV5	55 C3	
Forge Leys. WV5	55 B3	
Forge Valley Way. WV5	55 B3	
Furnace Clo. WV5	55 B3	
Gardeners Way. WV5	55 C4	
Giggetty La. WV5	55 C2	
Gilbert La. WV5	55 E3	
Glendale. WV5	55 E3	
Gravel Hill. WV5	55 E2	
Green Acres. WV5	55 C4	
Greenfields Rd. WV5	55 D3	
Greenhill. WV5	55 E3	
Greenhill Ct. WV5	55 E3	
Greenhill Gdns. WV5	55 E3	
Greenlands. WV5	55 D2	
Griffiths Dri. WV5	55 E4	
Hatch Heath Clo. WV5	55 D2	
Hawks Well Av. WV5	55 D3	
Hazel Gro. WV5	55 E1	
Heath House Dri. WV5	55 B3	
Heath Mill Rd. WV5	55 B4	
Heathlands. WV5	55 A3	
High Meadows. WV5	55 E3	
High St. WV5	55 E2	
Highfields Dri. WV5	55 C4	
Hill Side. WV5	55 C3	
Holloway Dri. WV5	55 C3	
Honeybourne Cres. WV5	55 C3	
INDUSTRIAL ESTATES:		
Wombourne Enterprise Park. WV5	55 A4	
Jenks Rd. WV5	55 C4	
Kirkstone Cres. WV5	55 D3	
Ladywell Clo. WV5	55 D1	
Lamb Cres. WV5	55 D3	
Lear Rd. WV5	55 E1	
Lilac Dri. WV5	55 D3	
Lindale Dri. WV5	55 C2	
Link Rd. WV5	55 E1	
Lockside. WV5	55 C2	
Longford Clo. WV5	55 B3	
Manor Gdns. WV5	55 E2	
Marlburn Way. WV5	55 C3	
Meadow La. WV5	55 E1	
Mill La. WV5	55 E2	
Millers Vale. WV5	55 B4	
Millfields Way. WV5	55 B3	
Moises Hall Rd. WV5	55 F2	

Monks Clo. WV5	55 C3	
Mount Clo. WV5	55 D1	
Mount Dri. WV5	55 D1	
Mount Pleasant Av. WV5	55 D1	
Mount Rd. WV5	55 D1	
Neachless Av. WV5	55 D4	
Nursery Dri. WV5	55 D4	
Oaks Dri. WV5	55 E3	
Ounsdale Cres. WV5	55 C2	
Ounsdale Rd. WV5	55 C2	
Park Av. WV5	55 D4	
Penleigh Gdns. WV5	55 C2	
Pinewood Clo. WV5	55 C3	
Planks La. WV5	55 C3	
Pool House Rd. WV5	55 E3	
Poplar Clo. WV5	55 E3	
Quendale. WV5	55 B3	
Redcliffe Dri. WV5	55 D3	
Redhill Av. WV5	55 D3	
Rees Dri. WV5	55 F2	
Rennison Dri. WV5	55 D2	
Richmond Gdns. WV5	55 E3	
Rookery Rise. WV5	55 E3	
Rookery Rd. WV5	55 E3	
Rosebury Gro. WV5	55 C3	
Rushford Av. WV5	55 E2	
St Benedicts Rd. WV5	55 E2	
St Brides Clo. WV5	55 D2	
Sandringham Rd. WV5	55 C5	
Sandy Mnt. WV5	55 F2	
School Rd. WV5	55 F2	
Smallbrook La. WV5	55 F2	
Smestow La. WV5	55 A4	
Station Rd. WV5	55 D1	
Stoney Brook Leys. WV5	55 B3	
Stourbridge Rd. WV5	55 B3	
Sunny Hill Clo. WV5	55 F2	
Sunridge Av. WV5	55 B4	
Swinford Leys. WV5	55 B4	
Sytch La. WV5	55 D4	
The Broadway. WV5	55 E3	
The Celandines. WV5	55 C2	
The Croft. WV5	55 B3	
The Grange. WV5	55 D2	
The Hedges. WV5	55 D3	
The Longlands. WV5	55 D3	
*The Maltings, Walk La. WV5	55 E2	
The Meadlands. WV5	55 E2	
The Paddock. WV5	55 C3	
The Shales. WV5	55 B3	
The Warings. WV5	55 C4	
The Willows. WV5	55 A3	
Trysull Rd. WV5	55 C1	
Uplands Dri. WV5	55 E3	
Van Diemans Rd. WV5	55 E3	
Vicarage Dri. WV5	55 E2	
Victoria Gro. WV5	55 D1	
Walk La. WV5	55 E2	
Waterdale. WV5	55 B4	
Waverley Gdns. WV5	55 F2	
Wedgwood Av. WV5	55 D4	
Wesley Clo. WV5	55 D4	
Westbrook Way. WV5	55 D5	
Westfield Dri. WV5	55 D2	
Westleigh Rd. WV5	55 C4	
Whites Wood. WV5	55 E3	
Windmill Bank. WV5	55 E2	
Windsor Rd. WV5	55 D3	
Withymere La. WV5	55 F1	
Woden Clo. WV5	55 E1	
Wombourne Pk. WV5	55 D4	
Wood Hill Clo. WV5	55 D5	
Wood Rd. WV5	55 F1	
Woodford La. WV5	55 B3	
Woodford Way. WV5	55 B3	
Woodlands Rd. WV5	55 E3	